PHILOSOPHY IN FRANCE TODAY

PHILOSOPHY IN FRANCE TODAY

Edited by Alan Montefiore

Cambridge University Press
Cambridge
London   New York   New Rochelle
Melbourne   Sydney

Published by the Press Syndicate of the University of Cambridge
The Pitt Building, Trumpington Street, Cambridge CB2 1RP
32 East 57th Street, New York, NY 10022, USA
296 Beaconsfield Parade, Middle Park, Melbourne 3206, Australia

First published 1983

Printed in Great Britain at the
University Press, Cambridge

Library of Congress catalogue card number: 82–9730

British Library Cataloguing in Publication Data
Philosophy in France today.
1. Philosophy, French——20th century
I. Montefiore, Alan
194   B2421

ISBN 0 521 22838 7 hard covers
ISBN 0 521 29673 0 paperback

wv

Contents

ALAN MONTEFIORE

Introduction

If publishers' lists and sales are anything to go by, it seems as if French and English-speaking readers – or at any rate buyers – of books on philosophy are, after a long and notorious break, starting to find a renewed interest in what is going on in each other's world. To mention just two highly successful straws in this new and as yet somewhat fitful wind: Vincent Descombes's very personal account of *Modern French Philosophy*,* commissioned and written specifically for the English-speaking reader, and, in the other direction, the double number of the review *Critique*,† in which a variety of philosophers, mainly British or American, set out to present to French-speaking readers the present state of research and debate in the world of analytic philosophy, taking each some particular region of that world as they see it.

This present volume is not conceived as an exact counterpart to that number of *Critique*. The French philosophers contributing to it were not asked to try and divide up between them the overall terrain of contemporary French philosophy. Indeed, for a number of reasons which may become at least partially apparent to any reader of the whole book, this might have been an inappropriate or even unworkable request to make. There is, in principle, notably less agreement within that world, whatever it may be or be held to be, as to how or where its map and its boundaries should be drawn – whether in respect of its external frontiers, if, indeed, it has any, or in respect of its internal regions – or even as to the possibility of any such map-making venture at all.

* Cambridge: Cambridge University Press, 1980.
† Vol. XXXVI, nos. 399–400, August–September 1980.

What the authors of the eleven contributions that together make up this volume were asked to do was rather to present to the English-speaking reader their own view of their own work as they now see it in relation to the context in which they are working and, perhaps, to the reactions which they might expect it to provoke. In this way the resulting book offers, both by way of exposition and explanation and by way of direct exemplification, a very fair introductory, sample experience of the world of philosophy as it may be found in France today. But it is essential to any proper understanding, whether of that world or of this book as an introduction to it, to recognize also that there might be in principle many other introductory experiences that, though different, might be equally fair. Not only should none of those who happen to find themselves contributing to this book be taken as seeking to 'represent' anything or anyone other than themselves or their own work; there is an important sense in which anyone trying to respond to such editorial questions as those which lie at the origin of this book, is bound to certain pressures that may lead him to write in a way that may be, in certain important respects, *un*representative of his own 'normal' work as such. The most obvious of these pressures lies in the untypical nature of the situation of a French philosopher having to write with a non-French readership in mind. It is, after all, of the very essence of this book's interest that it is conceived out of the very recognition that the cultural contexts of contemporary French and English language philosophy are still in the main very different, and that what may be taken for granted in the one context will need to be explained or rendered otherwise accessible in the other. Other reasons will emerge in the course of this introduction and, no doubt, in the course of the book as a whole. But it is important to recognize at the outset that just as the questions of how, where and even whether there are any internal or external boundaries to be drawn within or around the world of French philosophy are themselves deeply and properly controversial within that world, whatever one may take it to be, so too are any questions of just how this writer, this current of thought, or that may or may not be related to what other.

It is an attempt to avoid the advance begging of any such questions that the contributions to this book have been placed with arbitrary simplicity in the mere alphabetical order of their

authors' surnames. But, it should likewise be noted at the outset,
there are also problems in the way of avoiding a rather different
form of question-begging in advance that could only too easily be
involved in the writing of any would-be introduction to a book
such as this. It is not just that it would be inappropriate for a
British philosopher to presume to be able to step in to tell the
'true' story of the present state of French philosophical affairs or,
by commenting one by one on each of the following contributions, to explain in more effectively Anglo-Saxon terms what
they are 'really' trying to say; it would be in principle wholly
misconceived to envisage the task in this way. Of course, every
reader, the writer of this introduction among them, will, it is
hoped, be able to form some sort of view as to the content and
point of each contribution and, if appropriate, to set down his
view in writing. But the nature of the relationship between such
views and those of the contributors themselves, or – to set the
matter in a different perspective – to the texts that constitute their
present contributions, is not simply to be judged in terms of
straightforwardly factual accuracy or inaccuracy. On the contrary, it itself presents a characteristically philosophical problem;
and one, moreover, on which these same contributors would,
one may suppose, themselves have very different views, or reactions. In other words, any attempt to make of an introduction to a
volume of this sort some kind of précis in advance, simpler and
easier of access than the texts themselves but still somehow unproblematically faithful to them, is virtually bound to end up by
being in one way or another misleading; misleading in as much as
it would involve – in some cases, significantly, very much more
than in others – a radical shift from the mode or modes of
presentation adopted by the contributors themselves, but above
all misleading in that it would in effect and inevitably constitute
an intervention in a complicated and deeply divided debate under
the guise of an apparently neutral explanation and report.

This said, it remains the case that the manner, as much as the
content and insofar as the two may be clearly distinguished, of
many of the following essays is different enough from that to
which most English-speaking readers will be accustomed as to be
liable to cause them a certain initial perplexity. An introduction
may not sensibly set out to tell them in advance just what they are
to read out of or into the texts themselves; but certain things may

be said which, whether they end up by endorsing them or not, may be of some provisional help to them in working out their own readings. And while it is, of course, true that no amount of disclaimers can succeed in altogether neutralizing an intervention that remains an intervention however its sense may have been modified or disguised by the disclaimers in question, it is proper that this too should be noted – by way of yet a further disclaimer? – in this introduction itself.

One of the things which may first strike, perhaps even surprise, the reader of these essays is their multifaceted and criss-crossing diversity. From this side of the Channel, no doubt, this diversity may still be perceived as existing within a certain indeterminate unity. But if unity there is, it is at most a unity of family history and resemblance; and even then one might in certain cases have to count mutual recognition as partners or contestants in an arena of common dispute as a family relationship, if kinship is to be extended to all. That such diversity is here made so explicit is surely a good thing, if for no other reason than that any collection that allowed the reader to carry away an impression of contemporary French philosophy as constituting one homogeneous bloc would be encouraging an illusion of major proportions. Such diversity within a family, however disparate and discordant it may be, must in principle allow of a certain number of generalizations; but they will be generalizations which virtually never extend to cover every member of the family, which lie in overlapping relations to each other and which, moreover, apply to such members as they do apply to with only varying degrees of precision. Nevertheless, such generalizations, imperfect though they may be, may still in their way be characteristic of the family to which they apply.

Among the generalizations which seem to apply in this way to the papers of this collection are the following:

(i) A significant number of the participants seem to find themselves somehow embarrassed by the personal or narrative nature of the request 'How do you understand the nature of your own (philosophical) work?'

(ii) A significant number of the participants are committed to a view of philosophy as having an indissociable, and perhaps never fully expressible, 'practical' dimension. Typically, but not invariably, an acute awareness of this dimension even of their own contribution to this volume may play a problematic part in the fashioning of that contribution. (Typically, too, this 'practical' dimension may be understood as including the political.)

(iii) A significant number of the participants seem to regard themselves as standing alone, or almost alone, in whatever part of the field it is that they occupy.

(iv) It should perhaps be repeated as a fourth generalization that none of the above generalizations would seem to apply to *all* of the contributors here gathered together and that, though there may well be certain links between one generalization and another, these links fall far short of constituting identity of application.

Why should one find anything problematic in the (apparently?) straightforward request to provide an account of how one sees one's own work and the context within and for which it is produced? The reasons go far deeper, and are of far greater interest, than any mere considerations of personal modesty or professional embarrassment. No doubt there will be (and in principle must be) an indefinite number of different ways in which these reasons may be articulated, classified, marshalled, presented and analysed; their proper study would demand the space of a whole book on its own. For the more limited sake of this introduction, however, we may try to bring them under some sort of provisional control by dividing them into two groups: (i) those that are bound up with the subject's loss of self-confidence in its own ability to understand itself, and, indeed, in its own intrinsic significance; and (ii) those that have more to do with a loss of confidence in the sense or security of the distinction between stating and other forms of practical expression or activity, together with a related loss of confidence in the sharpness of any distinction between what is or is not of properly philosophical significance or relevance.

What would one have to be sure of *not* to find anything problematic in the request to report on one's own view of the nature and point of one's own work in philosophy? One would need, of course, to have some idea of whether one's work, or which part of it, was 'really' to be counted as philosophical and why; one would in any case need to be confident in laying claim to or in acknowledging any work, or any body of work, as one's own; and thus, even more primitively no doubt, one would need to have some reasonably confident idea – or at least some reasonable confidence in the possibility of working through to an idea – of what is involved in any reference back to oneself. But, philosophically speaking at any rate, any such confidence has proved to be of a notoriously uncertain stability. Descartes may have thought that this at least, even if nothing else, was something that he could claim truly to know. But even in the fairly close Cartesian succession the nature of the self-subject of this certain knowledge of what it is to be oneself became more and more problematically distanced from the seemingly ordinary, everyday human being who might have to get up and go to work in the morning, make his way around the streets or, occasionally perhaps, find himself trying to read or even to write a book of what might be regarded as philosophy. By the time one gets to Hume, for instance, this distance has become, so to speak, unmeasurable. Hume himself, in that famous passage in the Appendix to his *Treatise*, was brought to recognize that within the framework of his philosophy the very notion of the 'self' had come, as it were, to pieces. And Kant was to need all his transcendental horses and king's men to put the temporally discrete fragments back together into some sort of unity again.

'All *his* transcendental horses and king's men . . .' But here we are caught up in a new version of the problem. For how unified after all was this new sort of unity? What, within the framework of '*his*' own philosophy, could Kant be justified in regarding as constituting himself as *Kant*? 'How the "I" that thinks can be distinct from the "I" that intuits itself . . . and yet, as being the same subject, can be identical with the latter; and how, therefore, I can say: "I, as intelligence and *thinking* subject, know myself as an object that is *thought*, in so far as I am given to myself [as something other or] beyond that [I] which is [given to myself] in intuition, and yet know myself, like other phenomena, only as I appear to myself, not as I am to the understanding" – these are questions that raise no greater nor less difficulty than how I can be an object to myself at all, and, more particularly, an object of intuition and of inner perceptions.'* Nor do the difficulties stop here. Behind the self that is intuited, observed, met with in experience lies perhaps, unspecifiably but in the end ineliminably, a self-in-itself. Is this (unknowable and even strictly unsayable)

---

* *Critique of Pure Reason*, 'Transcendental Deduction', B155. Translation by Norman Kemp Smith, London: Macmillan, 1929.

self to be identified straightforwardly with the self that thinks, that is conscious of itself? Not *straightforwardly* at any rate. For – among other possible reasons – the self-in-itself, thought of simply as the putative ground of the self-that-appears, is from the standpoint of the theory of knowledge at best a mere object of thought and at worst nothing more than a limiting or negative concept to which no positive content can even be meaningfully ascribed. The self-that-thinks, on the other hand, is a transcendentally necessary presupposition of any conscious experience, any intentional action, whatsoever.

With which if any – or all? – of these selves is Kant to identify himself? The critical philosophy as a whole seems to provide no satisfactorily consistent answer, even, it may be argued, to rule out any such answer as in principle impossible. Not least of the difficulties lies in the fact that the principle of individuation of persons as a plurality of inhabitants of a common world of experience would seem to have to lie in the body and its spatio-temporal history; but this means, of course, that Kantian persons, inasmuch as they *are* individually distinct from one another, are so under that aspect of their dual nature which is necessarily subject to laws of a mechanical or efficient causality, a strictly deterministic causality of a sort which is seen as incompatible with that freedom of rational autonomy which is equally inseparable from the idea of persons as persons. For persons as persons, that is (necessarily) to say as rational agents, self-conscious of themselves as such, cannot but think of themselves as, precisely, autonomous and free. Indeed, as rational thinker and synthesizer of the discrete inputs of sensory awareness into a knowable experience, I (or that principle of active thought and synthesis within me) am (or is) the source of causally determinate order itself. How, indeed, can the two, the 'I' that thinks and the 'I' that is met with in experience, be one and the same, or different aspects of one and the same, thing?

Furthermore – for these problems have their own momentum – the question will also have to be faced of how, on this understanding of the matter, any other thinking subject or self can be observed or known to appear, or even be consistently thought of as possibly appearing, in a world of experience that is constituted as such by 'my own' activity of categorial synthesis. Or to put the same difficulty another way: how could any two materially distinct embodiments of this world-constituting principle of activity of transcendental synthesis both inhabit the same constituted world as each other? Unless perhaps, and supposing that one can make adequate sense of this suggestion, the world-constituting principle in both of us is numerically distinct only in its embodiments, but not in its capacity for conscious and self-conscious thought. Perhaps, indeed, such thought is only able to achieve any determinate consciousness of itself through its self-recognition as dispersed and separated from itself throughout and by the diversity of its different experiential situations and perspectives, while still having to recognize itself as being throughout this diversity the thought or thoughts of the one and self-same subject; for how otherwise could this diversity of situation and perspective be understandable as a feature of one and the same world? But if this *is* the case, and if 'we' find 'ourselves' thus committed to thinking of the whole world of objective knowledge as related ultimately to only one thinking subject (as unity of the field of experience), whatever the empirical diversity of its embodiments might be, then the sense in which 'we', Hume, Kant or anyone else can consistently regard his own work or texts as 'his own' can only be very incomplete, partial and provisional. As productions of thought they, along with all other texts of whatever apparent significance, must all be considered to be the work of the one thinking subject – and hence, moreover, all related to each other as such.

By this time – by this line of thought – we have arrived at a position of recognizably Hegelian outline. In fact, Kant himself, in his incomparable efforts to pick up and, again and again, to reknit the ravelled threads of his own thought, had by the time of his old age travelled, in his *Opus Postumum*, a notable distance in this direction. But, of course, Hegel did not, as he himself had supposed, represent the crowning achievement of philosophy in the sense of its finality or end. Of subsequent thinkers some have raised primary objection to, for example, the exceedingly abstract (mentalist or 'idealist') nature of his characterization of the relations between the subject and object of experience. But while seeking to bring both subject and object 'down to earth' by identifying the subject with, say, man as a natural species or, in a different version, the proletariat, and the object with physical, or physical and social, nature, many have retained his vision of the subject as a transitionally dispersed but ultimately to be reintegrated unity; from this point of view the consciousnesses of individual men might be regarded as nothing but so many facets of this dispersion. Others, on the other hand, have objected primarily, or at least equally, to this assumption of overall unity, that is to say to the thesis according to which subjects in the plural (and as plural appearing, therefore, as objects for each other) have to be understood, together indeed with everything that is object as such, in the light of their ultimate reunification within the totality of the subject as One. For them, on the contrary, dispersal, diversity and irremediable lack of any guaranteed overall synthesis or unity have to be accepted as the condition of human thought, language and life.

The dissolution of the bonds of ultimate, systematic unity does not necessarily take us back, however, to a plurality of subjects each unproblematically located within the limited integrity of its own individual consciousness and secure at least in the possession and mastery of the meaning of its own thought. If, for instance, the possibility of a subject or agent conscious of itself as such is bound up with that of its own self-expression or articulation through concepts: if the possibility of the formation and meaningful employment of concepts has to be understood as in effect the possibility of language: if language has to be seen as essentially social or public in terms of its own primary possibility: and if the meaning of what is said or thought at any one moment lies as much in the ways in which it differs from what *else*, within the whole open range of possibilities that language may provide or suggest, *might* have been said or thought as in the words that have in fact been pronounced in the thoughts that have in fact occurred: then the networks of relations, both social and conceptual, on which the practical and constitutive possibility of language depend, or in which they consist, must always precede in order of both logical and temporal priority the formation of any individual consciousness as such. The subject, and *a fortiori* the subject as individual consciousness, is thus displaced from its role as source and author of meaning. It has to learn to look upon itself as a secondary or derivative phenomenon dependent for its own self-conscious existence on those networks of meaning that precede it – networks which are themselves, moreover, never completable, never closed, never definitively systematizable into assured and self-consistent unities. And if the meaning of 'my own' situation and 'my own' discourse resides primarily in such a ramifying network of relations, then there must always be more to this meaning than can possibly be made determinate or meet my own eye at any particular moment. It is only by an optical illusion that the meaning of 'my own' discourse, works, thought or texts can be regarded as being properly my own.

Philosophy in the English-speaking world has not in its mainstream development, of course, reacted to the Kantian dilemmas by following through on the paths opened up by the fathers of German Idealism and characterized subsequently by the reactions to which this speculative form of philosophy gave characteristic rise. This is not, very evidently, to say that the problems of self-identity, of self-knowledge and of other minds have not remained high on the agenda. But by and large – for once again broad generalizations cannot pretend to accuracy of detail – the dominant 'Anglo-Saxon' retreat from and consequent bypassing of the entanglements of transcendental philosophy, whether in the form of an attempted renewal, updating and refinement of the Cartesian tradition or, on the contrary, in that of a rejection of private consciousness as the basis of meaning and experience, has tended to take it robustly for granted that the world is inhabited by recognizably individual human beings, that 'we' are those beings and that it is such beings as 'us' who, under whatever influences, are, nevertheless and for example, the authors of the articles and books that 'we' write. One can and must ask, no doubt, on the basis of such an assumption, how it in fact comes about that 'we' use the concepts of 'self' and 'person' that we do. What is their precise – or imprecise – meaning? What is their basis in the facts of experience as it is and how, were this experience to become very different from what we now understand it to be, might concepts such as these also be expected to change? But these are to be understood as problems, however difficult, of conceptual analysis; I may be deeply unconfident as to the accuracy of my analysis of the concept (or concepts) of self-identity, but, even if I have, like Hume, to confess myself in the end unable to give any adequate account of what I may be justified in taking myself to mean when I refer to 'myself' or to what 'I' may think or have done, I may still take myself to be justified in affirming that it is I who has thought or has done it.

Indeed, it is tempting to add, this is surely the only reasonable assumption to make. It is only on this assumption that I can ever regard myself as responsible for anything that I may think, say or do; and only on this assumption that I can ever engage in any self-conscious learning process whatsoever. We might even seek to return via this route to Kant and to say with him not only that this assumption is reasonable but that, from the perspective of self-conscious thought, it is, *qua* assumption, inescapable. (Though it must also be noted that if we return to the Kantian form of the assumption, we return likewise to the Kantian problems concerning the nature of the subject to whom conscious thought has to attribute itself.)

It goes without saying, of course, that even those philosophers most deeply within the influence of the tradition of transcendental philosophy and its varied succession (of further transformation or of rejection that originates from within) are perfectly capable of using the whole range of personal pronouns and of reporting, when called upon to do so, the basic facts of their own everyday lives. What they may find problematic, however, is the 'philosophical' significance of so doing, and particularly problematic, therefore, any attempt to report on 'their own' philosophical activities. But if this has to be regarded as problematic, then any response to a request for such a report by an unself-questioningly first-person narrative could only be taken, if not as a sign of ignorance or refusal of this whole nest of issues, then as a deliberate and philosophically non-neutral device for confronting and dealing with them – and in its own turn, therefore, as correspondingly problematic. Alternatively, one might go to the opposite extreme of avoiding explicitly first-person reporting altogether and of responding by the provision of a sample, as it were, of the work attached to one's name, chosen or constructed in terms appropriate to the request and the context. Or one might seek to work out some more or less complex combination or interplay of these two modes of response, perhaps by way of the construction of a context of response within which the use of the personal pronoun might take on some more clearly delineated significance, which in more general contexts it might lack. In one way or another, at any rate, the subject, being thus problematic, may come to be treated within a text not simply as an object of discussion, but as belonging to the conditions of production of the text itself. And one way in which the subject (the author) of a text may respond to the problem of its own status in relation to what, before the problem is seen as a problem, may unproblematically be called its own productions, is, precisely, to disappear, to dis-integrate, to disperse into the play of words that gives to these productions *their* own characteristic 'texture'.

Considerations of this nature are not – of course – to be attributed as such to any of the contributors to this book. They may nevertheless form a background against which the subject's loss of confidence in the security of its own access to itself or in its certainty of the meaning of its own conscious thinking, even in the assured reality of its own autonomous status as subject, may be more readily understood. To them may be added those other (but partially related) considerations that lie behind the loss of confidence in the general sense or security of the distinction between stating or reporting and other forms of discursive activity. If I am asked to report on what I do as a philosopher, I also need to know with some reasonable confidence what is to count as a report.

One way in which these two sets of considerations may be connected is by reference to the at first sight unremarkable point that the very notion of a report carries with it that of some sort of distinction between a reporter, that which is reported and the audience to whom the report is addressed (even if in the limiting case this might be no other than the reporter himself). A report is only distinguishable from other forms of discursive activity insofar as it may in principle be either (or more or less) true or false. But how are the notions of truth and falsity themselves to be understood? In the context of a report, at any rate, they must surely have something to do with the degree to which – or the way in which – the report is 'adequate' to that which is reported. But this distinction between the reporter and the reported, even in the case where what is reported is some 'given' state or activity of the reporter, turns out to be but one more version of that earlier overall distinction between the 'subject' and the 'object', and must in consequence carry with it all the same problematic features. Insofar, anyhow, as one is thinking within the tradition that goes back to Kant, the tradition of transcendental philosophy, one is bound to follow Kant in asking how the 'I' that reports can be distinct from and yet at the same time identical with the 'I' whose state or activities are reported. If truth as 'adequation' or 'objectivity', and truthful or untruthful reporting, only arise as possibilities within the space of a distinction between subject and object, we find ourselves back with the question of how the subject as the principle of synthetic activity constitutive of the context of this distinction itself could ever hope to report on its own productive activity without either distortion or remainder. It may be, as has been most influentially argued, that behind this conception of truth as fidelity to its object must lie the prior activity of truth-as-disclosure, the disclosure of a world in which the subject finds itself already involved in ambiguous relations with an always redeterminable object; but how, in that case, is one to proceed to the disclosure of disclosure itself? Certainly not by way of a subject's straightforward report on the object of its own activity as subject, if the (perhaps cultural) matrix out of which both subject and object emerge must somehow precede them both. Any attempted report on *this* 'state of affairs' must of necessity be always both more and less than a report; and ways must be sought of revealing it other than through 'adequate' statement alone.

In following these (admittedly not very analytically philo-sophical) lines of thought we have already linked up with the second of my original by-and-large generalizations. 'A significant number of the participants are committed to a view of philosophy as having an indissociable, and perhaps never fully expressible, "practical" dimension. Typically, but not invariably, an acute awareness of this dimension even of their own contribution to this volume may play a problematic part in the fashioning of that contribution.' Of course, the deep but somewhat tortuous route signposted above is not the only one by which one may come to an awareness of this sort. A much more immediately recognizable route to those who have studied philosophy in the analytic tradi-tion might, for instance, pass by way of a reflection upon the implications of speech act theory.

It is by now almost a commonplace that whenever one pro-duces any unit of discourse, of speech or of writing, a word, a sentence, a whole allocution, article or book, one is necessarily doing many different things at once; that is to say, there are many, even an indefinite number of descriptions under which one's action may be brought. Indeed, it is one of the main preoccupations of speech act theory to try and provide some systematic characterization of the different types of circumstance – conventional, institutional, contingently causal – within which the production of different forms of writing or speech may result in different forms of speech act or action. Obviously enough, considerations of this sort must apply to the whole range of production of all the varied forms of 'philosophical' discourse itself. In doing philosophy, as one says, whether in speech or in writing, whether indeed on one's own or in relation to or with others, one is necessarily doing many other sorts of thing as well; and there is no reason to suppose that even all the most evidently possible descriptions under which his actions might appropriately be brought must have been present to the mind of the producer of any particular instance of discourse or even, if it comes to that, have been available to him. The subject, if one likes to put it that way, has no monopoly of or privileged access to the multiple significance of his own acts of discourse; nor is there any good reason for supposing that there could exist any such thing as the totality, systematic or otherwise, of all those descriptions under which, from one perspective or another, his actions might be brought.

So far, so commonplace. But what follows from these commonplaces may turn out to be both more complex and more controversial. Here, for the sake of brevity, we may sum up the questions that may arise as being, first, whether one can, while recognizing the multiple potential dimensions or aspects of one's actions in producing, say, a philosophical lecture or text, nevertheless make and maintain some fairly sharp distinction between those which are of properly philosophical relevance and those which are not; and, secondly, if such distinctions as can be made have to be regarded as neither sharp, hard, fast, fixed or determinate, what implication the recognition of this state of affairs might have for the further continuation of one's 'philosophical' production?

Even for the sake of brevity, the answers to such questions cannot reasonably be argued out in so short a space. Happily, however, the needs of an introduction include no call to try and settle upon firm answers. It will be enough here to note one or two pertinent points and to follow through – in a merely preliminary way – one or two suppositions.

First, then, we may note that, nowadays and in the mainstream tradition of analytic philosophy at any rate, philosophy is to be reckoned among the cognitive forms of discourse. But the distinction between the cognitive and the non-cognitive forms, including, of course, except incidentally, the main forms of literary discourse, is tightly bound up with that between those which lay claim to assessment by reference to criteria of truth or validity and those which do not. If philosophy is essentially structured as *argument*, then indeed it must be a necessary condition of its success that the links in its chains be valid and its premises and conclusions true (and where the status of arguments is concerned, the truth which is at stake, the truth of the propositional elements which constitute its premises, its intermediary steps and its conclusions, is more naturally to be associated with 'adequation' than with 'world-disclosure'). No doubt, there are also many other criteria to be met; relevance to the matters in hand, generality, conceptual creativity . . . the list will be endless and inherently controversial. No doubt, too, other grounds of distinction must be at work. Neither all valid arguments nor all true statements are as such to be reckoned as philosophically relevant. And certainly one may reasonably regard the distinction between philosophical significance and non-significance as being essentially contestable in the sense that the attempt (as, indeed, the refusal) to make any such distinction must itself necessarily raise characteristically philosophical issues. It is true, too, that many forms of speech act or performance other than those of assertion and the production of arguments are to be found within the textures of what even the most analytically minded philosophers would nevertheless recognize as philosophical discourse; invitations (to imagine this or that), suppositions, questions and so on. Still, it also remains true – and this, significantly, is the second sentence in succession which starts thus with an appeal to truth – that the making of distinctions, the elaboration of arguments and the construction of theories lies at the heart of contemporary analytic philosophy, and that where non-argumentative procedures are employed, it is virtually always in order to bring about certain forms of understanding, even in the case of those philosophers who would maintain that not all that can be understood can necessarily be stated.

Let us suppose, then, that these are distinctions which it is in general possible to make. No doubt, the very nature of the concepts concerned is not such as to admit of sharp or rigid boundaries, but let us suppose that we can distinguish confidently enough between, on the one hand, the validity of an argument, its pertinence to other arguments, the truth or falsity of its conclusions and the wealth or poverty of its insights and, on the other hand, all those other attributes which, in the contexts of its production or its reproduction, it may equally be recognized to have: its impact on political or moral circumstances, on institutional or personal relations, its contribution to the career prospects of its author, to the reinforcement or undermining of one set of structures of power and influence or another, its entertainment value, its educational function and so on. Clearly, it may form part of what is recognized to be the proper business of philosophy to draw attention to the existence (and conditions of existence) of all these aspects of discourse, including the varying productions of philosophical discourse itself. But what is not so clear – indeed, it is clearly controversial – is whether the recognition of all these potential features of his own philosophical production should be taken into account by the philosopher not only in the course of their diagnosis and analysis, but also and already in the very fashioning of what he produces.

What sorts of considerations might serve as a basis on which to answer this question? Evidently, there may well be, for instance, strong political reasons for shaping the direction of one's philosophical work towards the production of certain sorts of political effects. But the question is precisely whether these reasons should be understood as having any sort of relevance for the 'philosopher as such'. We have already agreed to suppose that we may be confident enough in our ability to distinguish between what it is to understand and what it is, say, to influence, to advise or to manipulate. If philosophy arises primarily in response to the demand for understanding, how can considerations of political import be of unmediated or direct philosophical import? But then understanding may have a practical as well as a theoretical dimension. Is not the performer's understanding of the nature of his own performance to be found as it shows itself not only in the explicit content, but also in the whole manner of his performance? If, for instance, I am to be taken as genuinely understanding that my philosophical performance is, in the time and context of its production, also and equally and in virtue of many of the very same conditions which determine its philosophical dimension, a performance of political significance, then whether I choose to stage it as if in ignorance of that significance or not, I must naturally be presumed to do so in full knowledge of what I am doing – including the knowledge that to act as if I could divest my action is not only a philosophical but also a political decision, with its own political as well as philosophical significance. In full knowledge (which must as always include the paradoxical self-recognition that it can never be total) . . . and therefore in proportionately full responsibility? For in what else, if in anything, could philosophical responsibility itself consist if not in the acceptance of responsibility for fashioning one's philosophical performances in the light of everything that one believes oneself to understand about the conditions and the nature of the performance?

This is, of course, no more than a sketch of one possible line of argument; nor, once again and equally of course, should it be attributed as such to any of the contributors to this volume. But, and whether one is inclined to accept it, or any of its possible modifications, or not, it may provide another possible perspective from which the transformation of philosophical argument into philosophical-and-more-than-merely-philosophical performance may itself appear more readily understandable. It is also worth noting that if one does find oneself led in the direction of such an understanding, one will by the same token be led towards some adjustment of the criteria by which philosophical performances or productions are to be assessed. 'Truth' and 'validity' will remain as important, even indispensable values; but they may no longer be seen as playing the same central, privileged and easily distinguishable role. The appropriateness of a performance to the context of its staging lies . . . precisely in its appropriateness. Insofar as the performance is one of statement or of argument, then this appropriateness must, in all paradigmatic cases at any rate, be assessable in terms of validity and truth. But if statement and argument are only aspects of the performance as an open, non-totalizable whole, then truth and validity can equally be no more than aspects of its overall appropriateness. One might say, perhaps, that insofar as the performance continues to demand assessment as philosophy, to that extent indeed it can never altogether detach itself from statement and argument and hence from considerations of truth and validity, and that, to this extent, these values retain after all a certain position of privilege; but also that, insofar as philosophy seeks to embody as full a self-understanding as possible, statement and argument, truth and validity, can no longer be seen as able to tell or to evaluate the whole of the story.

It should be repeated, no doubt, even in two paragraphs running, that neither the terms nor the peculiar intent of any of the above arguments are to be attributed as such to any of the contributors to this volume. (Nor should the arguments be taken as laying claim to unhesitating acceptance just as they stand; even in the best of cases, they would need much more and much more careful adjustment.) But it is noteworthy how many of the contributors – though by no means, of course, all of them – regard philosophy, in one way or another, as in part or even essentially performance, a performance produced in interrelationship with all sorts of adjacent performances and one that can only be understood in its own peculiar nature in the light of these interrelationships; and some of these have, or so it seems to me, to be understood as presenting their own contributions in the light of that self-understanding.

There remain for comment two of my four tentative generalizations, and already this Introduction is more than long enough; so further comment must be very brief. 'A significant number of the participants seem to regard themselves as standing alone, or almost alone, in whatever part of the field it is that they occupy.' If this *is* so, then the significance will not lie in any peculiar personal characteristic or circumstance of those of whom this generalization is more or less true, but rather in the nature of the institutions, in the most general sense of that term, in which they find or have found themselves working. These institutions include not only the *lycées*, the universities and other institutions of higher learning, considered in terms of their structures, organization and conventions (and the relations, within these contexts, between philosophy and other institutionally recognized disciplines), but also the institutions of access to publication, the media, the rules (formal and informal) of appointment and advancement, the relations between Paris and the provinces, those between the French and non-French-speaking worlds in general, and so on; they may include also, perhaps, the notably different and in France more openly intimate relationships between philosophy on the one hand and both politics and religion on the other than those which have generally prevailed, in recent times at any rate, in the English-speaking world. (It is further true, of course, that there is a very great numerical disparity between the potential world audience of any writer writing in English and of one writing in French; but what is striking here is the frequency of a sense of isolation within the Francophone context itself.)

It would be well beyond my present scope – or, alas, competence – to attempt anything like an analysis of the nature of these institutions or of the interplay between them and the very texture of the (very varied) forms of philosophy that is produced within or in relation to them. (Reference to this interplay is anyhow to be found among the contributions which follow.) But it is at least a worthwhile hypothesis that the conditions under which philosophical communication has both to take place and conceive of itself as taking place should, in their more or less imperfect coincidence, contribute very largely to the actual nature of its performance. It would, of course, be grossly caricatural to suggest that the most appropriate ways of taking certain texts could be simply (or even unsimply) read off from the institutional contexts of their production. But it may still be helpful to readers more familiar with a very different set of institutional contexts to remember not only that these differences may be very subtle as well as very great, but also that these very differences may play a part in determining how relatively close or remote may be the relations between text and context from one case to another.

As to the fourth generalization, it calls perhaps for no further comment, but only for yet a further warning repetition. 'None of the above generalizations would seem to apply to *all* of the contributors here gathered together and, though there may well be certain links between one generalization and another, these links fall far short of constituting identity of application.' It is surely one of the virtues of this collection of essays that it should demonstrate so clearly the vigorous and disputatious diversity of contemporary French philosophy; there is philosophy, if not for all, at any rate for many different tastes and interests. One can never reasonably expect to be able to step with instant understanding into the middle of an ongoing debate without having to devote some considerable effort to picking up the threads of its background. It is surely another of the merits of these essays that together they provide such strong indication of how worthwhile the effort could prove to be.

PIERRE BOURDIEU

The philosophical institution

In the beginning is the *illusio*, adherence to the game, the belief of whoever is caught in the game, the interest for the game, interest *in* the game, the founding of value, *investment* in both the economic and the psychoanalytic sense. The institution is inseparable from the founding of a game, which as such is arbitrary, and from the constitution of the disposition to be taken in by the game, whereby we lose sight of the arbitrariness of its founding and, in the same stroke, recognize the necessity of the institution. *Esse est interesse*: Being is being in, it is belonging and being possessed, in short, participating, taking part, according importance, interest. Interest in the broadest sense is, *a parte objecti*, what interests someone, what matters to (*interest*) him in a thing, a person, a situation, etc., and, *a parte subjecti*, the disposition of whoever feels concerned, touched, and who enters into the game, invests something in it, ascribes value, finds it 'worthwhile', hence whoever acts or reacts. The generalization of the tendency to think in terms of calculations called for by the logic of the economy makes us forget that interest is opposed not only to *disinterestedness*, whose manifestation is to be found in generosity, but also to *disinterest*, to the indifference which discerns no difference, shows no preference, for which 'it's all the same', Tweedle Dee or Tweedle Dum. One can therefore be interested, find an interest in something which is at stake, at issue, without being or seeming self-interested, that is, inspired by the search for economic profit: this is what La Rochfoucauld tirelessly repeats when he reminds us that generosity, free giving and pardon can have their source in a form of interest.

Social existence is dependence; it is participating in a game, which is social life, life itself. The principle that makes us enter into the race of all against all, the principle of competition, productive of agents who act, who are shaken out of their quietude, out of their apathy, out of inappetence, out of indifference, is nothing other than the game itself, or, more exactly, the field of struggle in which *illusio* arises, the involvement in the game, the belief in the game, investment, the principle of all truly social energy. Traditional wisdom says nothing other than this, but gives expression to it in a normative mode; involvement in the world is held to be the illusion *par excellence*, the digression which leads away and distracts from what is essential, and no way is seen of escaping from the world's grasp or from its temptations, such as ambition and the taste for honours, except by fleeing into the 'desert' like the hermit who retreats into solitude, thus leaving all social games behind. And if the 'vanities of this world' have been perceived more often than the other social stakes in their true status as products of collective illusion, this is doubtless because the arbitrary nature of the game is more easily revealed, especially to the eyes of those who are excluded, when, as in life at the court, the stakes are purely symbolic, that is, when they are almost entirely lacking in material substance, and so cannot become objects of physical scarcity, but are more directly and more completely tied to the competition which constitutes them as scarce goods, albeit of an arbitrary and artificial scarceness.[1] On the other hand, the material nature and the limited physical supply of what is at stake makes it easy to overlook the fact that the functioning of the economic game itself presupposes adherence to the game and belief in the value of its stakes. Materialism, which leads us to believe that material conditions determine belief, causes us to forget that belief – the belief in the primacy of material conditions – is also at the basis of materialism. Thus it is forgotten that materialism too is itself the product of material conditions, those very conditions which lead to the recognition of the primacy of material stakes (and material conditions). Whence the missing question, concealed by what is left of utopianism in 'scientific materialism': if investment in the economic game is itself the product of a certain economic game, how can this game be destroyed without destroying the investment? And if it is the same logic which both brings about investment and makes us enter into competition, as the race of all against all that gives rise both to the pursuit of personal interest and to individuation, how is it possible to produce that minimal investment which is the condition of economic production without resorting to competition and without reproducing individuation?[2]

As long as the logic of social games is not explicitly recognized as such (and even if it is, for mere conscious awareness is not sufficient to dissipate the illusion), even the apparently freest and most creative of actions is never more than an encounter between reified and embodied history, between habitus and the necessity immanent in a field, a necessity which the agent constitutes as such and for which he provides the scene of action without actually being its subject: to write the resolution of a musical chord is, as Adorno observes, to realize those tendencies immanent in the musical material which are constituted as 'natural' necessity by virtue of their relation with the musical competence of the composer. The most fundamental reasons for acting are rooted in the *illusio*, that is in the relation, itself not recognized as such, between a field of play and a habitus, as that sense of the game which confers on the game and on its stakes their determining or, better, their *motivating* power.[3] The arbitrary founding of value and of sense, an arbitrary founding which is unaware of itself as such and which is lived as the submission to a natural necessity or to universal values, *illusio*, investment, involvement, interest, all these are products of the logic of a field and serve, in turn, as the condition of its functioning. The establishment of history in things and in bodies causes the body politic, like the biological body, to be inhabited by a sort of tendency to persevere in its state of being, and to place individuals in the service of its own production.

In this way, sociology discovers at the source of social life, as a sort of founding *datum*, that which traditional wisdom has always denounced as an escape into worldly games and their stakes. But rather than leaving no other choice than one between the investment of utter commitment or an absolute detachment, which may either be lived as an experience of the absurd or be sublimated into a deliberately total quietude, sociology offers the possibility of a practical *epoche*, which can find its first and most urgent application in the very area where the specific interests and investments of the thinker are constituted, that is to say, in the intellectual field. Unlike practical or scholarly knowledge of the laws of the game, a mastery of the game and its stakes which presupposes actual alienation in the game, knowledge of the game *qua* game, provides the ability to dominate both the game itself (that is to say, to dominate the domination exerted by the laws of the game) and the *illusio* which is at one and the same time the effect and the principle of this domination.

If there is a question that philosophy, itself so questioning, manages to exclude, this is the question of its own socially necessary conditions.[4] Resembling the artist in this respect, the philosopher sets himself up as an uncreated creator, a creator whom there is no getting around and who owes nothing to the institution.[5] The distance from the institution (and, more precisely, from the socially instituted post) which the institution itself allows him, is one of the reasons why he finds it difficult to think of himself in the framework of an institution; and difficult to cease to be its instrument and its plaything, even in his institutionally directed games with the institution. Every attempt to bring philosophy into question which is not bound up with a questioning of the philosophical institution itself still plays the institution's game by merely playing with fire, by rubbing up against the limits of the sacred circle, while still carefully refraining from moving outside it.

To bring to light the mechanisms through which the philosophical game works on those who, by agreeing to play it, tacitly commit themselves to identifying the interest of philosophy with the interest that they have in philosophy, is to give oneself an opportunity for a real freedom in relation to determinisms which are left untouched by every methodological doubt and by every *epoche*. Freedom in relation to the censorships imposed by the hierarchies established in the way things are and in people's minds, by the hierarchy of canonical texts (which places Parmenides, for example, highest and Epicurus lowest), by the hierarchy of subjects, which relegates to the unnameable all those subjects that current tradition has not constituted as worthy of philosophizing upon, by the hierarchy of styles, which demands or recommends as suitably important this or that variant of discourse, this or that rhetoric of profundity or radicality; freedom in relation to those strategies of domination and of defence of the status of philosophy as the dominant discipline (strategies of classification of the sciences, of epistemology, etc.), which obscure its relation to the sciences and, in particular, to the social sciences.

Philosophers like to ask: 'What is thinking?' But they never ask what are the necessary social conditions for that particular way of performing the activity of thinking which defines the thinker, he who thinks the nature of thinking (by asking, for example, 'What is thinking?') or, to put it more simply, the philosopher as he is conceived of in the university, in fashionable circles or in the press? Does what philosophers think, what they can and especially what they cannot think (starting with the social conditions of thinking, of their own thinking and of their social being as thinkers), owe anything to these conditions? Is there any possible way of thinking which would allow one to think the possibility of *freedom* in relation to these conditions? Perhaps, instead of denying, as if by magic, the limits that every form of thinking owes to its social conditions of production and of operation, one should instead work to deny them in practice on the basis of a critical knowledge of these limits. It is in this way, for example, that the critique of intellectualism and of 'intellectualocentrism', which prohibits the intellectual from thinking practice as practice, is not in itself the end of this critique: it aims only to provide an orientation for the work required to free the intellectual from those limits that derive from his position as intellectual and, in particular, from all those that have their source in the illusion of intellectual freedom with respect to social conditioning. More precisely, the incapacity of both philosophy and social science to comprehend practice – and more especially a practice as fully and entirely practical as ritual practice – lies in the fact that, just as in Kant reason locates the principle of its judgements not in itself but in the nature of its objects, so the scholarly thinking of practice includes within practice the scholarly relation to practice. This is to say that the critique of intellectualism which is at one and the same time epistemological and sociological, is not just one moment in a social polemic leading to the relativization of all intellectual production, but is rather the most radical form of a critique of theoretical reason, which aims at grasping, in order to transcend them, the limits inherent in all scholarly knowledge.[6]

Thus, to objectivize the conditions for the production of producers and consumers of philosophical discourse, as well as those

necessary for this discourse itself to function as properly authorized discourse, as a discourse of authority, is to give oneself an
opportunity to perform a true *epoche* with regard to the founding
belief inherent in participation in the philosophical game, that is
to say, not only the belief in the value of philosophy as such, of the
philosopher and of philosophical activity, but also the adherence
to all that is unreflectingly inscribed in the very logic of the field,
and which provides the basis of tacit agreement on the subjects
worthy of disagreement, on the themes and problems worthy or
unworthy of discussion, etc. etc. This is likewise to give oneself a
chance to apprehend all that philosophical discourse may owe to
the social conditions that make it possible, such as the inclination
to logocentrism and to theoreticism which is inscribed in the
scholè of the schools, or that propensity to deny the social and
political world which is encouraged by the way in which the
academic world shuts itself up in itself, with its protected market
(with a clientèle regularly guaranteed by examination subjects,
etc.), with its extreme inertia, which is that of a body almost
entirely in control of its own reproduction, and so on. We can see,
for example, that there is surely less to be gained by going from
the philosophical ideas of university philosophers to their idea of
the University than from their ideas on the University to their
philosophical ideas, the latter being often the product of the
universalization of the presuppositions of a university world
which university professors tend to think of as coextensive with
the universe. And one could wager that the speculative categories
structuring the thought of thinkers owe a great deal, as I have
tried to show with regard to the *Critique of Judgement*, not only to
their position in the social realm, but also, as a reading of the
Conflict of the Faculties shows, to the structure of the university
world, whose own divisions and hierarchies tend to impose
themselves as structuring principles of the general world view.[7]

The science of the institution provides the polemics of science
against the institution, that is against reified history, history as a
thing, closed history, with all its strength. It permits a break with
the tradition of *cultured reading* (*lecture lettrée*) which, under the
guise of breathing new life into the letter of what is written by
supplying the variants and the variations allowed for by the
legitimate definition of what it is to read a text, assures the
perpetuation both of the letter and that of the sacralized rela-

tionship to it. If it is impossible for science ever to free itself completely from institutional acts and discourses (and from the correlative marks of authority and censorship), it at least allows of some control both over the motivations of the discourses or actions which are produced in the mechanics of the field and over the automatisms of dead thought (reified categories of thought, fossilized oppositions, etc.), whose real subject is the intellectual field and its history. Thus, it is on condition that they take what is indeed the greatest possible risk, namely that of bringing into question and into danger the philosophical game itself, the game to which their own *existence* as philosophers, or their own participation in the game, is linked, that philosophers can assure for themselves the privilege that they almost always forget to claim, that is to say their freedom in relation to everything that authorizes and justifies them in calling themselves and thinking of themselves as philosophers.

Translated by Kathleen McLaughlin

NOTES

1 The unreality of court life (one can think of Monsieur de Phaeneste, a man of seeming and appearance) is doubtless one of the bases of the baroque theme of life as 'dream', as theatre. And it is not by chance that literature expresses today the absurdity of worldly investments through the metaphor of the game, an occasion for extraordinary, even desperate, effort that may end in the null result of a draw; (cf. the rugby match in Claude Simon, *Gulliver*, Paris: Calmann-Levy, 1952, p. 43).

2 The social economy as such does not obey the laws of the economy in the narrow sense recognized by economists. In the economy of the most exclusively symbolic goods, smiles, esteem, affection, attentions, recognitions, kindnesses, etc., one can both 'have one's cake and eat it'. (The limits of absolute generosity reside not in what is given, as in the case of material goods, but in the time which is required for the giving and which can make up the entire value of the gift.) Whence perhaps derives the impression that, in the exchange of economic capital for symbolic capital, the one who gives economic capital is repaid in sham coin, in a thoroughly 'symbolic' fashion, as we also say. I give you a million and you give me your esteem; I can no longer give my million to anyone else, whereas you can once again accord your esteem. (There is no perfect system of accounting for exchanges between different types of capital.) From this perhaps stems also the

fact of the institution of exclusive exchanges: he who is paid in esteem, protection, etc., tends to insist on an exclusive right to the symbolic good he receives, not only because this good loses its distinctive value by being made public, but also because it is given in exchange for goods which cannot be given to others.

3 The relation to the sacred, whether of a religious or an artistic nature, is only one particular – and limited – case of the enchanted or fetishistic relation to the social world, which is the initial and primitive form of the experience of this world.

4 It is significant that the Marxist tradition is itself no exception: scientific studies of the socially necessary conditions for the production of the canonical texts and their successive interpretations are extremely rare and only partial – as if the competition for the monopoly of the legitimate reading, of which all the great philosophies are the object, above all of this particular tradition because of its political implications, had inhibited the turning back upon itself of the critical power which this theory contains.

5 The history of philosophy in its canonical form takes no account of the social conditions of the production of philosophical discourse and, especially, of the philosopher: indeed, the diversity of the philosophies of the history of philosophy which are involved, most often implicitly in this history (just as those that construe the various philosophies as but so many different historical realizations of the same *philosophia perennis*, or as so many incommensurable and incommunicable points of view on the world, etc.) must not obscure the basic consensus concerning the irreducibility of philosophical discourse to any social determination, the necessary correlate to the philosopher's ability to reflect upon himself better than anyone else.

6 Cf. P. Bourdieu, *Le sens pratique*, Paris: Les Editions de Minuit, 1980.

7 Cf. P. Bourdieu, 'Eléments pour une critique "vulgaire" des critiques "pures" ' in *La Distinction, Critique sociale du jugement de goût*, Paris: Les Editions de Minuit, 1979, pp. 565–85.

JACQUES BOUVERESSE

Why I am so very unFrench

I

In trying to meet the wishes of the editor of the present work I am, obviously, faced with a peculiarly difficult, if not to say insoluble, problem. My participation in a project of this nature has, at first sight, a totally paradoxical aspect in that (1) I can in no sense be considered a representative or influential contemporary French philosopher, (2) I do not claim, and have never claimed, any genuine originality in my manner of treating the questions that have interested me, and (3) what I have tried to do will certainly be much more comprehensible to the English-speaking philosophical public than to that to which I have addressed myself or which I have tried to help create in France. The only thing that would need to be explained to the English-speaking reader is, no doubt, the fact that I should have adopted from the start such an unorthodox position in relation to my own native philosophical milieu and that I should have shown so little interest in the productions most characteristic of contemporary French philosophy.

It is a fact that I have found a good part of the philosophical literature published in France since the 1960s quite simply unreadable and that its interest has seemed to me in many cases to be of a documentary or sociological rather than of a properly philosophical nature; I have found myself almost immediately disconcerted and put off by its highly idiosyncratic, astonishingly marginal and provincial character: a character which sticks out a mile whenever, for one reason or another, one is led to consider it from the outside, and which, moreover, explains to a large extent the remarkable fascination that it continues to exert abroad. For want of producing anything really important and lasting, French philosophy of today can at least flatter itself with producing things which resemble nothing else and which, indeed, do not seem possible anywhere else. Bearing in mind the central importance it explicitly attributes to 'seduction' in the art of writing and of pleasing, which, most often, takes the place of any theory of philosophical argumentation, I feel justified in saying quite simply that this so widely reputed seduction has, in general, had no effect upon me. This is, after all, a result that it is only fair to expect in certain cases, when such a systematic use is made of 'arguments' of this kind. Nietzsche said that France 'has always had a masterly aptitude for converting even the portentous crises of its spirit into something charming and seductive'.[1] At the risk of appearing unjust, even in the eyes of foreign readers, I must confess that French philosophy over the past forty years seems to me on the whole to have been remarkably successful in effecting the transmutation described by Nietzsche.

To be considered an 'analytic' philosopher in France is not an altogether comfortable situation, especially when one considers that the expression 'analytic philosophy' continues to be used most often as a synonym for 'logical positivism' and, moreover, that the ideas of logical positivism are generally caricatured in a most improbable way. I have even been told that my own works were practically unreadable by the French philosophical public because they were concerned essentially with 'logic' (which meant in addition that they were not in any event worth reading, inasmuch as they contained nothing that was properly philosophical). When Frege referred to the reaction of philosophers who, at the mere sight of a formula, exclaimed: *mathematica sunt, non leguntur*, he doubtless did not foresee that this same reaction would also be provoked by works which contain no formulae at all, that is, not only by logic as such, but also by the philosophy of logic, because of the relatively technical character which springs necessarily from the nature of its object, by all those philosophies which are inspired in various ways directly or indirectly by logic, and finally even by the commentaries and discussions, however nuanced and critical, to which these philosophies give rise. To understand what I mean one has only to note that Wittgenstein, for example, is still regularly classified here not only as a 'logical positivist', but also as a 'logician' (which says a great deal about the idea which the French have both of Wittgenstein and of contemporary logic).

If I speak of things I have 'heard said' about myself, this is because I have, all in all, no real indication by which I could tell whether my works have exerted any sort of positive or negative influence, inasmuch as they have occasioned only a certain purely formal and inconsequential approbation, certain objections on principle (in particular political ones) unrelated to their content, and, for the rest, a total lack of interest or reaction one way or the other. A French philosopher who openly displayed his sympathy for the analytic tradition at the time I began to do so – I do not believe that, in my case, one could speak exactly of belonging to it – could, even in the best of cases, never hope to be considered as anything but marginal or eccentric by the French philosophical milieu or as anything more than a mere chronicler or a more or less gifted imitator by the official representatives of the tradition in question. It is obvious that someone working on his own and almost entirely self-taught, and who is forced to confront an indifferent or hostile environment, can hardly hope to entertain the ambition of obtaining results in any way comparable to those of philosophers benefiting from the decisive advantages offered by the fact of belonging to a well-established tradition and by their use of proven methods of research and discussion, methods which have long formed part of their philosophical consensus.

As regards analytic philosophy, it is certain that the situation in France is today incomparably better than it was when I first started to become interested in it. But I do not think that the efforts made by a few 'eccentrics' have contributed a great deal to this change in attitude. The interest it appears to generate at the present time is basically due to the relative vacuum that has prevailed during the past few years and to the temporary openness to new ideas that has resulted from it. There is every reason to believe that if it really manages to win a place on the market or, rather, in what could more crudely and appropriately be called 'the bordello of ideas', to use Pierre Boulez's expression, this will once again be thanks to a passing fashion, probably just as superficial and ephemeral as those that have preceded it.

It has, indeed, been possible to read in the Press on a number of occasions that analytic philosophy has now become 'fashionable' in France. This has reminded me of the epoch in the not so distant past when someone had only to succeed in publishing a modest article on Carnap or Quine, without any particular apologetic intention, for the guardians of the integrity of our national philosophical culture to rush to warn the innocent public against the secret invasion of logical positivism. When it is said that analytic philosophy has become fashionable, this must be understood as meaning simply that to speak about it is no longer absolutely forbidden – which, for those for whom even this relaxation seems already much too much, is more or less tantamount to saying that no one any longer talks about anything else. The truth is that the way in which it is talked about at the present time could provide serious reasons for those who did not wait to be authorized by the current philosophical situation to take an interest in analytic philosophy, to regret the days when it was not talked about at all.

It is to be remarked, moreover, that, even before the public's curiosity concerning an as yet strange and little-known reality might have had time to transform itself into a real effort of understanding, voices of authority on all sides are to be heard remarking ironically on the characteristic tendency of French philosophy to discover only after thirty to fifty years' delay things which, by the time of their discovery, no longer present any real interest. On this point the scenario is always the same: at the moment when new things appear, all sorts of good or bad reasons are found to prevent their importance from being recognized; and when there is no longer any apparent obstacle to acknowledging it, then the decisive argument becomes, precisely, that they are by now *no longer* of any importance. There is nothing more comical, and at the same time more distressing, than the self-assured way in which the people who make news always claim to have passed beyond that which they have never passed through: without ever having made the slightest effort to understand anything at all about what philosophers like Frege, Wittgenstein, Russell or Carnap tried to do, they preserve their good conscience with the banal and reassuring observation that even those who are taken to be the successors of these philosophers have long ago ceased to do exactly the same thing and are indeed, for the most part, engaged in something quite different. In other words, the earlier stages of this movement can safely be ignored because they belong nowadays only to past history or to prehistory; and the latter can be ignored just as well either because, despite a few minor changes, they represent an inexplicable persistence in the initial error, or because they consist essentially in the rediscovery of certain self-evident truths, truths which had always been known to those lucky enough to have avoided this useless experience entirely. In short, one might as well say, as much from an historical as from a philosophical point of view, absolutely nothing has happened that merits reflecting upon.

The only important change in this domain is that there exists today in France a certain number of young philosophers who have stopped taking for granted the generally accepted ideas and customary clichés concerning analytic philosophy and who have applied themselves to reading the philosophers in question in exactly the same way as any others, that is, with the same sort of attention and with the same conviction of having something to learn just as much from their failures as from their successes. The only merit that I should claim for myself personally is that of having contributed to a certain extent, both in writing and in teaching, to this evolution. One must not underestimate the importance of this first step, which is always the most difficult to take, and make the mistake of requiring those who are coming into contact for the first time with a foreign tradition to judge it straightaway from the necessary historical and critical distance. Since any hope of modifying the opinions of those already in place is completely vain, one must count, for a long-term improvement, essentially on the change which seems to have occurred in the attitudes of the younger generation and which at least means that the case is no longer judged entirely in advance.

Ever since I began to be interested in analytic philosophy, I have heard people who are almost completely ignorant of it repeat that it is in the process of dying or that it is perhaps already dead. There was a time when it was reproached above all with having what was held to be an anti-philosophical character. Today what is in question is, it seems, more its 'anti-scientific' orientation and its lack of interest in 'true' problems, that is, those which have to do with the knowledge of reality in general and, more precisely, the consequences that can be drawn from the most recent developments in contemporary science. This more 'Popperian' variation on the classical theme of the death of analytic philosophy at least has the merit of posing a problem that is perfectly real. If the analytic tradition arose, as Dummett thinks, out of the dismissal of the theory of knowledge as the fundamental part of philosophy in favour of the theory of meaning or, more broadly, the philosophy of language, it will never find favour in the eyes of those who have renounced once and for all not only any effort to seek a new paradigm for first philosophy, but also any idea that there exists some sort of domain reserved for philosophy alone, that is to say, a range of philosophical problems specifically different from those that are posed elsewhere, in particular in the sciences.

The analytic tradition can in fact be considered one of the last ways of safeguarding the relative autonomy of philosophy and of upholding its claim to the status of a 'fundamental' discipline, at the very time when there is a general tendency to contest the pre-eminent position it is supposed to occupy within our culture as a whole and the special prerogatives it continues to demand. For those who are in favour of a systematic elimination of conventional boundaries and of hierarchical distinctions between the most diverse manifestations of culture and who consider, for example, the sciences, philosophy and literature itself as so many different exercises of the same creative imagination in the service of the same will to 'knowledge' in the broadest sense of the term, a conception such as that of analytic philosophy has every chance of seeming as unsuitable and as obsolete as those which it has supplanted.

However this may be, there is no reason to consider the defence and the promotion of analytic philosophy as constituting, for the moment, the major problem presenting itself in France. For example, it cannot be said that the current situation of philosophy in Germany is itself, despite a traditional prejudice in its favour, much better known or appreciated in any more exact manner. And it is noteworthy that the exchanges and characteristic movements of mutual convergence that have for some time now been taking place between contemporary Anglo-Saxon philosophy and currents that are as specifically 'continental' as phenomenology or hermeneutics, provoke scarcely more curiosity and interest than do the hard-core analytic productions. Everything leads one to believe that the opposition between the analytic and continental traditions is gradually being transformed into a marked anachronism. But it is probable that France will for some time to come continue to make itself ridiculous by combating as a threat that which the philosophy of most other countries will have long ago integrated as a positive and essential contribution. What is considered just about unanimously everywhere else as the current state of philosophy is, it seems, always too modern for our university teaching and too traditional for our avant-garde.

In a comment on a celebrated passage in Hume's *Treatise on Human Nature*, Musil makes the following observation about the situation of philosophy in the contemporary world:

Consequently, one could, in an epoch like that of today, unconcernedly affirm that which one does not know to be objective fact and one would be justified, if the thing is done with an elegant hand, in counting on a greater success than would one who hesitates. Since in Germany, moreover, we have the ideal of a specialized philosophy, written for professional philosophers and removed from any contact with the blissfully loquacious joys and sorrows of real life, one cannot even grumble too much about the fact that there has developed, alongside this, a sort of newspaper and magazine philosophy, a philosophy of 'lighting to the best advantage' in which, thanks to the juggling of literary hands, one sees floating around just about everything that one could shake out of the volumes of an international philosophical library if one were to break their binding. I shall have more to say about this later; for the moment it is enough for me to say that it can be more modest to talk about oneself than to talk about ideas.[2]

The tendency to talk about oneself (with a disconcerting lack of modesty) rather than about ideas has undeniably been encouraged in France by the fact that philosophy is considered here as an essentially literary discipline and the philosopher as being first and foremost a writer who is to be judged principally as such. The avowed aim of some of our most gifted and most influential 'theorists' is, moreover, to erase as far as may be possible the distinction which is supposed to exist between philosophy and literature, without being overly concerned with the practical consequences, which are, to my mind, already most disturbing. We are witnessing, in particular, the proliferation of a type of work which attempts, with a very relative degree of success, to compensate for the absence of properly philosophical argumentation by means of literary effects and for the absence of properly literary qualities by means of philosophical pretensions. In general, contemporary French philosophers are past masters in the art of making themselves quite impossible to grasp, that is to say, they are never to be found at the precise point where criticism might possibly reach them. In particular, they are always doing something other than 'philosophy' whenever they are suspected of doing it poorly, namely literature, science, politics or something else which has as yet neither name nor status and which cannot be judged in terms of habitual criteria. One may note in this connection that, by a paradox by which it seems only the naive are astonished, structuralism, which constituted in principle a return in strength of 'scientific' objectivism and which had made the disappearance of the 'subject' and of the 'author' one of its favourite themes, has given rise to the most detestable forms of narcissistic self-celebration, of unconditional submission to the master, of the cult of the personality and of the star system, along with an almost total inhibition of the most elementary of critical reflexes. In this regard, I must confess that despite all the psychological, sociological, historical and other explanations that may have been proposed, the remarkable conformity of my generation and the astonishing docility with which it has generally allowed its convictions and its orientations to be dictated to it by undisputed intellectual masters, by circumstances and whatever may be in the news still constitutes for me even today a fairly incomprehensible phenomenon.

Apart from its intrinsic interest, which appeared to me at once to be considerable, analytic philosophy has attracted me in large part because of the instinctive aversion that the opinions of the majority have always inspired in me and because of my tendency to consider that a philosophical idea diminishes in value in proportion to its success. As Vincent Descombes remarks: 'In the recent evolution of philosophy in France we can trace the passage from the generation known after 1945 as that of the "three Hs" to the generation known since 1960 as that of the three "masters of suspicion": the three Hs being Hegel, Husserl and Heidegger, and the three masters of suspicion Marx, Nietzsche and Freud.'[3] At the time I began my studies in philosophy, the Holy Trinity Marx–Nietzsche–Freud was in the course of being enthroned in the Pantheon (whence, it seems, it has for some time now been seriously threatened with ignominious expulsion). It has not taken much more to make a hardened disbeliever of me. It is always fascinating to observe the unimaginable forms of blindness and idolatry to which authors reputed essentially for their exceptional mastery in the art of stripping off masks and casting down idols can in their turn give rise. One of the reasons why I have never really been attracted by Marxism and psychoanalysis has been simply the fact that everything that counted at the time as reflection and creation had necessarily to refer to them.

As for me, I have never been able to bring myself to submit to the constraint of externally imposed interests and subjects, as described by Pierre Bourdieu in his works on the sociology of the intellectual milieu. It is as difficult to believe in theory as it is incontestable in practice that a privileged minority, holding symbolic power and innocently exerting the ·violence which this power authorizes, may determine arbitrarily and at every instant what is and is not to be discussed, for the sake of a crowd of followers persuaded that they are wholly free in choosing their subjects on the basis of their intrinsic importance alone. The consequence for France, where the phenomenon is, like the influence of fashion, clearly more perceptible and more spectacular than in most other countries, is that only a minute fraction of the information relevant to philosophical reflection on the world of today is actually considered or used. The most significant example is certainly that of psychoanalysis which, despite the fact it has for some time been thought to be, as one says, 'in crisis' (or perhaps, more precisely, because of this), continues to occupy a place out of all proportion in relation to other disciplines that are just as important and, in certain cases, distinctly more promising.

II

Spengler wrote in *The Decline of the West*: 'And I can only hope that men of the new generation may be moved by this book to devote themselves to technics instead of lyrics, the sea instead of the paint-brush, and politics instead of epistemology. Better they could not do.'[4] The only possibility remaining, according to him, for philosophy today, and which it must resolutely adopt by making a virtue of (historical) necessity, is *history*:

Systematic philosophy, then, lies immensely far behind us, and ethical philosophy has been wound up. *But a third possibility, corresponding to the Classical Scepticism, still remains to the soul-world* of the present-day West, and it can be brought to light by hitherto unknown methods of historical morphology. That which is a possibility is a necessity. The Classical scepticism is ahistoric, it doubts by denying outright. But that of the West, if it is an inward necessity, a symbol of the autumn of our spirituality, is obliged to be historical through and through. Its solutions are got by treating everything as relative, as an historical phenomenon. . . . Whereas the Sceptic philosophy arose within Hellenism as the negation of philosophy – declaring philosophy to be purposeless – we, on the contrary, regard the *history of philosophy* as, in the last resort, philosophy's gravest theme. This *is* 'skepsis' . . .[5]

If one adds that for the author of *The Decline of the West* the politics of a civilized epoch, in contrast with those of a cultivated epoch, are represented today by journalism, whereas in Antiquity they were represented by rhetoric, one is tempted to say that the idea of an historicist, political, rhetorical and journalistic philosophy, which has been so remarkably illustrated by the case of France, corresponds as a whole rather well with the prognostic formulated by Spengler. If I have mentioned his name, knowing well that it is enough to set off unanimous reactions of horror and indignation on the part of French philosophers, this is first because contemporary French philosophy has produced, in a different manner and style, a certain number of false prophets of the same species as Spengler, and secondly because I have always had the feeling that there was something typically Spenglerian in the historicism – whether explicit or latent – of French philosophy, with its obsession with the decline and exhaustion of possibilities, its recurrent pessimism concerning the future of philosophy in general, its submission to the *fait accompli* and to what is unavoidable in the development of philosophical thought, its haste to give in to the necessity of the epoch and its resolve not to go beyond what it considers to be its limits and its historical obligations. It is rare indeed to find a philosopher who, in addition to his philosophy properly speaking, does not offer a sort of historical plea *pro domo*, which allows him to make his philosophy appear as the only one possible and necessary and to transform the mood of the time into an imperative of world history. Every philosophical enterprise that wishes to have any chance of success must be accompanied by a sort of certificate of 'uncircumventible' and 'untranscendable' topicality, that guarantees both its conformity to the exigencies of the historical moment and its having been imposed by them, to the point of exclusion of every other possibility. In the selection of the mandatory subjects, the appeal to sovereign history and the more or less terrorist invocation of 'modernity', considered as *index sui et antiqui*, naturally plays a wholly fundamental role.

Today, we are, at least in France, obviously far from the period when Nietzsche reproached philosophers with a fundamental lack of a sense of history and a sense of relativity. History has become, in a certain sense, our *Darstellungsform*, to such an extent that it is from now on difficult to envisage classical philosophical problems from an angle that is not above all and in essence historical, or to imagine that these problems may have any sort of present or future existence as such. This type of historical thinking is, moreover, applied more and more systematically to the immediate present itself, so that, as Musil remarked with irony, one has nowadays the impression that with each new academic (or publishing) year a new 'ism' or a new epoch commences. This disastrous custom is further aggravated by an 'heroic' conception of the history of ideas as constituted by a series of more or less spectacular ruptures or revolutions, which in principle forbid any kind of return to earlier problems or solutions. As we have seen in the structuralist episode, philosophical 'revolutions' are openly assimilated to scientific revolutions and are supposed to imply the same kind of irreversibility, a move which authorizes treating the recalcitrant as though it were a matter of imposing a new science in the face of prejudices and questions belonging to another age. One not infrequently hears it said that, after the 'definitive' work of X or Y, one can no longer pose this or that problem or employ this or that philosophical concept, in much the same way as we would say that, after Einstein, we can no longer speak of the ether or of absolute simultaneity. The only way to reconcile this view of things with the periodical reappearance of the same basic philosophical problems which were believed to have been settled definitively is, of course, to claim that one invents them at the time at which one rediscovers them.

I have laid stress on this aspect because the absence of an historical sense, which here is considered to be one of the major weaknesses of analytic philosophy, and its characteristic tendency to make the traditional philosophical questions topical by retranslating them directly into its own language, a tendency which professional historians of philosophy generally find so shocking, did a great deal, at the beginning, to make analytic philosophy appealing to me, so excessive and so frustrating did I find the importance accorded by French university philosophy to erudite historical research and its attitude of deferential neutrality towards the great authors and the great controversies of tradition. As, in its own way, by virtue of a more audacious – if not more convincing – utilization of history, the avant-garde tended to the conclusion that we are, in one way or another, already in the era of post-philosophy, so analytic philosophy offered the image, doubtless somewhat naive but distinctly more reassuring and encouraging, of a philosophical universe in which the great traditional problems preserve a certain contemporary relevance and can be treated in a relatively fruitful way through the application of new methods.

The major advantage of analytic philosophy, especially if seen as Dummett – rightly or wrongly – interprets it, in the fundamentally positive and progressive perspective of a sort of revolution in the history of philosophy brought about by Frege, was, in the eyes of the rare French philosophers of my generation who discovered it at a moment decisive for their future orientation, precisely that it presented itself as a philosophy which was really suited to the present in a philosophical context outrageously dominated, on the one hand, by a nostalgia for the 'grand' philosophical tradition and, on the other, by futurist speculations concerning 'unheard of' modes of thought that were to be those of the post-historical and post-philosophical era into which, without realizing it, we had already entered.

Today still, even though I am entirely convinced by his arguments, I cannot bring myself completely to share Michael Ayers's severity concerning the analytical type of history of philosophy,[6] for its errors and historical misunderstandings seem to me, all things considered, less scandalous than the tendency to make the historical understanding of authors and of doctrines – which, moreover, by definition, one can never actually attain – a philosophical aim in itself rather than an indispensable means or preliminary step. This is the reason why I am not sure whether I have ever quite managed to do justice to historical works as exemplary and as indispensable as those of Martial Gueroult, which have always given me the impression of offering stones to someone who is asking for bread.

It is at the least surprising to see an author like Carnap regularly denounced by contemporary French philosophers as a paradigm of anti-philosophical dogmatism, while they themselves practise their own forms of intellectual terrorism and censorship of bothersome questions in such a natural and candid way that one is quite taken aback. As Putnam writes: 'The school to which Carnap belongs – the so-called Logical Empiricist school – has often been criticized for oversimplification and dogmatism. Oversimplification it has, indeed, been guilty of; but dogmatism seems a highly unfair accusation. I know of no group of philosophers who have been more willing to abandon their own cherished beliefs when careful logical analysis showed those beliefs to be untenable.'[7]

It is true that 'the importance of the Logical Empiricist contribution is often overlooked (or, worse, deliberately played down) today because the real contribution has turned out to be entirely negative'.[8] Now, the idea that philosophy could consist in formulating theses and in trying to see whether or not these can, in the final analysis, hold up when confronted with the facts involved, and the by no means negligible interest to be found in even clearly negative results obtained in this way, all this is manifestly foreign to contemporary French philosophy, to such an extent indeed that rational argumentation, critical discussion and the custom of replying to objections tend to be considered as old-fashioned and incongruous practices. (Those who are sceptical or recalcitrant are generally treated by the representatives of the orthodoxy of the moment as an anomaly to be explained rather than as an honourable opposition one might possibly attempt to win over.) And yet, as Putnam notes concerning the 'failure' of logical positivism: 'While the sense of disappointment is, humanly speaking, all too understandable, and so is the desire to "try something new", it still remains a great historical contribution to have shown us how to make philosophical propositions more precise. And if the propositions all turn out to be false – well, getting agreement on even that is surely an important progress.'[9]

Although I have certainly never been in any sense an adept of logical empiricism and although reading Wittgenstein has made me fairly sceptical regarding the possibility or the necessity of making philosophy more 'scientific' than it generally is, I have always been extremely grateful to Carnap for having revealed to me the existence of a way of doing philosophy incomparably more satisfying to a rational mind than that to which I was accustomed. And even today I continue to hold him in great admiration not only for the substantial contribution he made to numerous areas of exact philosophy, but also because of the remarkable serenity and total absence of proselytism or fanaticism that characterizes his philosophical efforts and style. One must, doubtless, have been acquainted with the extraordinarily pretentious, provocative and disdainful tone of some of the most typical productions of French philosophy and the aggressive militantism – not to say the militarism – of certain politico-philosophical programmes, which have experienced a success as surprising as it was ephemeral, in order to appreciate fully an enterprise conducted with as much measure, method and perseverance as was that of Carnap.

Generally speaking, logic continues to be considered here as a purely technical discipline, with no privileged relation to philosophy properly speaking, since it is supposed, in fact, to have become a mere part of mathematics; and it is disqualified *a priori* by philosophers of science themselves (including philosophers of mathematics) essentially because of the 'guilt by association' of which Hao Wang speaks,[10] that is because of the tendency to take logic purely and simply for logical positivism or, at the very least, to consider the latter as the (spontaneous) philosophy of logicians. Contemporary French epistemologists have always categorically opposed any philosophy of science more or less directly inspired by logic. At the time I was a student, one had to choose once and for all between the 'logic of the sciences' (as it used to be called) and historical epistemology, explicitly identified with epistemology as such and thought of as an exclusively French speciality. Inasmuch as the efforts to clarify or to explain fundamental meta-scientific concepts made by the logical positivists and their more or less direct descendants seemed to me not only interesting from a purely philosophical point of view but also to be dictated more or less directly by scientific practice itself, one would surely have just as much right to judge historical epistemology in terms of the contribution it may make towards the solution of questions of this sort; and I have never really understood why the sole response to such questions acknowledged as permissible by French epistemologists consisted in simply decreeing that they were not to be raised.

If the partisans of an exclusively historical approach implicitly considered the distinction between the 'context of discovery' and the 'context of justification' to be entirely illusory, they were manifestly prepared neither to provide any sort of argument in favour of this evident fact, nor to make explicit and to confront, as Feyerabend does today, the extremely disagreeable epistemological consequences resulting for scientific rationalism and realism, which they defend in principle and refuse in practice. Feyerabend himself finally concludes that the philosophy of the sciences should not be reformed but simply allowed to die its own death. This type of declaration, which I have heard repeated as a *leitmotiv* by the epistemologists of my generation, would obviously be much more comprehensible and more plausible if it were only explained in what way the case of the philosophy of the sciences, considered as the bastard and parasitical discipline *par excellence*, is fundamentally different from that of the philosophy of morality, of religion or of art and finally from that of philosophy as such.

However regrettable it may be, ignorance of mathematical logic and of the contribution it has made to contemporary philosophy certainly does not constitute the most disturbing phenomenon. What is far more disturbing is the general tendency denounced by Musil as early as 1921 in his critique of *The Decline of the West*: there exists today in intellectual circles (in particular in philosophical circles) 'a favourable prejudice with regard to infractions against mathematics, logic and exactitude; among the crimes against the mind, these are willingly placed under the category of political offences which do honour to their author, the public prosecutor finding himself, strictly speaking, in the role of the accused'.[11]

French philosophers who display a rather too pronounced taste for precision and accuracy (I dare not say rigour, since every philosopher is convinced of being rigorous in his *own* way) are well acquainted with this sort of situation. Exact philosophy, which cannot be said to have occupied a position of high prestige in France for the past forty years or so and whose representatives might rather have the impression of being on the whole in a state of legitimate intellectual self-defence, is nevertheless regularly treated as a potential aggressor threatening the most fundamental of philosophical freedoms. The same type of favourable prejudice naturally works to the benefit of obscurity and hermeticism with the result that an insistence on clarity and intelligibility finishes by being itself considered as a sort of abuse of inquisitorial power.

The critique of rationalism (regularly confused with positivism and with scientism) is naturally always accompanied by formal protestations of respect for the sciences and logic, with regard to which the question is, in principle, simply one of limiting their more abusive claims by bringing them to recognize their own presuppositions and limitations. But the practical consequences of this purely reactive and defensive attitude, by virtue of which the sole manner in which scientific knowledge can directly interest philosophy lies in the clarification and denunciation of its unavowed (and unavowable) presuppositions, are always the same. From Sartre to the 'new philosophers', contemporary French philosophy has been largely dominated by an instinctive refusal and a panic-like fear of scientific and technical culture and by an exasperated resolve to affirm its radical heterogeneity and its absolute superiority in relation to a discourse whose platitude, vulgarity, pre-critical easy conscience, utilitarian preoccupations and compromises with the political powers-that-be are too obvious to give rise to anything but mistrust and disdain.

The diversity and the subtlety of the reasons invented by the fox of this fable in order to decree the grapes he cannot reach to be too green, will doubtless be rewarded with the astonishment and admiration of future generations, especially if they recall that as a good disciple of Marx, Nietzsche and Freud, he more or less pledged himself never to be taken in by the bad reasons given by others. The intellectual masters who have dominated the French philosophical stage over the past few decades may be, in general, little disposed to assume the objective consequences of their explicit or implicit teaching; but it is difficult not to see anti-scientific, anti-rationalist and anti-analytical bias as partly responsible for the disastrous weakening of the critical sense, the progressive transformation of the knowledgeable (or presumed to be knowledgeable) public into a sort of religious community dedicated to the cult of a few consecrated stars, the uniformly admiring, not to say out-and-out dithyrambic, style of authorized criticism, the regrettable disappearance of intermediary ranks between genius and pure and simple nonentity and the tendency systematically to absolve errors of reasoning and method (to the extent that these are still actually perceived) in order to retain only what is essential, namely the literary qualities. In a context such as this, the mere fact that it continues to conceive of philosophy as an *argumentative* discipline already constitutes by itself a weighty argument in favour of analytic philosophy.

III

As Descombes remarks: 'In France the development of a political position remains the decisive test, disclosing as it does the definitive meaning of a mode of thought. It is as if the heart of the matter had not been reached until, from suppositions about the One and the Many, or about the nature of knowledge, the subject shifted to the issue of the next elections or the attitude of the Communist Party.'[12] The collapse of Marxism, the 'discovery' of the cause of human rights and the replacement of theoreticism and scientism by moralism and the rhetoric of prophecy have obviously changed nothing of any consequence in this state of affairs, since commitment to the service of a great political or humanitarian cause continues to be considered capable in and of itself of taking the place of philosophy and of dispensing one from the necessity of observing the most elementary rules of argumentation and of critical discussion.

There are two important observations to be made concerning this situation. The first is that this omnipresence of politics in philosophy has always gone hand in hand with an almost total absence of any philosophical reflection worthy of the name on the subject of politics. The second is that the accumulated disappointments and errors, notably in political matters, do not appear capable of really bringing into question the characteristic tendency of French philosophers to attribute to themselves a sort of monopoly of critical lucidity, considered once and for all as their basic professional virtue, so that in the end it would be altogether small-minded and out of place to ask them for any concrete proof of it. The resistance to any type of refutation by results shown by the postulate according to which philosophy is considered to be *the* critical discipline *par excellence* is nothing short of astounding.

Putnam reports that, at Princeton, he has heard a certain

number of literary colleagues discussing the case of scientists in general and denouncing, with a remarkable unanimity, their lack of culture, their narrow-mindedness, their arrogance and the danger represented on the social and political level by their 'simplistic' conceptions, in view of the presumption in their favour shown by those in power, who allow themselves to be too easily impressed by their scientific titles and their supposed expertise. One probably has to admit that the refined conceptions of literary men, and in particular those of philosophers, have never made, and never could make, humanity run risks of this sort. (It is true that this tendency can also, on occasion, be reversed, to the extent that, as we have recently witnessed in France in the case of the 'new philosophy', the 'intellectual masters' in philosophy and literature are in their turn considered to be more or less directly responsible for totalitarianism and oppression.) In France, where philosophy is a discipline which is supposed at one and the same time to participate actively in the transformation of society and to represent, in relation to the scientific and political establishment, the vigilant and disinterested awareness of the stakes and the risks involved, it is not surprising that it is constantly torn between the determination to be taken seriously and the fear that this will actually happen.

If it were not for the phenomenon of immunization against every kind of potential counter-example, which I mentioned above, the adequate response to the remarks reported by Putnam would consist in remarking, as he does, that, generally speaking, literary scholars are not to be outdone by scientists when it comes to making declarations and taking up positions in thoughtless and irresponsible ways, and that one cannot see why these should be ascribed to the whole of the community in question when they come from the scientific world and yet, on the contrary, be considered completely marginal and representative of only a minority point of view when they are made by people from the world of literature.[13]

Putnam very justly remarks that the protests heard increasingly today against the professionalism, academicism, esoterism and the growing technicality of philosophy are by no means new, each philosophical generation having been suspected for more or less the same reasons of not dealing with the 'true' questions, 'whose discussion would, of course, interest one and would never become technical',[14] but that things have been made undeniably worse by the excessive inflation of the problematic of language, an inflation which, in any case, is not limited solely to analytic philosophy: 'This perennial tendency to criticize philosophy as "too technical" is very much reinforced by the "linguistic" character of contemporary philosophy. For language . . . is thought by the layman to be uninteresting in itself and irrelevant to the Great Questions.'[15]

If, for obvious reasons, it is considered entirely normal that science should rapidly become a matter for specialists, whereas philosophy should in principle remain to the end everybody's business, still it is not certain that professional philosophers do not give in a bit too quickly to the temptation to reply to questions which have perhaps not been put to them and to provide justifications for which it is not always sure that the uninitiated public has really asked. In an interview published in *Le Monde*, Desanti has contrasted two sorts of philosophy, one which is concerned with the problems and reflections of each and every one of us and another which he characterizes in the following way:

alongside this, and in opposition to it, there is what I shall call the philosophy of professionals. Now this philosophy, if one considers the dominant philosophy today, Anglo-Saxon language philosophy, known as 'analytic philosophy' (but the name matters little) is presented as an institutionalized body of knowledge. It includes various schools, often competitive but also often working together, with strict forms of learning and with initiation rituals. Out of this come extremely important, subtle and useful works: but these works remain academic. They are developed within the field of the discipline, just as algebra or differential topology are developed within their own field. This inevitably gives rise, in ordinary people, in the worst case to a feeling of intimidation or exclusion and in the best case to a reaction of disinterest, of not being concerned.[16]

For Desanti, with whom everyone will surely agree on this point, 'it is . . . essential to see clearly that philosophy would write its own death warrant if it did not seek to connect up with the needs of everyday man, if it were to shut itself up in a new "clergyship" '.[17]

These reflections, intended for the general public, are of a type which is quite common in France, and seem to me particularly interesting for three main reasons: (1) because analytic philosophy is presented as the 'dominant' philosophy, although it is taught almost nowhere in France (which is most indicative of the general tendency of contemporary French philosophers to take their fears for realities), (2) because the professionalization and the institutionalization of philosophy as an organized body of knowledge are described as *new* phenomena, posing a problem specific to contemporary philosophy and liable seriously to compromise its future, (3) because the philosopher who denounces this sort of peril would probably be the first to recognize that the really important and lasting part of his own production comprises works which are particularly austere, specialized and esoteric, dealing essentially with the history and the philosophy of mathematics and which can really be of interest only to a very restricted public.

The solution which he himself has adopted is that of many other French philosophers; it consists in doing simultaneously both of the types of philosophy he distinguishes, that is to say, in proffering at one and the same time a discourse reserved for the professional public and another intended for the general public, to which correspond two conceptions of philosophy and its exigencies, two philosophical styles and two completely different types of publications. The problem then inevitably reappears within philosophy itself, in the form of the connection which has now to be made between the two types of discourse, that of the 'clerk' who speaks as a professional and that of the 'popular' philosopher who uses a language reputed to be in principle accessible to everyone.

Certainly, no one asks what sort of reaction 'ordinary people' of the period might have had with respect to preoccupations such as those of Plato, Aristotle, Descartes, Kant or Hegel, nor whether it could simply be a question of this sort of reaction. Morever, even if it is true that the great moral and political questions are more directly related to the preoccupations of the ordinary person, one may easily realize that any serious philosophical discussion of this sort of question ends up being hardly less technical and esoterical than questions dealing with the theory of knowledge or epistemology. The true problem would, in fact, be to know why the gap between the philosophy of the professionals and the presumed expectations of the general public (which, by definition, is never consulted) gives the impression of having become today more radical and more intolerable than in the past, from a point of view which in reality is essentially that of the professionals themselves.

It is obvious that the public of philosophers who specialize in dealing with questions which, as Desanti says, 'concern life and death, and the ordering of desires, and the evils of society' and others of the same sort, even if it is no doubt much larger, is not necessarily much closer to what Desanti calls 'ordinary people' than the public of a logician or an epistemologist. But there is indisputably a great difference between philosophers who, like Sartre, Marcuse or Foucault, give the impression of having more or less transformed the mentality of their time in their respective areas, and others, like most analytic philosophers and, in fact, philosophers in general, who address themselves almost exclusively to the members of their confraternity. And it is entirely understandable that the former give the impression of more closely corresponding to what philosophy today can and should be if it is to remain faithful to its traditional vocation (or perhaps, more precisely, to the idea we form of it).

It remains nevertheless the case that the unformulated demands of the general public with regard to professional philosophers are determined much less by what one really knows about these demands than by what philosophers themselves believe them to be or, for various reasons, judge that they should be and would wish them to be. Moreover, it is clear that when philosophers claim to deal with the problems which we all have, they are actually dealing, in a good many cases, with nothing but *their own* individual and collective problems, such, for example, as has been seen in a number of recent cases, as the problem of *their own* relation to politics. Finally, if it is normal to require of philosophy that it deepen our reflection on the great moral, social and political questions of the age, it would certainly be wholly unreasonable and absurd to require of any given philosopher that he justify his position by a contribution of this sort which would probably, in most cases, be fairly trivial and of no great interest.

Rather than incriminating, as does Desanti, a certain propensity of contemporary philosophers to overlook their fundamental obligations to the unspecialized public in order to confine themselves to purely technical tasks, it would no doubt be preferable to recognize that their apparent capitulation on this point corresponds also to an objective situation, a situation constituted by the fact that the professionals are today in many respects the last to be able to provide what society generally demands of them under the name of 'philosophy'. Those who propose any sort of reply at all obviously have a better chance, in any case, to make themselves heard than those who would feel themselves constrained, not, as is ordinarily supposed, by pusillanimity but by a sense of 'professional' honesty, to confess their own ignorance. As Musil notes, *quod licet bovi non licet Jovi*; that is to say, 'The epoch in which the wise doubt their ability to arrive at a world-view has made of world-views a possession of everybody.'[18] This is why 'nowadays there is a terrifying amount of philosophizing done in small slices, so much so that shops are the only places where one can still get anything without a philosophic view being involved. There is, on the other hand, a definite mistrust of philosophy in large chunks, which is simply considered impossible.'[19]

For my part, I have never been convinced that the practice of analytic philosophy or, more generally, of a relatively technical and specialized type of philosophy, should of itself lead to a lack of interest in the important questions of everyday life or to a particularly conformist or conservative attitude on questions of this sort. I even tend to think that 'ordinary language philosophy' itself, despite the absence of an explicitly normative point of view with which it is constantly reproached, could help substantially to improve our manner of formulating and discussing the most practical philosophical questions (including political ones). But the benefit that one can expect in such cases from this type of philosophy is, whatever way you look at it, incomparably more indirect, more ambiguous, less substantial and, to be blunt, frankly more disappointing than that which the majority of French philosophers have recently acquired the (to my mind most regrettable) habit of immediately requiring of the most abstract philosophical reflection. An analytic philosopher would probably find it a great deal more difficult to realize 'the abrupt leap from the Idea of good to palpable good' mentioned by Descombes.[20] And one must not forget that what French philosophers mean when they reproach analytic philosophy with encouraging submission to established opinion and authority is most of the time simply that it runs the risk of making people a little less self-assured, a little less eloquent and a little more circumspect re-

garding what are at once the most important and the most difficult questions.

I have been reproached with not being entirely fair towards
contemporary French philosophy, the brilliant superiority of
which has been expounded to me by students at Oxford, Cambridge and Harvard, to whom it had opened entirely new horizons and far more exalting perspectives. It would obviously be
absurd to deny that it has produced extremely brilliant individuals
and works of such specific originality that one can at least
acknowledge, as I have done at the beginning of this essay, the
merit French philosophy is due for having made a totally novel
contribution to contemporary philosophy, one probably incon-
ceivable in any other context. But the individual successes that the
entire world is supposed to envy us cannot completely hide the
dramatic fragility, instability and inconsistency of its deep structures of thought, the lack of taste for intellectual enterprises that
are not likely to lead to immediate and rather spectacular results
which are then to be echoed and amplified on the level of the
general public, the eclecticism, the superficiality and the confusion of interests and crazes, the rather infantile predilection for
systematic excesses and provocations, the profound indifference
concerning reasons and consequences, which explains the levity
and the irresponsibility with which ethical and political choices
are made. So far as I am concerned, I have never managed to
consider as altogether secondary and trivial the most irritating
faults of the 'Gallic' style of thinking, in particular the childish
chauvinism and nationalism, the political megalomania, the ver-
satility – confused with critical sense and mental flexibility – and
the repetition, at ever-increasing intervals, of the same heroic–
comic episodes consistently interpreted in the tragic mode (by
this I mean the constant oscillation of the pendulum between
more or less blustering subversive attitudes and pitiful returns to
the most commonplace self-evidence). Nor do I consider that to
come belatedly to a recognition of the nature of one's situation or
to produce resounding pieces of self-criticism is enough to make
us forget the time that has been lost, the injustices committed and
the deep wrongs done to the cause of philosophy itself.

It is true that, if the mentality of the 'new mandarins' in Amer-
ica really corresponds to Chomsky's unflattering description of it,
the French intelligentsia has the right to boast of a distinctly more

developed critical sense and consciousness of its moral responsibilities, at least if we are to judge according to the frequency and the nature of their declarations and the positions they take up. However, this indisputable advantage to which French intellectuals are so ready to refer in their own support, is in fact probably much more symbolic than substantive, to the extent that talkative bad conscience is too often substituted for effective action, verbal denunciation of abuses and injustices for the resolve really to contribute to their abolition, and the production of a political mythology intended essentially for domestic consumption for the elaboration of a political thought capable of bringing any weight to bear on the ways in which things actually evolve. For a French intellectual, to take up a political position is generally nothing more than a sort of statutory obligation that has to be fulfilled at every moment, without there being any need either to justify it by means of real arguments or to answer for it later. To consider things in the way of Desanti, is not the paradox precisely that what is or should be everyone's business can give rise to the constitution of a semi-professional category whose principal function is to formulate a 'specialist' opinion on questions of which it is declared that everyone must resolve them with the help of his own knowledge and at his own risk?

After having believed during the preceding period in political violence and revolution, French philosophy seems today to have returned quite simply to morality and to right, apparently forgetting that it had adopted and celebrated the first solution because of the real or presumed insufficiencies of the second. It is not impossible, after all, that the next 'revolution' may consist in a rediscovery of the discreet charms of truth, eclipsed for some time past by the more obvious seductiveness of rhetoric. We must give fashion the credit for giving a chance, one day or another, to all ideas, including those which may appear to contradict it most directly. In other words, if the worst is never entirely certain, the best is probably never entirely impossible.

Translated by Kathleen McLaughlin

NOTES

1 Friedrich Nietzsche, *Beyond Good and Evil*, in *The Philosophy of Nietzsche*, New York: Modern Library, 1927, 1954, pp. 508–9.

2 Robert Musil, *Tagebücher*, ed. Adolf Frisé, Reinbeck bei Hamburg: Rowohlt Verlag, 1976, Vol. 1, p. 664.

3 Vincent Descombes, *Le Même et l'autre: quarante-cinq ans de philosophie française (1933–1978)*, Les Editions de Minuit, 1979, p. 13. Trans. L. Scott Fox and J. M. Harding, *Modern French Philosophy*, Cambridge: Cambridge University Press, 1980, p. 3.

4 Oswald Spengler, *The Decline of the West*, trans. Charles Francis Atkinson, London: George Allen and Unwin, 1934, p. 41.

5 *Ibid.*, p. 45.

6 Cf. Michael Ayers, 'Analytical philosophy and the history of philosophy', in Jonathan Ree, Michael Ayers and Adam Westoby, *Philosophy and its Past*, Hassocks: Harvester Press, 1978.

7 Hilary Putnam, 'Language and philosophy', in *Philosophical Papers*, Vol. 2, *Mind, Language and Reality*, Cambridge: Cambridge University Press, 1975, p. 20.

8 *Ibid.*

9 *Ibid.*

10 Cf. Hao Wang, *From Mathematics to Philosophy*, London: Routledge & Kegan Paul, 1974.

11 'Geist und Erfahrung. Anmerkungen für Leser, welche dem Untergang des Abendlandes entronnen sind' (March 1921), in *Gesammelte Werke* (9 vols), ed. Adolf Frisé, Reinbeck bei Hamburg: Rowohlt Verlag, 1978, Vol. 8, *Essays und Reden*, p. 1043.

12 *Le Même et l'autre*, p. 17; *Modern French Philosophy*, p. 7.

13 Cf. Putnam, *Meaning and the Moral Sciences*, London, Henley and Boston: Routledge & Kegan Paul, 1978, p. 88.

14 Putnam, 'Language and philosophy', p. 2.

15 *Ibid.*

16 'Entretien avec Jean-Toussaint Desanti', *Le Monde*, 8 March 1978, p. 2.

17 *Ibid.*

18 *Gesammelte Werke*, Vol. 7, *Kleine Prosa, Aphorismen, Autobiographisches*, p. 932.

19 *The Man Without Qualities*, London: Secker and Warburg, 1953, Vol. 1, p. 300.

20 *Le Même et l'autre*, p. 17; *Modern French Philosophy*, p. 7.

The time of a thesis*: punctuations

Should one speak of an epoch of the thesis? Of a thesis which would require time, sometimes a great deal of time? Or of a thesis whose time would belong to the past?

In short, is there a time of the thesis? And even, should one speak of an age of the thesis, of an age for the thesis?

Allow me to begin by whispering a confidence which I shall not abuse: never have I felt so young and at the same time so old. At the same time, in the same instant . . . and it is one and the same feeling, as if two stories and two times, two rhythms were engaged in a sort of altercation in one and the same feeling of oneself, in a sort of anachrony of oneself, anachrony in oneself. It is in this way that I can, to an extent, make sense to myself of a certain confusion of identity. This confusion is, certainly, not completely foreign to me and I do not always complain about it; but just now it has suddenly got much worse and this bout is not far from leaving me bereft of speech.

Between youth and old age, one and the other, neither one nor the other, an indecisiveness of age, it is like a discomfiture at the moment of installation, an instability, I will not go so far as to say a disturbance of stability, of posture, of station, of the thesis or of the pose, but rather of a pause in the more or less well-regulated life of a university teacher, an end and a beginning which do not coincide and in which there is involved once again no doubt a

---

* This is the text of a presentation which was given, according to custom, at the opening of a thesis defence (based on published works), 2 June 1980 at the Sorbonne. The jury consisted of MM Aubenque, De Gandillac, Desanti, Joly, Lascault, Levinas.

certain gap of an alternative between the delight of pleasure and fecundity.

This anachrony (I am, obviously, speaking of my own) has for me a very familiar feel, as if a rendezvous had forever been set for me with what should above all and with the utmost punctuality never come at its appointed hour, but always, rather, too early or too late.

As to this stage on which I here appear for the defence of a thesis, I have been preparing myself for it for too long, I have doubtless premeditated it, adjourned it and finally excluded its possibility, excluded it for too long so that when, thanks to you, I at last find myself engaged upon it, it is impossible for it not to have for me a slight character of phantasy or irreality, an air of improbability, of unpredictability, even an air of improvization.

It is now almost twenty-five years ago that I committed myself to working on a thesis. Or rather, it was scarcely a decision; I was at that time simply following the course that was taken to be more or less natural and which was at the very least classical, classifiable, typical of those who found themselves in a certain well-determined social situation upon leaving the Ecole Normale and after the *agrégation*.

But these twenty-five years have been fairly peculiar. Here I am not referring to my modest personal history or to all those routes that, after starting by leading me away from this initial decision, then brought me deliberately to question it, deliberately and as I honestly thought, definitively, only to end up, just a very short while ago, by deciding in a context which, rightly or wrongly, I believed to be quite new to take the risk of another evaluation, of another analysis.

By saying that these twenty-five years have been peculiar, I am not first thinking, then, of this personal history or even of the paths my own work has taken, even supposing that it could, improbably, be isolated from the environment in which it has moved through a play of exchanges, of resemblances, of affinities, of influences, as people say, but also and especially, more and more indeed, through a play of divergences and of marginalization, in an increasing and at times sheer isolation, whether as regards contents, positions, let us just say 'theses', or whether more especially as regards ways of proceeding, socio-institutional practices, a certain style of writing as well as – regardless of the cost, and today this amounts to a great deal – of relations with the university milieu, with cultural, political, editorial, journalistic representations, there where, today, it seems to me, are located some of the most serious, the most pressing, and the most obscure responsibilities facing an intellectual.

No, it is not of myself that I am thinking when I allude to the span of these twenty-five years, but rather of a most remarkable sequence in the history of philosophy and of French philosophical institutions. I should not have the means here and now, and in any case, this is not the place, to analyse this sequence. But as, for reasons that are due not only to the limited amount of time available to me, there can be equally no question of putting together the works that have been submitted to you in something like a presentation in the form of conclusions or of theses; and as, on the other hand, I do not want to limit the discussion that is to follow by making an overly long introduction, I thought that I might perhaps hazard a few fragmentary and preliminary propositions, indicating a few among the most obvious points concerning the intersections between this historical sequence and some of the movements or themes that have attracted me, that have retained or displaced my attention within the limits of my work.

Around 1957, then, I had *registered*, as one says, my first thesis topic. I had entitled it 'The ideality of the literary object'. Today this title seems strange. To a lesser degree it seemed so even then and I shall discuss this in a moment. It received the approval of Jean Hyppolite who was to direct this thesis, which he did, which he did without doing so, that is as he knew how to do so, as in my opinion he was one of the very few to know how to do so, in a free and liberal spirit, always open, always attentive to what was not, or not yet, intelligible, always careful to exert no pressure, if not no influence, by generously letting me go wherever my path led me. I want to salute his memory here and to recall all that I owe to the trust and encouragement he gave me, even when, as he one day told me, he did not see at all where I was going. This was in 1966 during a colloquium in the United States in which we were both taking part. After a few friendly remarks on the paper I had just given, Jean Hyppolite added: 'That said, I really do not see where you are going.' I think that I replied to him more or less as follows: 'If I clearly saw ahead of time where I was going, I really don't believe that I should take another step to get there.' Perhaps

I then thought that knowing where one is going may doubtless help in orientating one's thought, but that it has never made anyone take a single step, quite the opposite in fact. What is the good of going where one knows oneself to be going and where one knows that one is destined to arrive? Recalling this reply today, I am not sure that I really understand it very well, but it surely did not mean that I *never* see or *never* know where I am going and that to this extent, to the extent that I do know, it is not certain that I have ever taken any step or said anything at all. This also means, perhaps, that, concerning this place where I am going, I in fact know enough about it to think, with a certain terror, that things there are not going very well and that, all things considered, it would be better not to go there at all. But there's always Necessity, the figure I wanted recently to call Necessity with the initial capital of a proper noun, and Necessity says that one must always yield, that one has always to go where it calls. At the risk of never arriving. At the risk, it says, of never arriving. Calling it even, prepared for the fact that you won't make it. (Quitte à ne pas arriver. Quitte, dit-elle, à ne pas arriver. Quitte pour ce que tu n'arrives pas.)

The ideality of the literary object; this title was somewhat more comprehensible in 1957 in a context that was more marked by the thought of Husserl than is the case today. It was then for me a matter of bending, more or less violently, the techniques of transcendental phenomenology to the needs of elaborating a new theory of literature, of that very peculiar type of ideal object that is the literary object, a bound ideality Husserl would have said, bound to so-called 'natural' language, a non-mathematical or non-mathematizable object, and yet one that differs from the objects of plastic or musical art, that is to say from all of the examples privileged by Husserl in his analyses of ideal objectivity. For I have to remind you, somewhat bluntly and simply, that my most constant interest, coming even before my philosophical interest I should say, if this is possible, has been directed towards literature, towards that writing which is called literary.

What is literature? And first of all what is it 'to write'? How is it that the fact of writing can disturb the very question 'what is?' and even 'what does it mean?' To say this in other words – and here is the *saying otherwise* that was of importance to me – when and how does an inscription become literature and what takes place when it does? To what and to whom is this due? What takes place between philosophy and literature, science and literature, politics and literature, theology and literature, psychoanalysis and literature? It was here, in all the abstractness of its title, that lay the most pressing question. This question was doubtless inspired in me by a desire which was related also to a certain uneasiness: why finally does the inscription so fascinate me, preoccupy me, precede me? Why am I so fascinated by the literary ruse of the inscription and the whole ungraspable paradox of a trace which manages only to carry itself away, to erase itself in marking itself out afresh, itself and its own idiom, which in order to take actual form must erase itself and produce itself at the price of this self-erasure.

Curious as it may seem, transcendental phenomenology was able, in the first stages of my work, to help me sharpen some of these questions, which at the time were not as well marked out as they seem to be today. In the fifties, when it was still not well received, was little-known or too indirectly understood in the French universities, Husserlian phenomenology seemed to some young philosophers to be inescapable. I still see it today, if in a different way, as a discipline of incomparable rigour. Not – especially not – in the versions proposed by Sartre or by Merleau-Ponty which were then dominant, but rather in opposition to them, or without them, in particular in those areas which a certain type of French phenomenology appeared at times to avoid, whether in history, in science, in the historicity of science, the history of ideal objects and of truth, and hence in politics as well, and even in ethics. I should like to recall here, as one indication among others, a book which is no longer discussed today, a book whose merits can be very diversely evaluated, but which for a certain number of us pointed to a task, a difficulty and no doubt to an impasse. This is Tran Duc Tao's *Phénoménologie et matérialisme dialectique*. After a commentary which retraced the movement of transcendental phenomenology and in particular the transition from static constitution to genetic constitution, the book attempted, with less obvious success, to open the way for a dialectical materialism that would admit some of the rigorous demands of transcendental phenomenology. One can imagine what the stakes of such an attempt might have been and its outcome was of less importance than the stakes involved. Moreover, some of Cavaillès's dialectical, dialecticist conclusions proved of interest to us for the same reasons. It was in an area marked out and magnetized by these stakes, at once philosophical and political, that I had first begun to read Husserl, starting with a *Mémoire* (Master's thesis) on the problem of genesis in the phenomenology of Husserl. At this early date Maurice de Gandillac was kind enough to watch over this work; twenty-six years ago he alone served as my entire examination committee, and if I recall that he was reduced to one-third of the committee for a *3e cycle* thesis (*De la grammatologie* in 1967) and that he has been further reduced to one-sixth of the committee today, I do so not only to express my gratitude to him with that feeling of fidelity which is comparable to no other, but to promise him that henceforth this parcelling out, this proliferating division will cease. This will be my last thesis defence.

Following this first work, my Introduction to *The Origin of Geometry* enabled me to approach something like the un-thought out axiomatics of Husserlian phenomenology, its 'principle of principles', that is to say, its intuitionism, the absolute privilege of the living present, the lack of attention paid to the problem of its own phenomenological enunciation, to transcendental discourse itself, as Fink used to say, to the necessity of recourse, in eidetic or transcendental description, to a language that could not itself be submitted to the *épochè* – without itself being simply in the world – thus to a language which remained naive, even though it was by virtue of this very language that all the phenomenological bracketings and parentheses were made possible. This un-thought out axiomatics seemed to me to limit the scope of a consistent problematic of writing and of the trace, even though the necessity of such a problematic had been marked out by *The Origin of Geometry* with a rigour no doubt unprecedented in the history of philosophy. Husserl indeed located the recourse to writing within the very constitution of those ideal objects *par excellence*, mathematical objects, though without considering – and for good reason – the threat that the logic of this inscription represented for the phenomenological project itself. Naturally, all of the problems worked on in the Introduction to *The Origin of Geometry* have continued to organize the work I have subsequently attempted in connection with philosophical, literary and even non-discursive corpora, most notably that of pictorial works: I am thinking, for example, of the historicity of ideal objects, of tradition, of inheritance, of filiation or of wills and testaments, of archives, libraries, books, of writing and living speech, of the relationships between semiotics and linguistics, of the question of truth and of undecidability, of the irreducible otherness that divides the self-identity of the living present, of the necessity for new analyses concerning non-mathematical idealities.

During the years that followed, from about 1963 to 1968, I tried to work out – in particular in the three works published in 1967 – what was in no way meant to be a system but rather a sort of strategic device, opening onto its own abyss, an unclosed, unenclosable, not wholly formalizable ensemble of rules for reading, interpretation and writing. This type of device may have enabled me to detect not only in the history of philosophy and in the related socio-historical totality, but also in what are alleged to be sciences and in so-called post-philosophical discourses that figure among the most modern (in linguistics, in anthropology, in psychoanalysis), to detect in these an evaluation of writing, or, to tell the truth, rather a devaluation of writing whose insistent, repetitive, even obscurely compulsive, character was the sign of a whole set of long-standing constraints. These constraints were practised at the price of contradictions, of denials, of dogmatic decrees; they were not to be localized within a limited domain of culture, of the whole encyclopedia of knowledge or of ontology. I proposed to analyse the non-closed and fissured system of these constraints under the name of logocentrism in the form that it takes in Western philosophy and under that of phonocentrism as it appears in the widest scope of its dominion. Of course, I was able to develop this device and this interpretation only by according a privileged role to the guideline or analyser going under the names of writing, text and trace, and only by proposing a reconstruction and a generalization of these concepts: writing, the text, the trace as the play and work of *différance*, whose role is at one and the same time both of constitution and of deconstitution. This strategy may have appeared to be an abusive deformation – or, as some have cursorily said, a metaphorical usage – of the current notions of writing, text or trace, and have seemed to those who continued to cling to these old self-interested representations to give rise to all sorts of misunderstandings. But I have untiringly striven to justify this unbounded generalization, and I believe that every conceptual breakthrough amounts to transforming, that is to deforming, an accredited, authorized relationship between a word and a concept, between a trope and what one had every interest to consider to be an unshiftable primary sense, a proper, literal or current usage. Moreover, the strategic and rhetorical bearing of these attitudes has never ceased to engage me in numerous subsequent texts. All of this was grouped together under the title of deconstruction, the graphics of *différance*, of the trace, the supplement, etc., and here I can only indicate them in an algebraic manner. What I proposed at that time retained an oblique, deviant, sometimes directly critical, relationship with respect to everything that seemed then to dominate the main, most visible, the most spectacular and sometimes the most fertile outcrop of French theoretical production, a phenomenon which, in its various different forms, was known, no doubt abusively, as 'structuralism'. Certainly, these forms were very diverse and very remarkable, whether in the domains of anthropology, history, literary criticism, linguistics or psychoanalysis, in the rereadings, as people said, of Freud or of Marx. But regardless of their indisputable interest, in the course of this period which was also in appearance the most static period of the Gaullist republic of 1958–68, what I was attempting or what was tempting me was of an essentially different nature. And so, aware of the cost of these advances in terms of their metaphysical presuppositions, to say nothing of what was, less evidently, their political price, I buried myself from this time on in a sort of retreat, in a solitude which I mention here without pathos, as simply self-evident, and merely as a reminder that increasingly in regard to academic tradition as well as to established modernity – and in this case the two are but one – this solitude has been and often still is considered to be the well-deserved consequence of an hermetic and unjustified reclusiveness. Is it necessary to say that I do not think this is so and that I interpret in an entirely different manner the reasons for this verdict? It is also true that the living thinkers who gave me the most to think about or who most provoked me to reflection, and who continue to do so, are not among those who break through a solitude, not among those to whom one can simply feel oneself close, not among those who form groups or schools, to mention only Heidegger, Levinas, Blanchot among others whom I shall not name. It is thinkers such as these to whom, strangely enough, one may consider oneself most close; and yet they are, more than others, other. And they too are alone.

It was already clear to me that the general turn that my research was taking could no longer conform to the classical norms of the thesis. This 'research' called not only for a different mode of writing but also for a work of transformation applied to the rhetoric, the staging and the particular discursive procedures, which, historically determined as they very much are, dominate university discourse, in particular the type of text that is called the 'thesis'; and we know how all these scholarly and university models likewise provide the laws regulating so many prestigious discourses, even those of literary works or of eloquent political speeches which shine outside the university. And then, too, the directions I had taken, the nature and the diversity of the corpora, the labyrinthian geography of the itineraries drawing me on towards relatively unacademic areas, all of this persuaded me that the time was now past, that it was, in truth, no longer possible, even if I wanted to, to make what I was writing conform to the size and form then required for a thesis. The very idea of a thetic presentation, of positional or oppositional logic, the idea of posi-tion, of *Setzung* or *Stellung*, that which I called at the beginning the *epoch* of the thesis, was one of the essential parts of the system that was under deconstructive questioning. What was then put forth under the heading – itself lacking any particular status – of dissemination explicitly dealt, in ways that were in effect neither thematic nor thetic, with the value of the thesis, of positional logic and its history, and of the limits of its rights, its authority and its legitimacy. This did not imply on my part, at least at that particu-lar time, any radical institutional critique of the thesis, of the presentation of university work in order to have it legitimized or of the authorization of competence by accredited representatives of the university. If, from this moment on, I was indeed con-vinced of the necessity for a profound transformation, amounting even to a complete upheaval of university institutions, this was not, of course, in order to substitute for what existed some type of non-thesis, non-legitimacy or incompetence. In this area I believe in transitions and in negotiation – even if it may at times be brutal and speeded up – I believe in the necessity for a certain tradition, in particular for political reasons that are nothing less than tradi-tionalist, and I believe, moreover, in the indestructibility of the ordered procedures of legitimation, of the production of titles and diplomas and of the authorization of competence. I speak here in general and not necessarily of the *universitas*, which is a powerful but very particular, very specific, and indeed very recent, model for this procedure of legitimation. The structure of the *universitas* has an essential tie with the ontological and logocentric onto-encyclopedic system; and for the past several years it has seemed to me that the indissociable link between the modern concept of the university and a certain metaphysics calls for investigations such as I pursued in my teaching or in essays that have been published or are in the course of being published on *The Conflict of the Faculties* by Kant, and on Hegel, Nietzsche and Heidegger in their political philosophy of the university. If I insist on this theme, it is because, given the circumstances and the impossibility in which I find myself of summing up or presenting thetic conclusions, I feel that I should attend first and foremost to what is happening here and now, and I should wish to assume responsibility as clearly and as honestly as possible from my very limited place and in my own way.

In 1967 I was so little bent on questioning the necessity of an institution such as this, of its general principle in any case, if not its particular university structure and organization, that I thought I could make a sort of compromise and division of labour and time, according its share to the thesis, to the time of the thesis. On the one hand, I would have let the work in which I was engaged develop freely and outside the usual forms and norms, a work which decidedly did not conform to such university requirements and which was even to analyse, contest, displace, deform them in all their rhetorical or political bearing; but at the same time, and on the other hand, the transaction and the time or the epoch of the thesis would have amounted to setting apart one piece of this work, a theoretical sequence playing the role of an organizing element, and treating it in accordance with one of those acceptable forms which are, within the context of the university, so reassuring. This would have involved an interpretation of the Hegelian theory of the sign, of speech and of writing in Hegel's semiology. It seemed indispensable to me, for reasons I have discussed especially in *Marges*, to propose a systematic interpretation of this semiology. Jean Hyppolite gave me his consent yet once again and this second thesis topic was in its turn – registered.

This, then, was in 1967. Things were so intertwined and over-determined that I cannot even begin to say what was the impact on me, on my work and my teaching, on my relationship to university institutions and to the domain of cultural representation of that event which one still does not know how to name other than by its date, 1968, without ever having any very clear idea of just what it is one is naming in this way. The least that I can say about it is this: something I had been anticipating found its confirmation at that time and this confirmation accelerated my own movement away, as I was then moving away more quickly and more resolutely *on the one hand* from the places where, as early as the autumn of 1968, the old armatures were being hastily recentred, reconstituted, reconcentrated, and *on the other hand* from a style of writing guided by the model of the classical thesis, and even directed by a concern for recognition by academic authorities who, at least in those bodies in which were to be found gathered together, officially and in terms of built-in majorities, their most effective powers of evaluation and decision, seemed to me, after '68, to be both overreactive and too effective in their resistance to all that did not conform to the most tranquillizing criteria of acceptability. I had numerous indications of this; certain concerned me personally, and if I say that politics was also involved it is because, in this case, politics does not take only the conventional distribution along an axis running from left to right. The reproductive force of authority can get along more comfortably with declarations or theses whose content presents itself as revolutionary, provided that they respect the rites of legitimation, the rhetoric and the institutional symbolism which defuses and neutralizes whatever comes from outside the system. What is unacceptable is what, underlying positions or theses, upsets this deeply entrenched contract, the order of these norms, and which does so in the very *form* of works, of teaching or of writing.

The death of Jean Hyppolite in 1968 was not only for me, as for others, a moment of great sadness. By a strange coincidence, it marked at that date – the autumn of 1968 and it was indeed the autumn – the end of a certain type of membership of the university. Certainly, from the first day of my arrival in France this membership had not been simple, but it was during these years no doubt that I came to understand better to what extent the necessity of deconstruction (I use this word for the sake of rapid convenience, though it is a word I have never liked and one whose fortune has disagreeably surprised me) was not primarily a matter of philosophical contents, themes or theses, philosophemes, poems, theologemes or ideologemes, but especially and inseparably meaningful frames, institutional structures, pedagogical or rhetorical norms, the possibilities of law, of authority, of evaluation, and of representation in terms of its very market. My interest for these more or less visible framework structures, for these limits, these margin effects or these paradoxes of edgings continued to relate to the same question: how is it that philosophy finds itself inscribed, rather than itself inscribing itself, within a space which it seeks but is unable to control, a space which opens out onto another which is no longer even *its* other, as I have tried to make apparent in a *tympanum* as little Hegelian as possible. How is one to name the structure of this space? I do not *know*; nor do I know whether there can even be what may be called *knowledge* of such a space. To call it socio-political is a triviality which does not satisfy me, and even the most indisputable of what are said to be socio-analyses have often enough very little to say on the matter, remaining blind to their own inscription, to the law of their reproduction performances, to the stage of their own heritage and of their self-authorization, in short to what I will call their writing.

I have chosen, as you can see, to confide to you without circumlocution, if not without a certain simplification, all the uncertainties, the hesitations, the oscillations by way of which I sought the most fitting relationship with the institution of the university, on a plane that was not simply political and that concerned not only the thesis. It was at first a somewhat passive reaction: the thing no longer interested me very much. I should have had to come up with a new formulation, come to an understanding with a new supervisor, etc. And as doctorates based on published works, theoretically possible, were evidently not encouraged, to say the very least, I turned away, at first somewhat passively, I repeat, from those places which seemed to me less and less open to what really mattered to me. But I have to admit that in certain situations, most notably those in which I am writing and in which I am writing about writing, my obstinacy is so great as to constitute a compelling constraint upon me, even when it is forced to take the most roundabout paths. And so beyond the three works published in 1972, I kept worrying away at the same problematic, the same open matrix (opening onto the linked series formed by the trace, *différance*, undecidables, dissemination, the supplement, the graft, the hymen, the parergon, etc.), pushing it towards textual configurations that were less and less linear, logical and topical forms, even typographical forms that were more daring, the intersection of corpora, mixtures of genera or of modes, changes of tone (*Wechsel der Töne*), satire, rerouting, grafting, etc., to the extent that even today, although these texts have been published for years, I do not believe them to be simply presentable or acceptable to the university and I have not dared, have not judged it opportune, to include them here among the works to be defended. These texts include *Glas*, despite the continued pursuit there of the project of grammatology, that is the discussion with the arbitrary character of the sign and the thesis of onomatopoeia in Saussure as well as with the Hegelian *Aufhebung*, the relation between the undecidable, the dialectic and the double bind, the concept of generalized fetishism, the pull of the discourse on/of castration towards an affirmative dissemination and towards another rhetoric of the whole and the part, the re-elaboration of a problematic dealing with the proper noun and the signature, with the testament and the monument and many other themes besides; all of this indeed was an expansion of earlier attempts. I should say the same thing with respect to the other works that I have deliberately left aside from this submission, works such as *Eperons, les styles de Nietzsche* or *La Carte postale*, which, each in their own way, nevertheless extend a reading (of Freud, of Nietzsche and some others) begun at an earlier stage, the deconstruction of a certain hermeneutics as well as of a certain way of theorizing about the signifier and the letter with its authority and institutional power (I am referring here to the whole psychoanalytic set-up as well as to the university), the analysis of logocentrism *as* phallogocentrism, a concept by means of which I tried to indicate, in my analysis, the essential indissociability of phallocentrism and logocentrism, and to locate their effects wherever I could spot them – but these effects are everywhere, even where they remain unnoticed.

The expansion of these texts dealing with textuality might seem anamorphic or labyrinthian, or both at once, but what in particular made them just about unsubmittable as a thesis was less the multiplicity of their contents, conclusions and demonstrative positions, than, it seems to me, the acts of writing and the performative stage to which they ought to give rise and from which they remained inseparable and hence not easily capable of being represented, transported and translated into another form; they were inscribed in a space that one could no longer, that I myself could no longer, identify or classify under the heading of philosophy *or* of non-fiction, etc., especially at a time when what others would call the autobiographical involvement of these texts was undermining the very notion of autobiography, giving it over to what the necessity of writing, the trace, the remainder, etc. could offer of all that was most baffling, undecidable, wily or despairing. And since I have just alluded to the performative structure, let me note in passing that, for the same reasons, I have held back from the thesis corpus, along with a good many other essays, a debate that I had in the United States with a speech act theorist, John Searle, in an opuscule that I entitled 'Limited Inc'.

During an initial period, then, from 1968 to 1974, I simply neglected the thesis. But during the years that followed I deliberately decided – and I sincerely believed that this decision was final – not to submit a thesis at all. For, besides the reasons I have just mentioned and which seemed to me to be more and more solid, I have been engaged since 1974 with friends, colleagues and university and high school students in a work which I should dare to call a long-term struggle which directly concerns the institutions of philosophy as they exist, especially in France. The context of this work is to be found first and foremost in a situation whose nature has been determined by a long history, but which was seriously aggravated in 1975 by a policy which could – or, one may fear, will – lead to the destruction of philosophical teaching and research, with all that this implies by way of consequences for this country. For all the women and men who, like me, worked to organize the Groupe de Recherches sur l'Enseignement Philosophique (GREPH) and who participated in its rough draft, its works and its actions, from 1974 until the meeting of the Estates General of Philosophy in this very place just one year ago, for all of us the task was of the utmost urgency, and the responsibility ineluctable. I must specify: this task was urgent and ineluctable in the places which we occupy – those of teaching or research in philosophy – the places to which we cannot deny that we belong and in which we find ourselves inscribed. But of course, other things are urgent too, this philosophical realm is not the only one available to thought; it is neither the first one in the world, nor is it the one with the greatest determining influence on, for example, politics. We dwell elsewhere as well, and this I have tried never to forget; nor indeed is it something that allows itself to be forgotten. What we in GREPH were questioning with respect to philosophical teaching could not be separated, and we have always been attentive to this point, from all of the other cultural, political and other contending forces in this country and in the world.

In any case, as far as I was concerned, my participation in GREPH's works and struggles had to be as consistent as possible with what I was trying to write elsewhere, even if the middle terms between the two necessities were not always either easy or obvious. I have to say this here: although among the works presented to you I have included neither the texts I have signed or those that I have prepared as a militant of GREPH nor, *a fortiori*, the collective actions in which I have participated or which I have endorsed in that capacity, I consider them to be inseparable, let us say in spirit, from my other public acts – most notably from my other publications. And the gesture I make today, far from signifying that I have abandoned anything in this respect, will, on the contrary I hope, make possible other involvements or other responsibilities in the *same* struggle.

It remains the case that during this second period, beginning around 1974, I thought, rightly or wrongly, that it was neither consistent nor desirable to be a candidate for any new academic title or responsibility. Not consistent given the work of political criticism in which I was participating, not desirable with regard to a little forum that was more internal, more private and upon which, through a whole endless scenography of symbols, representations, phantasies, traps and strategies, a self-image recounts all sorts of interminable and incredible stories to itself. So I thought I had decided that, without further changing anything in my university situation, I would continue for better or for worse doing what I had done up to then, remaining in the place where I had been immobilized, without knowing anything more about where I was going, indeed knowing less no doubt about it than ever. It is not insignificant, I believe, that during this period most of the texts I published placed the greatest, if not the most novel, emphasis on rights and on what is proper, what is one's own, on the rights of property, on copyright, on the signature and the market, on the market for painting or, more generally, for culture and all its representations, on speculation on what is proper, one's own, on the name, on destination and restitution, on all the institutional borders and structures of discourses, on the whole machinery of publishing and on the media. Whether in my analyses of the logic of the parergon or the interlacing stricture of the double bind, or in my discussions of the paintings of Van Gogh, Adami or Titus Carmel, of the meditations on art by Kant, Hegel, Heidegger or Benjamin (in *La Vérité en peinture*), or again in my attempts to explore new questions in conjunction with psychoanalysis (for example, in relating to the works of Nicolas Abraham and Maria Torok, works that are so alive today) – in all of these cases I have been increasingly preoccupied with the necessity of making a fresh start in working on questions said to be classically institutional. I should have liked in this respect to have been able to shape both my discourse and my practice, as one says, to fit the premises of my earlier undertakings. In fact, if not in principle, this was not always easy, not always possible, at times indeed very burdensome in a number of ways.

Of the third and final period, the one in which I find myself here and now, I can say very little. Only a few months ago, and after taking account of a very wide number of different factors which I cannot analyse here, I came to the conclusion, thus putting an abrupt end to a process of deliberation that was threatening to become interminable, that everything that had justified my earlier resolution (concerning the thesis, of course) was no longer likely to be valid for the years to come. In particular, for the very same reasons of institutional politics which had until now held me back, I concluded that it was perhaps better, and I must underline the 'perhaps', to prepare myself for some new type of mobility. And as is often, as is always the case, it is the friendly advice of this or that person among those here present, before or behind me, it is other people, always others, who effected in me a decision I could not have come to alone. For not only am I not sure, as I never am, of being right in taking this step, I am not sure that I see in all clarity what led me to do so. Perhaps because I was beginning to know only too well not indeed where I was going, but where I had not so much arrived as simply stopped.

I began by saying that it was as if I was bereft of speech. You recognized, of course, that this was just another manner of speaking;

nevertheless it was not false. For the *captatio* in which I have just indulged has been not only excessively coded, excessively narrative – the chronicle of so many anachronies – it has been also as impoverished as a punctuation mark, rather, I should say, an apostrophe in an unfinished text. And above all, above all, it has sounded too much like the totting up of a calculation, a self-justification, a self-submission (as of a thesis), a self-defence (in the United States one speaks of a thesis defence for a *soutenance de thèse*). You have heard too much talk of strategies. Strategy is a word that I have perhaps abused in the past, especially as it has been always only to specify *in the end*, in an apparently self-contradictory manner and at the risk of cutting the ground from under my own feet – something I almost never fail to do – that this strategy is a strategy without any finality; for this is what I hold and what in turn holds me in its grip, the aleatory strategy of someone who admits that he does not know where he is going. This, then, is not after all an undertaking of war or a discourse of belligerence. I should like it to be also like a headlong flight straight towards the end, a joyous self-contradiction, a disarmed desire, that is to say something very old and very cunning, but which also has just been born and which delights in being without defence.

Translated by Kathleen McLaughlin

JEAN-TOUSSAINT DESANTI

A path in philosophy

The situation in which I find myself here rather disturbs me. I do not like talking about my own work: the proper distance is lacking and, of course, one must beware either of appearing presumptuous or of seeming too humble. Yet I must get on with it, as I have, perhaps rashly, committed myself to doing so.

1. In order to begin, I shall, therefore, make use of such detours and devices as history affords, and ask myself this question: just what was involved in deciding to become a philosopher in France in the mid-thirties (to be exact, in 1934, the year I turned twenty), and what fate was one thereby embracing? And why take such a decision after all? I had done my secondary schooling in Corsica, my birthplace, at Ajaccio college, a place sheltered from the currents of contemporary culture to an extent that is today quite unimaginable. I had really learned only three things: Latin, Greek and mathematics (or rather their prehistory; I had had to learn algebra in Serret and calculus in Joseph Bertrand!). But I had never heard of Proust, Joyce, Gide, Nietzsche (certainly no new-comer, even then!), Freud and so on . . . In short, our insularity re-stricted us to the past. With regard to what I could suspect as to the existence of contemporary works, I felt no curiosity at all: only an icy disdain. So that at the end of adolescence, I had reached the point of believing that human culture included two regions: one ancient, serious, fundamental and with deep roots; the other recent, insignificant, unstable and at most capable only of enter-taining the 'continentals'.

Thinking about it now, at a distance of half a century, it seems to me that these circumstances were not unrelated to my choice in favour of philosophy. On the continent away from home, in the Paris of 1934, I sought in Plato, Spinoza and Kant something like another homeland: a place to retreat to, a shelter against modernity, which, since I understood it poorly, I took to be futile – in short, I sought a place to put down roots and in which to discover something serious to think about. It has taken me time, and a great many experiences, many of which were far from intellectual, to rid myself of this disdain.

In deciding in favour of philosophy in the academic year 1934–5, to what, then, was I committing myself? Of course, one may choose to be a plumber, a shoemaker, a mason, while being a philosopher to boot. But the times did not allow for marginal living. We lived in well-structured surroundings. And our most serious adventures were political ones – that is, structured, organized. I had to follow the path laid down by the university institutions: the *cursus* leading to the *agrégation* which, in France, makes a profession of philosophy and a professor of the philosopher. At the time this offered, for most of us, no prospects other than that of teaching philosophy in the final year of the *lycée* (in the best of cases, in the 'Philosophy' section). None of this was free from constraint or from the danger of distortion. We had to confine ourselves to the obligatory forms of a tradition-bound rhetoric, and to follow the venerable models whose memory was perpetuated by the 'Inspection Générale': the 'great professors' who, it was said, had formed generations of 'free citizens', and also, on occasion, other professors, who followed in their footsteps. Caught in this reproductive mechanism, which is today very familiar, we could not, without damage to ourselves, comply with it completely, and yet were unable to withdraw from it. For my part, I solved this problem quite crudely. I had learned once and for all, during my years of preparation for the Ecole Normale, how to manipulate this sort of rhetoric. So I decided, once I was admitted to the Ecole, to allow this side of my training to lie dormant, ready to bring it to life the week this would be necessary, for three seven-hour periods. For some unknown reason, after 'trials and errors', this finally worked.

Two influences were to leave their mark on me at the Ecole Normale – that of Jean Cavaillès, philosopher and mathematician, and that of Maurice Merleau-Ponty. For me, Gaston Bachelard's influence came later; it dated from the 1940s.

At that time there was no methodical teaching of what the philosophers called, not without a certain scorn, 'logistics'. The situation in France was, in this regard, thoroughly distressing. It had nothing in common with what was going on in Göttingen, Cambridge or Warsaw. In our generation, there are a number of us that owe a debt to Jean Cavaillès for having opened this field to us, and for having introduced us to mathematical philosophy. Cavaillès was rigorous, exacting, deeply philosophical (after the manner of Spinoza, it seemed to us); any sort of trickery was immediately uncovered and confronted. In order to follow him, one had to educate oneself anew. With whatever means at hand, one had to learn this so much disparaged 'logistics' (basically in *Principia Mathematica*). And, so far as I was concerned at least, this included revising my background in mathematics, starting all over again from the very beginning. This I could never have done but for the constant company of my mathematician friends. They helped me avoid many needless detours. This resulted in the formation of a small, mathematical-philosophical community, numbering only a handful of individuals, but nonetheless alive. We taught one another how to decipher mathematical texts, how to elicit the concepts concerned, how to analyse the relevant operations. But, of course, with regard to the *cursus* all this led nowhere.

Merleau-Ponty, for his part, was not inclined towards what he called '*mathesis*'. And he was surprised at my taste for it, gently reproaching me in his role of benevolent mentor. Being responsible for our philosophical training, he was afraid that it would be my undoing, that I would become neither fish nor fowl. Yet he opened up another field for us, which we entered one step at a time – and not without some resistance: the field of transcendental phenomenology. In order to follow him too, we had once more to start our education all over again – situating ourselves anew in relation to the tradition of 'French philosophy', breaking out of the artificial dilemma within which, since the *lycée*, it had confined us: Kant or Bergson (if not, as was the case for many of us, Hamelin or Bergson!). Hegel was absent from this horizon, Marx too, at least at the beginning. So it seems to me that my early training was that of an apprentice phenomenologist working away at deciphering philosophical and mathematical texts side by side. I have since abandoned transcendental phenomenology. And yet I do not believe I have ever really broken with (but should I have?) the ways of thinking, the methodological requirements or the language habits acquired during this period.

As far as my philosophical education in the academic sense of the word is concerned, it was basically classical: that is to say, it was mainly centred for us (to each person, his own classicism) around Plato, Descartes, Spinoza and Kant. This was the result of Léon Brunschvicg's teaching, which, if it was centred around this quartet, was not thereby limited solely to it. However, in this sequence Brunschvicg accustomed us to see something like an internal logic according to which these names represented the high-points in Reason's Odyssey, necessary reference points along the unfolding of philosophy as manifested in history. Taken in this sense (as the unveiling of the rational) the history of philosophy and the history of the sciences (in my case, the history of calculus since Cauchy) formed, for many of us, the fertile soil and the mediation necessary to encourage us towards philosophical reflection. Were we to learn to rid ourselves of this tradition or should we, on the contrary, commit ourselves completely to it? This is one of the questions that I have to examine, for it is at the heart of the problems that have always bothered and that continue to bother me still. It is all the more perturbing inasmuch as a long-lasting political commitment, born out of the war and the Resistance, brought me, up to the end of the 1950s, into serious and at one moment even dramatic confrontation with certain theoretical and ethical problems which, as a result of Marx, the contemporary period has been constrained to face.

If I find it useful to recall these historical points, it is not only out of a concern to continue to skirt around what I am reluctant to talk about, namely what I have been able to accomplish in the epistemology of mathematics and – especially in my teaching – in the history of philosophy (textual analysis). My historical reminders are intended rather to point up the fact that, for people of my generation in France, what is termed 'exact philosophy' was not at all self-evident. Nor did we have any direct contact with mathematical logic. This was not part of our heritage. We had to move against the current, against the pervasive culture, and forge our own relationship to mathematical logic for ourselves, on the basis of what our tradition – which was basically historicizing – had already made of us. I can still recall today the feeling of desolation that I had (a kind of despair arising from a sensation of being excluded) the first time (which was, if I remember well, in 1937) that I read the *Tractatus Logico-philosophicus*. I assuredly did not feel any complicity with it. But this, I had to acquire.

Just one more word, however, before going on to the subject that I have to deal with here. It would be dishonest for me to pass over in silence the decade (1947–58) during which I was a militant philosopher in the ranks of the French Communist Party, which I joined during the Nazi occupation. The expression 'militant philosopher' may seem shocking. And yet this is the appropriate term. The workers' parties that claim adherence to Marxism (and this has been the case since Karl Kautsky and German Social Democracy) have a tendency to reproduce, by turning them upside-down, the institutions of 'bourgeois society'. If in the university philosophy is a profession, in the Communist Party it is a militant function; or at any rate it was at the time that I was involved, during the 'cold war'. What was expected of this philosophical function in the P.C.F. (Parti Communiste Français)? The same as what was generally expected from intellectuals and nothing more: to perform an ideological service. Develop theory? Contribute to the production of that 'Marxist philosophy', which Louis Althuser at the start of the sixties was to say, quite correctly, did not even exist? Of none of this did the question even arise. The 'theory' was there, ready-made, the 'philosophy' had been codified. And anyway, only the recognized political leaders, starting with the General Secretary, had any right to take a look at theory. Only they were entitled to 'enrich Marxism', as it was put. And first among these – actually the only one institutionally endowed with this right – supreme in the elaboration of theory, was J. Stalin. The most important question was, therefore, not what I, J.-T. Desanti, might think about Marx or Lenin, not how I was to situate myself within this textual corpus, making my way within it according to my own criteria. No one would have prevented me from asking myself these questions (and I did in fact put them to myself). But they were of no interest to the Party; they remained my own private concern. They fell outside my activity as a militant philosopher. In this capacity, the essential question I had to answer, at once and on the spot, was the following: taking into account its strategies and the ideological and political situation confronting it, what does the Party demand of me? In the Party jargon (which employed military metaphors) this was called 'occupying one's post on the ideological front'. We made up a sort of counter-society within society. We considered ourselves as if in a state of siege. On our borders it was important to keep the most vigilant of watches. And in the Party it was precisely this border area that was the business of the philosopher. One of his main functions was the pedagogical and critical task of preserving a clear and distinct outline: no contamination, the demarcation and safeguarding of the difference.

What happens to someone with a philosophical background when he plays this game? I can speak here only for myself. One tries first of all to constitute for oneself a unitary philosophical consciousness: to hold together both the 'public' side (the requirements of a militant) and the 'private' side (the need to clarify, for oneself, the choices and the things one is not prepared to give up). The only path open is that of putting oneself firmly within the framework of 'Marxism' (by this I mean within the framework of the writings of Marx and Lenin) as if in a place of origin from whence one could discover something like the foundation and intelligible source of one's own practice as a militant. In so doing, the heterogeneous strata which form 'the private philosophical consciousness' (in my case, phenomenology and mathematical philosophy) are reworked, and, so to say, reconsidered, rethought and reformulated in a different language – at certain points, even repressed or at least covered over. What one aims at here, ideally at least, is the formation of a totality in which all the areas one knows something about would be held together in a strong interconnection: an interconnection of which the method elaborated by Marx would enable all the links to be joined one to another. It does not take long, however, to see that this work is futile, inasmuch as it leads nowhere and remains closed in on itself, serving only the self-gratification of the 'philosopher', as he may here call himself, or, if one prefers to put it that way, serving to bolster his philosophical security. This work is foreordained to be solitary. Only the militant productions of the public consciousness ever see the light of day. However far this effort of clarification is pushed, it remains private; compared to the needs of the Party, it is neither wished for nor even acceptable. And even if it were, the requirements of totalization appeared no less an illusion. The strong interconnection that was desired proved itself in actual experience to be weak and full of holes, and this to such an extent that the preservation of the totalizing project became an article of faith, or better, something like an Idea in the Kantian sense of the word, towards which one continues to strive knowing all the while that it can never be reached. The collapse of this beautiful mythical totality was, for many of us, an historical fact, which I shall not discuss further here. In any event, following this collapse, at the end of the 1950s, I went back to epistemology. But, of course, as a result of the historical events I had lived through, this now involved other demands on the subject than those I had made on it when I was young.

2. The only book of mine to which I attach some importance is entitled *Les Idéalités mathématiques*. Begun in 1964, it was published in 1968. The title is somewhat misleading. The book is actually a monograph whose material is drawn from the state of the theory of real variable functions at the end of the 1920s. For the sake of convenience I had taken as my reference point Hobson's well-known treatise, which, despite its rather archaic style, had the advantage of offering at once a panoramic perspective and a detailed account of the theory. I have been reproached for choosing this topic for a work written during the 1960s. To this I can make but one reply: everyone is free to choose his own field of analysis, and this depends essentially on what one intends to show (or, at least, on what one believes oneself capable of showing).

As for myself, when I undertook this work my philosophical situation was most uncomfortable:

(1) I could not resign myself to 'Platonism' for at least three reasons: (a) If one were to be a Platonist, one must be so in all seriousness, or not at all. It seemed very strange to me to practise a selective Platonism, involving only mathematical entities. Plato himself, and Plotinus, were more consistent. One has only to reread Plotinus's famous Ennead *On Numbers* (VI, 6), especially Chapter 6. He raises the following question: if there is a number in itself, aside from those here below, and if the intelligible objects themselves include numbers, what can be the nature of these numbers and how can we conceive of their generation? Plotinus asserts that this generation can be accomplished through the

reason immanent in intelligible beings (*logos*). This leads him to a strong reaffirmation of Platonic 'realism': 'The essence of forms does not come into existence because a thinking being conceives of each of them and confers existence on them as a result of this conception . . . It is not because one thinks of the essence of justice that justice is born.' And again later: 'It is the object itself (the intelligible object), because it is without matter, that is at once intelligibility and thought. It is not a thought in the way its definition, or the representation we may have of it, would be, but being in the intelligence it is itself nothing but intelligence and science.' This is what I call a serious Platonist. If there are truly real numbers, then they are contemporary with intelligence and with the intelligible. In that case, one cannot speak of them without describing the structure of this intelligible world and without showing the way in which these numbers behave there and the function they perform. However, to retain of Platonism nothing but the realism of mathematical forms and to avoid the problem of the structure of the world of forms, this, it seemed to me, could be nothing but an *ad hoc* hypothesis, serving only to reassure the mathematician as to the degree of consistency of his objects. I should perhaps here plead guilty and accuse myself of reading too much Plato and Plotinus. But in truth I have always found quite insufficient the mutilated Platonism of those who, in the profession, are called 'Platonists'. The only one who (in my estimation, and to my knowledge) was truly serious about this was A. Lautman. He attempted to describe, in dialectical terms (in Plato's sense of the dialectic), the intelligible structures which are embodied in actual mathematics. But were not these intelligible structures (belonging to the order of Being) worked out on the basis of the mathematical structures elicited at the end of the 1930s? I fear so. In short, for these reasons, I was suspicious of 'Platonism'. And after all, I told myself, did this not amount to repeating the words of Parmenides of old: 'No, never will you find thought outside of Being, where its expression lies.' No doubt. But if such 'thought' is precisely that of the 'body of the real', then it becomes a very unclear task to discover in Being in general the mode of being of this or that particular body, or of its intelligible 'matrix'.

(b) Another reason for my mistrust was that my twofold education in mathematics and in (Husserlian) phenomenology had convinced me (perhaps mistakenly) that one had to hold together, without ever being able to separate them, mathematical objects and the series of acts which established their properties and maintained their unity. Thus, I took mathematics to be an activity developing in history, involving a specific form of experience articulated according to the series of acts and motivations concerning 'objects' whose invariance and omnitemporality were part and parcel of this experience itself and something like its own work. Under the circumstances it appeared to me gratuitous to refer to some 'intelligible world', to an 'in itself', homogeneous with the object that is thought and actually manipulated, and yet 'ontologically' prior to this very object. This kind of ontological primacy of the mathematical entity over the series of acts making it available as an object has always been a mystery to me. And, one mystery for another, I prefer those inherent in history and in time.

(c) There was a final reason for my mistrust, and one quite unrelated to mathematics: I hold men to be essentially mortal and humanity to be transitory, just like other species now extinct. I see no reason that could make me believe in some domain reserved for 'eternal truths'. The logical categories themselves, however transtemporal they may appear, must, it seems to me, be understood as essentially tied to the life of that historical being, doomed to die without recourse, which is man himself, '*Homo sapiens*'. That such a being should crave eternity to the point of wanting to confer it upon some of the 'entities' he has managed to conceive of or to construct, this, of course, calls to be understood. It remains that that which is called 'true' achieves existence only inasmuch as it is thought, said and proved, in other words, only in time. This at any rate was one of the convictions that led me away from 'Platonism'. It was not a matter of establishing a system of 'reasons' capable of 'refuting' the Platonizing hypothesis. What was involved was rather a mental disposition, born out of my experience, which, when faced with the conditions required to take such a hypothesis seriously, led me irresistibly to declare '*non possumus*'.

(2) The same suspicion drove me away (though I am not able to develop this point here) both from empiricism (at least in its classical forms) and, at the opposite extreme, from any form of 'transcendental philosophy'. What worried me about empiricism

was its ground, whatever the name that may be given to it ('impressions', 'sense data' etc.). It appeared to me to be a 'construct', an abstraction resulting from representation, thought and posited *ad hoc*, precisely to serve as a ground. However, upon examination it seemed to give way, much like a pocket of quicksand in which one slowly sinks. As for transcendental idealism, even in the form with which I was familiar, Husserlian phenomenology, it seemed to me to rest upon the exorbitant hypothesis of a primordially constitutive *ego*, a fixed point, around which the constitution of every experience capable of being presented to consciousness has to organize itself, and, consequently, the constitution of every 'objectivity' capable of being posited and maintained. Having tried my hand over a long period of time at the phenomenological method, I had, it seemed to me, experienced the futility of seeking this fixed point. In truth, I had always seen it flee at my approach, unceasingly presupposed, never reached in itself. Like the 'ground' of the empiricists, it always slipped away. In the light of this exercise, I eventually (this was still in the early 1960s) came to consider as chimerical both the hypothesis of the constitutive *ego* and the task required by this hypothesis – 'to organize all experience around the sources of transcendental subjectivity'. I explained my position on this question in a work entitled 'Phénoménologie et praxis'.[1] Although today I no longer agree with the positive part of this essay (it was, indeed, but barely begun), I have nothing to add to the critique of transcendental phenomenology as it is sketched out there.

Such was the seemingly discouraging situation in which I found myself in the year 1964. Like the man who had lost his shadow, I wandered, deprived of philosophy in free motion, so to speak. And, when deciding to begin work on a small fragment of the development of analysis (that is, of the theory of real variable functions around 1930), I had no advance idea of what sort of 'philosophy' would come out of it, nor even if there was any point in trying to extract one.

(3) All of this made for an uncomfortable situation which I had to try to turn to my advantage. I found myself free of the task of having to look in my field of analysis for examples (or counter-examples) by which to 'verify' (or 'invalidate') this or that 'philosophy'. In the state of philosophical vacuity to which I was reduced it seemed to me thoroughly futile – and anyway quite

impracticable (except as a sort of game)[2] – to treat this mathematical fragment as the stake in a '*disputatio*', a closed arena in which philosophical rivals were to cast objections and counter-objections at each other.

Morever, as it was now impossible for me to assume any sort of 'originary', primordial basis, either that of a fundamental ground or that of a self-constituting subject, I found myself swimming against two tides, so to speak, having neither the opportunity of climbing out to enjoy a panoramic view of this expanse of liquid nor that of diving down to the bottom to seek, it might be, the original well-spring. This meant that I could do nothing other, in the state in which I found myself, than plunge into the midst of the theory in question and find therein something to say that might show the sense of it all, and demonstrate (at least partially) the constitution and status proper to it. Should this sort of approach be termed 'philosophical'? In the ordinary sense, certainly not. It in no way involves an effort to come to terms with the traditional problems of what is called 'the philosophy of mathematics', that is, to seek, through the attempt to analyse a particular theoretical field, some basis of decision for determining and possibly testing the degree to which current theories (or points of view – Platonism, formalism, intuitionism, constructivism. . .) may be adequate to its living mathematical content. Nor was it a matter of setting out from this, all in all, rather limited material to raise the problems of the foundation of mathematics or to try to delimit some sort of fundamental material (a 'minimal ontology', so to speak) on the basis of which one could undertake the reconstruction of the theory on an entirely explicit basis. These kinds of investigation seem to me to be wholly legitimate and fruitful. However, they did not form part of my own project, nor could I at that time undertake any such commitment, due mainly to the 'philosophical' state into which my own history had led me and to the nature of my apprenticeship. For lack of any other available word I had to resign myself to calling the type of work to which I was committing myself 'epistemology'. And in fact, to take this word 'epistemology' in the strict sense of the term, my task was simply to try to 'say' something sensible about this fragment of '*episteme*' which I had decided (arbitrarily, of course) to set out to examine.

But, how was I to 'say' anything and what 'language' was I to speak? Mathematics has its own (more or less formal) language. There were here a number of stumbling blocks to be avoided: that of purely and simply repeating the theory in question in its own specific language, which would have been useless; that of limiting myself to retracing the history of the theory, which would have only postponed (or, at least, bypassed) the problem that concerned me; that of reconstructing it in an adequate, formal language, something which others – professional mathematicians and logicians – could do far better than I could ever have hoped to do, and who have indeed done so. There remained only my own natural philosophical language, that of phenomenology, which I had practised on my own account before as well as (when I come to look back on it) during my 'militant' period; there is here a phenomenon of 'double consciousness', or, rather, of a stratification of languages, whose analysis I am unable to undertake here. This situation was paradoxical: I could speak nothing but the language of a philosophy whose fundamental project I had deemed unrealizable. In the beginning, the use of this language seemed to me to be nevertheless more or less adequate for my aims. In fact, I was testing it out, as one would a machine or a set of tools, even though it might mean switching along the way, in the event that the topics to be analysed should become too complicated for this language. And this proved, indeed, to be the case as soon as the problem arose of untangling, except for certain 'simple' objects, the complex interplay of intratheoretical mediations proper to a highly stratified state of theory – for example, if one bases oneself on Lebesque's study, *Sur les fonctions représentables analytiquement*, the problem of analysing the oblique target which Lebesque himself failed to reach, but which was taken up again by Lusin based upon the very same study, concerning the screening process which enables one to obtain nonmeasurable sets (B).

It is important to note that in the expressions that were available to me at the start ('consciousness of an object', 'act constituting an object', 'intentional structure of an object', all fabricated out of Husserlian terminology), the word 'object' was in no way understood in the sense that has become common (if not entirely clear) since the work of Frege. By 'object' I then meant the unity of an ideal pole held invariant and of an open field (i.e. not necessarily given *ne varietur*), of procedures providing access to its domain of properties. In this way, for instance, the entity designated by '$\sqrt{2}$' appeared to me to refer to a unitary pole sighted across an open field of procedures – 'breaks', following Cauchy, the apogogic demonstration attributed to the Pythagoricians . . ., it seemed wise to leave the list open-ended. Although I did not sketch out a 'theory' of the hierarchical constitution of 'objects' (and this was a lacuna), I did permit myself to apply the term 'object' to 'entities' of differing degrees of complication, provided that I could in each case distinguish the pair: field of procedures – ideal pole. Thus, the term 'object' designated for me the thematic unity offered in each instance to mathematical contemplation and action, and this regardless of the degree of complication of the field or the degree of complexity of the pole. This was simply a convenient way of getting into the thick of the constituted theory in an attempt to exhibit its mode of production on the basis of the analysis of one of its states.

It is important here to attempt to clarify two points in this regard: (1) what is to be understood by 'ideality'; (2) what may be understood by 'production'.

(1) The use of the term 'ideality' seems to me to be called for as soon as one rejects every sort of realism. And this rejection is twofold. It concerns on the one hand the temptation to imagine a *place* in which the 'entities' involved in mathematics might be held to reside. On the other hand, it concerns what I will call the 'naturalism of interiority': imagine an inner man, a 'consciousness', containing or capable of containing 'representations' ('images', 'ideas'). This means that neither 'in nature', nor 'in a heaven of ideas', nor in what we call 'the human psyche', are the 'objects' in question here to be found, as if in a place of residence (some sort of 'conservatory'). The fact that these objects are simply thought of does not necessarily imply that they be *in* thought. To exist *for* thought and to exist *in* thought are two absolutely different things, especially in that it is not clear what 'thinking' could mean apart from 'speaking', 'writing', 'communicating', 'expressing', 'computing' and so on. To seek the relevant sense within the range of these acts, within the historically constituted practice of the exchange of information among men, constituted in my view the point of the rejection of 'psychologism' common to Frege and to Husserl; even if this point was not a particularly deep one, it was at least acceptable to me as compatible with the kind of theme

I was treating. To say that mathematical 'objects' are 'idealities' meant for me that they acquire existence and consistence only insofar as they refer to the fully realizable and verifiable acts of thinking – verifiable at the very least in intuition – which constitute them. 'Thinking' here does not designate some 'faculty' inherent in the human 'psyche', but instead nothing other than the effective intending of the object itself.

(2) As for the term 'production', we understand this in a very broad sense. If we admit that a mathematical theory is a 'product', that is to say, that it is introduced within a tradition-bound cultural domain such as a series of written texts whose meaning one needs to grasp and the procedural indications contained within which one needs to reactivate, then the following question cannot be avoided: in what way, by what acts of constitution, in response to what motivations, in what already available theoretical field, following what intended (ideal) objects, was the meaning we have to reactivate deposited there where it is offered to us, that is, in the mathematical 'text'? To raise this question is to try to reconstruct through a study of the product (which we have to decipher) the organization of the acts that have formed it, an organization which, at the outset, is hypothetical. Is this not what we ordinarily call history? Should we not say that an exhaustive 'history' of the domain in question would be fully enlightening here, and that if it were carried out, there would be no need to raise such problems? I doubt it, at least if we take the word 'history' in its ordinary sense which does not appear to me wholly to suit a 'science of idealities'. In a case of this particular type, the question will always arise as to how to grasp both the status of 'ideal objects' and the modalities of the acts that lead to them. This means that in such a case a 'history' could be enlightening only if the steps it involved were structured around the data provided by a prior analysis of this basic problem.

It remains that the reference to 'positive' historiography is doubtless always necessary, no one having the right to turn the succession of studies and treatises upside down as he pleases, nor to ignore their contents. However, the task of epistemology, understood in the way it is practised in *Les Idéalités mathématiques*, does not consist in substituting an ideal history for the raw materials of empirical historiography, that is, a linked chain of concepts (of 'ideas that follow one another', as one says) reconstructed on the basis of the present state of mathematics (a sort of 'philosophy of history' of mathematics reconstituting the 'stages' of a development that is posited as progressive). Rather, it is a matter (and herein lies the whole difficulty) of grasping in a regional and specific product (such and such a theory, in such and such a state, in such and such a series of texts) the ways of access to the constitution of the meaning of the 'ideal objects' which are to be recognized therein and which there remain deposited, just as the sense of an inscription is desposited in the marble. This means that an epistemology such as this requires, at least initially, that he who speaks (in this instance, the 'epistemologist') place himself, with no presupposition other than that of being able to re-realize and to reactivate the procedures, in the intratheoretical complex with which he is dealing. His problem is then to work from the inside, to re-do what is presented as already done, to strive to elicit in this operation the theoretical fields, the positing of explicit objects, the implicit references (and here the reference to histori-ography is necessary) to which the actual progress of the living mathematical thinking, which is at work in the only thing available to us, namely the product, was a response. It remains that this 'living mathematical thinking' (that which we attribute to Archimedes, Riemann or Cantor) cannot be said to 'exist' or to 'have existed' except inasmuch as it continues to address itself to someone capable of deciphering its products.

A few words in conclusion, since I have reached the limits of the space allotted to me. It happens that I have set out my position (or have attempted to) in a work entitled *La Philosophie silencieuse* concerning the way in which I conceive of epistemology and the traditional relationship of the sciences to philosophy (or at least to certain philosophies that have in common the project of develop-ing a form of discourse that would express the truth by way of a self-grounding movement; it is for this reason that I call these 'silent' philosophies with respect to the positive sciences).

I would draw here the 'moral', so to speak, of *Les Idéalités mathématiques*, to wit:

(1) I cannot conceive of a 'general epistemology', understood as an investigation aimed at defining the conditions of 'scientificity' for every domain of knowledge. It seems to me that it is up to those who actually work in a particular science to define the conditions of scientificity proper to it. If we take the word

'epistemology' in this sense, then it seems fair to me to say that we have reached the point where each science is capable (if those who practise it are to the slightest degree attentive to the methods of logic) of producing its own 'epistemology'.

(2) As far as I myself am concerned, I should make even more modest claims. I do not feel entitled to legislate in any domain. On the other hand, I believe it my duty, in a few domains that I do know somewhat, to attain for myself a clear comprehension of the mode of existence and the 'mode of production' of the theoretical fields concerned by these areas. And to try to share with others this 'clear comprehension' to the extent that I myself attain it. This is my only ambition. To call this work 'epistemology' is merely a matter of convention.

Translated by Kathleen McLaughlin

NOTES

1 Paris, 1963. Republished in the collection *Idées* (Gallimard) under the title, 'Introduction à la Phénoménologie'.
2 For example, a dialogue of the dead: Plato, Aristotle, Hume and Frege converse in Hell about the status of logical categories, assuming Hell to be a place of relative transparency where each knows all that each other knows, but not what he thinks or decides.

An essay in philosophical observation

(1) *To say what I do*

'To do philosophy' is, in French, an expression vague enough to allow me to say, without committing myself unduly, that I am indeed one of those who do philosophy; I rank among all those who, in doing what they do, find themselves doing that which is commonly understood by the phrase, 'to do philosophy'.

In the preceding sentence (and admittedly by means of some-what convoluted wording) I have managed to avoid having to say:

(1) here is what 'to do philosophy' means for me;

(2) here is how I personally proceed to do philosophy.

I have thus managed to avoid saying perhaps the very thing that I am expected to develop here. For the agreement is that each contributor to this volume should reply in his own way to a question bearing upon his way of doing philosophy.

Since, according to the programme, I am *to say what I do*, is it legitimate for me to transcribe this as follows: I say what I do by qualifying my activity (e.g. as 'philosophical'), and in order to qualify my activity (e.g. as 'philosophical') I must compare it to that which others than myself do whenever they do that which others than themselves consistently include within the range of activities answering, in one form or another, to that qualification? It would appear not, for in any description I may offer of what others do, I have not yet started upon the description of what I myself do; likewise, in recording what is generally said about this type of activity, I leave out of consideration the fact that for every philosopher 'worthy of the name', philosophical activity consists among other things in self-explanation, and in replying to such a questioning as 'In what sense can what I do be said to be philosophy?'

It is best, then, to reject the temptation to reduce a description of what I do under the name of philosophy to an account of what others are doing under that name. Instead, I would define the programme as follows:

(1) to say what I do (not only what others do)
(2) to say what I say about what I do (and not only what others say about it).

But in that case, why did I not begin with this simple, straightforward announcement: I am now going to say how I do philosophy, and give reasons why what I do counts, in my opinion, as philosophy? The answer is that one cannot announce an intention to do something unless one is in a position to explain how one is going to do it. That is why this preliminary question, whether someone is able to say what he does, is not an idle one.

Although I am as well placed as anyone else to describe what others than myself are doing around me, I am by far the worst-placed observer of my own activity; indeed, my account of what I do will inevitably consist of a record of the series of choices whereby I have ultimately done this rather than that. For I cannot say, *I do this*, except precisely to the extent that I might be doing something else; and I can only say that *I do it in this way* if I could be doing it otherwise. For example, 'I *give my lecture* from such and such a time to such and such a time' only insofar as I might be able to do so according to a different timetable. Otherwise, we will say that 'my lecture *takes place* from such and such a time to such and such a time', a fact for which I can claim no responsibility. Supposing that my timetable is laid down by the administration, my lecture will only fail to take place at that time if I do not give it at all, as a result of serious illness, for example.

And yet the description of what I find myself in the end to have done each time I have undertaken to do something, can never consist in a mere enumeration of my decisions. Initiatives of mine only effect others insofar as they are given weight by our common world. For example, an external observer will not initially be struck by the distinction, so crucial in my view, between 'I give my lecture at such and such a time' and 'my lecture takes place at such and such a time'. Transcribed into the third person, the two statements become equivalent: if 'X gives his lecture at such and such a time', then 'such and such a time is the time at which X's lecture takes place'. Only if this observer should wish to know, say, whom he must approach in order to have X's lecture-time changed, will he begin to be concerned by the difference between what X says that he does (to give his lecture, as opposed to being ill) and what follows from X's actually doing what he says he does. The statement 'X gives his lecture at such and such a time instead of being ill at such and such a time' would be an odd one; it would show the illness to be an alibi for not giving lectures under the conditions which are imposed. From a straightforward description of a person's behaviour, our observer would already have moved towards an interpretation of his conduct in the light of the motives he ascribes to him. Of course, the description given by the external observer should likewise be based on the assumption that a person does something insofar as he could do something else. But for the external observer, 'something else' suggests a comparison of different protagonists. Referring to me in the third person he will say that I do *this* like Jones, and unlike Brown who does something else; and that I do it *thus* like Brown, but unlike Jones, etc.

The instruction to *describe what I do* turns out to be inapplicable unless the description is to include what others are doing. In any case, it would seem preferable to request such a description from another than myself. On the other hand, it is up to me to say what I am trying to do – philosophy, for instance – or again, what I ought to be doing – for instance, in order to be doing philosophy. The answer is that I should be striving to end up by having done what I observe others doing when they do philosophy. The whole problem is now that of my own observation. For the question remains, who is to say what ought to be considered as philosophy? Is it not up to me, as a reasonable being, to say whether it is valid for one activity to be dubbed philosophical, while another is not? (For example, one might regard it as philosophical to teach the 'history of philosophy', but not so to teach the 'history of ideas'.) If philosophy must answer for itself – a view endorsed by all philosophers 'worthy of the name' – then anyone who does, or seeks to do, philosophy, should be able to answer for that which he does or seeks to do. It would thus appear legitimate that I should be asked *what meaning philosophy has for me*. And yet I have no intention of replying to a question put in this way. I am in no way disposed to concern myself about some meaning that the word 'philosophy' might have especially for me, or even that it might in any case have for me, whether it had the same sense for others or not. This would be to accept my own responsibility for 'giving a meaning to it', as they say; whereas I maintain, rightly or wrongly and certainly until I see proof to the contrary, that the meaning, for me, of the word 'philosophy' is exactly the meaning which it ought to have for everyone. There is nothing extravagant in itself about such a claim: it is only a way of saying that I myself wish to understand the word 'philosophy' in the sense that it should have for everyone, that is, the sense which it has in the end for anyone who puts himself under the same constraints. Hence the question 'what sense does it have for me?' is ambiguous. If this sense refers to the meaning of the word, it is not so much my business to give it as to discover it in order to conform to it. If, rather, I take 'mean' to refer to the significance that philosophical activity has for me personally, then it is indeed up to me to give such a meaning. However, I should not be giving this meaning to the word 'philosophy', or to philosophical activity as such, but rather to my own activity. I have no say in the meaning of 'to philosophize', but I do choose to invest certain of my activities with that meaning. In other words, in making my activity correspond to what I should have to do in order to be doing philosophy, it is I who *cause* my activity to earn the qualification of 'philosophical'. It follows from this that the concept of philosophy must already have been determined independently both of my activities and of my interests for me to be able subsequently to say whether what I would wish to do is indeed philosophy.

However, if I cannot say what is the sense that philosophy has for me, then no more can another than myself say what sense it has for him. There exists, in short, no oracle to which we may appeal for a common definition of the concept of philosophy. But who is then to say, if it is to be neither myself nor any of those who in the saying would have to use the phrase 'for me . . .'? Since no one is able simply to turn to himself, the only possibility left to each is that he turn towards the others to observe what they are doing. For the position is as follows: on the one hand, the concept of philosophy is not going to drop from the sky as and when we need it, and each of us (myself included, therefore) has to go out and look for it for himself; but it is worth remembering, on the other hand, that neither you nor I are the inventors either of the Greek word or of that which it serves to qualify. The name has been handed down to us by tradition, and it represents something. Our task is, therefore, to observe what is being done under this name, and to discover in what ways that which is done under the name of philosophy is in fact 'philosophical'. At the same time, we shall find out in what ways it is not. So doing, we presuppose nothing; we do not prejudge the sense of the word in order then to assess what is being done, but nor do we simply equate the sense of the word to what is being done without further ado. We observe on the basis of no presuppositions. This is, perhaps, a way of proceeding which in itself deserves to be called 'philosophical'.

(2) *To say what is being done*

The simplest course is to turn first to the institutions which transmit philosophy (both the name and the idea of a type of activity). In France, as elsewhere, the university brings together the majority of those who say that they are doing philosophy, either because they are studying philosophy there (sometimes with the intention of going on to teach it, most usually in the *classes terminales* of the *lycées*), or because they are already engaged in teaching these students. A first hypothesis may be derived from this regarding the content of the concept of philosophy: whatever is done within the French university under the name of philosophy constitutes the very prototype of what may properly be called 'philosophy'. Is this hypothesis confirmed by observation?

In order to find a place in the university, philosophical activity had to take on the forms of an academic subject leading to the conferral of degrees (e.g. a Doctorate in Philosophy) after examination. Whatever may be the case in actual practice, university examinations invoke the ideal of a public assessment of competence. The value of the answers given to the questions set must be capable of being established in indisputable fashion. These questions must, therefore, be questions either of fact or of right. Ideally, any philosophical perplexity would be reducible by analysis to one or the other of the two following types of question:

1. Is it true that, on a given line of a given page of a given work (consulted in an 'authoritative' critical edition), a given sequence of words is to be found?
2. Is it true that proposition x may be inferred from proposition y?

That is to say that once philosophy has been integrated into the institution of the university, it is apt to be compressed into two disciplines only: the history of philosophy and logic. It is common knowledge that the style which prevails in French universities is historical, a product no doubt of the importance given to 'classical studies' in the syllabuses of the various competitive examinations for recruitment to the teaching profession.

Those who give in to French academic tendencies may adopt one of two attitudes. The first is to determine the concept of philosophy in accordance with the university idea. In this case, 'to do philosophy' will mean to teach the great authors, and to 'teach a great author' will consist in showing how to justify everything that he wrote. The digestive capacities of each teacher will be the decisive factor in determining whether all authors are *ipso facto* great, or whether there are not on the contrary a handful of 'lesser authors' who might, for their part, have been mistaken (sophists, sceptics, assorted eccentrics, etc.). But if each great author is justified individually, then all are justified. Yet how can this be, seeing that they all expressly contradict one another? If all are right, then everyone must be saying essentially the same thing; but if all are right when some profess to contradict others, then no one can really be saying anything at all. Thus the university, left to itself, tends towards the destruction of philosophy; for 'to do philosophy' can hardly consist in speaking in order to say nothing at all. The lesson to be drawn from all this is that although the university affords it a home, perhaps indeed its only possible refuge, philosophy does not wholly belong there.

There are many, in France, content simply to adopt the reverse of the above academic formula. No longer is it said that *everyone is right*; one says instead that *everyone is wrong*. Once again, moreover, 'lesser authors' constitute an exception, but this time, it may be, to the general illusion. The history of philosophy now becomes the history of one long error. But just as the earlier, optimistic version held that all great authors were repositories of truth, without being able to specify the exact nature of this truth, so the pessimistic version finds fault with all and sundry without being able to specify the exact nature of this fault. If we term the first version 'university philosophy', it would be fair to call its negation, 'university subversion'.

Nothing that I have mentioned so far is an exclusive feature of French institutions. The peculiarity of these is that they constitute a State university. Just as there is no more than one State, so there can be no more than one university, whose potential audience must therefore be synonymous with the community as a whole.[1] This creates a risk of confusion between the ideals of the teacher and those of the 'citizen-cum-civil servant', suggesting a new hypothesis with regard to the sense in which what is done under the name of philosophy is 'philosophical'. University ideals are those of freedom of research, guaranteed by the system of a public verification of findings. Republican ideals are those of the free coexistence of citizens, guaranteed by the secular distinction between that to which all are bound for the sake of the common good, and that which is properly a matter for each individual conscience. Officially, all secular universities in the world share the principle of non-imposition of any one philosophy;[2] but the reasons for this differ according to whether the university is independent or State controlled. In the first case, philosophical neutrality corresponds to a scholastic ideal; it is as if no one philosophy can yet be imposed because none has as yet produced public evidence of its truth. In a State university, this same neutrality contains a political significance. No single view may be imposed upon the public, because the State must allow public opinion to form in the course of free discussion; philosophy is seen as the practice of precisely this discussion. 'To do philosophy', according to this hypothesis, would be to engage in discussion about all kinds of issues of common concern, no matter what they were. Such discussion would serve the political function of contributing to the formation of public opinion.

I believe that a sizeable number of French teachers of philosophy would recognize themselves in this sort of definition of an attitude that might be called the 'enlightened' conception of philosophy (by way of reference to the Age of Enlightenment), according to which philosophy is equated with critical activity as

such. For example, this concept is often put forward in the
controversy aroused by the government's plans to cut back on
philosophy in secondary education.★ The teaching of philosophy
aims at developing the critical faculties of those who enjoy this
singular advantage: this, according to some, is why such a study is
essential to a democratic society, and, according to others, why it
seems superfluous to technocrats.

But there is very little that is enlightening in this 'enlightened'
concept; it does not tell us what to do in order to find ourselves
doing philosophy. In a definition of philosophical activity, to
point to its critical effects is not enough; it remains to be said how
such effects are obtained. Advocates of the 'enlightened' definition appear to believe that an activity is positively characterizable
by such features as the dissolution of prejudice, the overthrow of
what seems obvious but is false, the denunciation of the arbitrary
that presents itself as merely natural, etc. Philosophy may indeed
produce effects of this order, but we would like to know exactly
in what way the act of philosophizing brings about the discredit-
ing of false solutions, the dissolution of prejudice, and so on. The
'critical' edition of a text is critical inasmuch as it is the outcome of
a series of steps that can be described positively (assessing manu-
scripts in the light of certain rules, etc.); similarly, philosophy can
only be critical inasmuch as it proceeds *in a certain way*; but it is
precisely this way that here remains indeterminate.

In order to emerge from this vagueness, one might say the
following: philosophical activity produces critical effects in that it
confronts mere opinions with a rational ideal. This ideal must in
turn assert itself in the discussion, failing which it would remain a
prejudice. But such an ideal can never be a consequence of discussion; indeed, we have just used it in a positive definition of the
latter. It remains to define it as a purely formal *a priori*: the ideal of
rationality is the pure form of free discussion, that is to say the
whole set of rules of free debate. In this way the 'enlightened'
concept ceases to be indeterminate. Yet it emerges from its vagueness only to fall into naivety. According to this hypothesis, the
function of free discussion is to contribute to the formulation of
public opinion. Consequently, philosophy is critical in the sense
that it confronts opinions with a certain model of human coexis-

★*Editor's Note:* This was written before the election of François Mitterand in
succession to Valéry Giscard d'Estaing as President of the Republic.

tence drawn from societies enjoying freedom of discussion, a model held up by it as the ideal of the community as a whole (which constitutes, it may be remembered, its potential audience). The good society is presented in terms of a scholarly colloquium, where each is free to say his piece, accepting contradiction, and forbidding himself any means other than persuasion in the promotion of his views. The naivety here consists in regarding free discussion as a universally applicable model of social relations. The prerequisites for a colloquium are that the participants should be gathered together, whilst at the same time the collectivity as such should remain quiet so that each person may make himself heard. Free discussion thus presupposes collective silence; it is a social relation in which the social aspect has been neutralized. However, this silence is artificially induced, and would not be kept for long if the participants were not assured of periodic breaks during which they may revert to other social relations giving rise as a result to collective noise. The 'enlightened' definition thus overlooks the fact that the emergence of societies permitting free discussion is never itself the consequence of such discussion, and that their peaceful operation implies a world outside, one in which social relations are not those of free discussion held in a context of collective silence.

Two hypotheses have now been set aside. In France, that which is done under the name of philosophy is often confined to the teaching of great authors – but it is not as such that this teaching can count as a philosophical activity. Alternatively, that which is done may well have (in the French context of a teaching carried out in a public university) certain critical effects, themselves serving a political purpose. But philosophical activity cannot consist in the pursuit of such effects. A third hypothesis now suggests itself, which we must test as before. Philosophical activity might consist – perhaps in the course of the study of great authors, or through the discussion of personal opinions – in allowing the noise of the world to make itself heard. Let us take as our starting point the fact that through the naivety of the 'enlightened' definition, any activity conforming to this definition would be deprived of its alleged critical effects. In order to correct this naivety, we may propose giving the floor to that barbarous element which had excluded itself from the arena of free discussion by its very incapacity to take part in it. We may then go on to say that the formation of public opinion through the channels of free discussion requires people to accept certain constraints. If we call *forms* those constraints aimed at stifling, within a collective whole, the noise of the collectivity (in the sense in which we speak of 'the noise of the city', or 'the noise of the sea', which is not the same as the sum of the sounds made by each wave) it follows that the respect of these forms (formality) will amount to the exclusion of everything that is unable to conform to them, and which we may therefore call *formless* (informal). By the same token, this formlessness can never be taken into account; respect for the forms thus creates a mental barrier, to which we must attribute the naivety of the preceding definition.

But to go further, we must discover a bit more about this 'formlessness' or 'informality', however paradoxical it may be to seek to fix the contours of that which eludes form. The difficulty of this task allows us to qualify the new, emerging definition as 'obscure' – in antithesis to its predecessor, and with no pejorative intent.

It is decreed by the forms of public and secular discussion, that one should never refer in public to anything to which a public as such might reasonably object. The respect that the State has to show to every shade of opinion or creed forbids the teacher-cum-civil servant ever to express any view except by way of an *example*. This maintenance of secular neutrality towards all convictions is but one instance of the restraint to be observed by anyone speaking within a society of free discussion. To take a non-philosophical example, one can hardly imagine a doctor of medicine at the meeting of a learned society devoting his entire paper to the description of his own stomach pains, unless he intends to use them as a 'case-study' or 'example' of some general point of interest to his listeners. The same would apply to a jurist telling a conference on divorce-law about his own divorce, to an economist listing his own operations on the stock exchange, to a psychologist talking about his own dog or his own children as anything but experimental subjects, etc. Failing the transformation or formalization, which good manners dictate, of personal discomfort into theoretical utterance, the doctor's words would sound no less incongruous, in the context of a learned meeting, than would the illustrative rumblings of the very stomach concerned. However, no one expects a doctor of medicine to mount the rostrum in order to declare that he has a stomachache, and if the scene were ever to occur, it would be like witnessing the break-down of his persona.

It seems to me that, in what is done under the name of philosophy in France, one can detect two variations on the 'obscure' conception: one may be termed *populist*, the other *literary*. Both set out to allow something barbarous to make itself heard, in other words something which theoreticians respectful of form would dismiss as a meaningless noise. In the populist version, the noise excluded by an institution devoted to theoretical discourse is the din of men fighting each other and fighting together against other elements. In the literary version, it is the noise of the speaker's own body that the institution sees as barbarous. This is why the term 'literary' is appropriate here; indeed the baring of oneself has been the hallmark of a literary career ever since the crystallization of the modern conception of literature (that is to say, roughly, since Rousseau's *Confessions*). However, the word 'body' must not here be interpreted to mean a mere object about which there might be free discussion at some learned meeting. We are here concerned with a body able to make itself heard (although without going so far as to speak in conformity with the rules). It does this, sometimes to express dissent from the lifestyle of its incumbent (by means of 'symptom'), at other times to let him or her know its will, and to prescribe the line of conduct to be followed (by means of imperatives known as 'drives').

The two versions are separated by a difference of emphasis rather than one of doctrine. Under any name, sound and fury will always be banned from the forum of reasonable discussion. Although some will tend first to hear in this general noise the clash of arms and the uproar of the mob, while others will be more attuned to the inaudible clamour of the body, these are merely two different scales by which one may measure one and the same noise. Let us imagine a scholar, in the middle of a conference, revoking the writ of silence served upon his own body: he will give vent, perhaps, to a bellow of rage, or quell an opponent with a blow of his fist. This will be enough to send the hall into an uproar, with some crying shame, and others throwing themselves on the guilty party in order to eject him.

However, none of this takes us beyond the planning stage of this project to dispel the systematic failure to recognize what actually happens outside reasonable discourse. As before, we now want to know how exactly this blindness is to disappear.

Contemporary philosophical texts abound in declarations of the following kind:

Reason is only effective within the bounds of the reasonable; it cannot but fail to grasp the irrational.

A representation is always that of something representable, and so it cannot but fail to grasp the unrepresentable.

Consciousness is conscious only of that which is conscious; therefore it cannot but fail to grasp the unconscious.

Common to all these formulae is the evocation of an ungraspable object which resists any ordered form of discourse, and which the 'obscure' conception of philosophy holds to be the object *par excellence* of philosophical activity. Now, how are we to deal with such an object? Obviously not by means of any formal discourse, since it has been posited as essentially ungraspable. And since it is form, in the discourse, which is held to be responsible for the object's exclusion, this form will have to be modified so as to bring to awareness that which by its exclusion has enabled discourse in due and proper form to exist as such. In other words, the discourse must undergo a change of style. But how can a change of style produce an evocation of the very thing about which one cannot actually speak? Will it be enough, in order to bring this about, to make any noise no matter what? Might the philosopher be somebody who, instead of telling his colleagues that their learned discussions are predicated on the provisional suspension of the noise of the world, chooses rather to slap his neighbour, for example, or to laugh in his face? Even allowing for the possible existence of an advocate of 'obscure' philosophy ready to indulge in such uncivilized behaviour, he would need great skill to ensure that his philosophical gesture be not mistaken for an act of brutality pure and simple. A mere noise would teach nothing to the 'obscure' philosopher's colleagues (who are obviously aware that such violence is a common occurrence *outside* their meetings). Rather he must show, by some incongruous device of calculated effect, that contrary to appearances noise is indeed present within the meeting itself; that what takes place in the meeting is nothing other than noise artificially turned into meaningful, reasonable discourse through the imposition of certain constraints (listening in silence, speaking in turn, etc.). Thus violence is neither suppressed nor transcended by the *logos* (in the terms of idealist philosophy), that is to say, by a context of free discussion – it is merely in disguise as polite controversy. The 'obscure' philosopher, then, by no means makes a noise (as he is often wrongly accused of doing); he is only pretending to make a noise. His stylistic incongruities are so many feints, so many ways of miming the violence done by the noise of the world to discourse in due and proper form, or of showing that such discourse is none other than the noise of the world muffled by certain conventions.

Our third hypothesis has now acquired a content: 'to do philosophy' is to import the noise of the world into discourse in due and proper form (where it could not genuinely make itself heard without drowning out that discourse), by producing, within the discourse itself, a simulacrum of noise through the deliberate transgression of certain rules governing formal discourse.

But if this is the case, the 'obscure' concept of philosophy is also unsatisfactory. For the above description defines nothing more than a pedagogic procedure; and a pedagogic procedure is a device for getting across or explaining the same thing in another way, without being able to tell us exactly what this thing consists of. The stylistic transgressions of the 'obscure' philosopher are not mere noises, but are signifying noises – noises which signify noise, in the same way that a given onomatopoeia is not an animal cry, but only the name of one. By these stylistic procedures form has not been 'transgressed' into something else; one form has merely slid into another. We have used what educationalists call a 'speaking' form, instead of a conceptual one, as when we say, 'the dog goes "woof woof" ' instead of saying, 'the dog barks'. Thus each stylistic transgression admits of a translation back into regular forms of argumentative discourse. Any appeal to mime or drama is for this reason purely pedagogical (a pedagogue must bring his subject-matter to life).

Here, then, is the fourth and last hypothesis as to what one should do in order to find oneself 'doing philosophy': that is, evoke, within formal discourse, the noise of the world, while proceeding in that discourse to give a name to that noise. (By 'giving a name' I mean the assignation of a common noun to a type of phenomenon, as opposed to the assignation of a proper name or cognomen to a particular instance of this phenomenon.)

However, such a description will be rejected by those who consider that the philosophical object *par excellence* – that is, that noise which, if it should prevail overall, would prevent us from speaking, but without which we should be altogether deprived of the signifying vociferation that is speech – is essentially un-nameable. According to the 'obscure' philosophers, it was precisely because it was impossible to speak of this 'object', or noise, that it had to be mimed. They would thus also reject the characterization of their mime as a mere pedagogical method, that is, another way of speaking or of representing the same thing. Likewise, it was because the philosophical object *par excellence* was thoroughly obscure that these philosophers resorted to a degree of obscurity in their own work. In their view, only negative designations would be suitable for this object (irrational, unrepresentable, unconscious, etc.). It could never be represented by an image, described by a concept, determined by a proposition, or analysed in a discourse.

Yet is seems that an error of logic has been committed here. The noise has been designated by negation. But this cannot be seen as the assignation of a *negative predicate* – for as Aristotle points out, an undefined predicate is not, properly speaking, a predicate at all. On the other hand, the *negation of a predicate* carries positive descriptive force insofar as the predicate expresses a potency (in the sense of 'able to be'): everyone acknowledges that in saying 'this glass is unbreakable', or 'that army is invincible', we are actually ascribing a property to an object. But to do this is to use a concept within a judgement in order to form a proposition which subsequently requires to be justified in a discourse. Yes, but here the negative predicate is 'can be named'. Is it not a contradiction to seek to name the unnameable? By no means (what could one seek to name, after all, except something with no name already and which is as yet unable to be named for lack of a name by which to name it?). Just as a glass is unbreakable because it can withstand any shock, so a phenomenon is unnameable because one does not know how to accommodate it within the description one gives of the whole set of phenomena – either because it offers an excess of characteristics (like a hybrid monster) or because it does not offer enough (like an 'unidentified flying object'). It is, then, this overall description that will have to be overturned and reordered before a single new phenomenon can be named. This, in my opinion, is what all philosophers have done, to one degree or another, in doing what they have called 'philosophy'.

Translated by Lorna Scott Fox

NOTES

1 The 'autonomy' of the French universities has produced no genuine plurality among them, since the nomination of teachers and the definition of degrees, fees and examination procedures are all outside their control.

2 Secularism (*laïcité*), in the French sense, excludes not only State-established religion, but also any philosophy established by the State. It is not limited simply to freedom of worship (which might still leave the citizen with the obligation to choose some form of worship or another), but actually prohibits the State from intervening in order to settle, for example, a dispute between 'theism' and 'atheism'. If the teaching of any particular philosophy was to be made obligatory, this could no longer count as secular teaching in the true French sense of the word (nor, no doubt, as philosophical teaching in the eyes of any teacher attached to the principle of secularism).

CLAUDE LEFORT

'How did you become a philosopher?'

Recently, somebody asked me, 'How did you become a philosopher?' It was an apparently commonplace question, and this was
not the first time I had heard it. Indeed, everyone, whatever his
field of activity, has been asked this sort of question. On this
occasion, however, I felt a particular unease. I had the impression,
not so much of having side-stepped the answer, as of having fled
in the face of a different question. Later, this tiny event started me
thinking along lines that led me a long way from my starting-
point. Since I had for some time been pondering the nature of my
contribution to the present volume, I thought that this could
provide me with a subject-matter.

How had I become a philosopher? The question had put me in
something of a quandary. Why? No doubt because it took for
granted something that was not, in fact, self-evident. My answer
would imply that I was prepared to take upon myself the identity
of a philosopher. It is true that I do not much care to be referred to
as a sociologist or a politologist merely on the grounds that my
thinking has been largely directed towards social or political facts.
I have sometimes had to disavow such appellations. Even less
could I represent myself as an historian, although I have often
drawn upon works of history. Broadly speaking, I have always
wanted to insist that my way of proceeding does not belong to
what are called the human sciences. But I have never found it easy
to count myself a philosopher. On that particular occasion, indeed, the word had aroused in me a new and surprising resistance.
It seemed easier to describe how I had come to choose my

profession – to say how I had decided to embark on the study of philosophy and upon a teaching career in the subject.

I take no particular pride in being a teacher; I find the academic species far from delightful. My unenthusiastic opinion of it was formed in the school classroom and as a student, long before I became one of its members. It does, of course, include a number of exceptions and I like to think that I figure among them. However, since it would be ridiculous to invoke my status as an exception, I have no alternative but to accept myself as falling under the rule of the common characterization. This profession is, after all, my own; there is no getting round the fact. In any case, of all the criss-crossing classifications that combine to define me, this one, so I wish to believe, is the least essential. For have I not always enjoyed – and maintained, though it becomes less with time – the freedom to change my job? On the other hand, I experience increasing difficulty in accepting the name of philosopher. My reservations in this respect do not, I tell myself, spring from any distaste at seeing myself ensconced in the common characterization; it must be that I fear to usurp a title which I may not deserve and which it demands an ever greater audacity to claim.

In the time of Socrates, as everyone knows, the word 'philosophy', in all the vigour of its primitive meaning, denoted the love of wisdom – something which it has become hard to translate, but which combined the search for truth with that for a way of life suitable to man's nature. For Socrates himself, philosophy was allied to the modesty of a questioning disposition, trusting to reason alone – in contrast with the assurance, not to say the arrogance of those who did not doubt their possession of the principles of upright judgement by virtue of Tradition, that is, through the religious teachings handed down by their ancestors. This primitive meaning has so degenerated that philosophy has increasingly been conceived of as a discipline having jurisdiction over the principles of knowledge – a particular discipline, while yet the science of the universal – and one whose progress might be measured by the degree of systematization reached in its conceptual operations. I have never been attached to this definition of philosophy. It too, however, now belongs to the past. Nowadays, philosophy has lost the credit that these ambitions had won for it, together with its place in the edifice of academic knowledge. But by the same token, it is on the way to losing its credit altogether. Its disappearance is heard proclaimed from all sides. In France at any rate, certain garrulous souls equipped with university degrees in lieu of authority argue over the date of philosophy's demise – now associated with Hegel or Fichte, now with Husserl, now with Heidegger (who himself, indeed, had opened the case against metaphysics).

Just as I have never espoused the characterization of philosophy as the ultimate system – a characterization whose outlines are discernible at the heart of the great classics and of German Idealism, but which turned into a caricature as a result of the development of the academic discipline known under the name of 'history of philosophy' – in the same way I am loath to join in the chorus of philosophy's detractors. I find it, indeed, somewhat amusing to note that those who flatter themselves that they are able to give an account of Hegel's alleged system in a few pages are often the very ones who proclaim that he marks the end of philosophy. But here we find the paradoxical consequence of this experience: it seems to me that, in the present conditions, to declare oneself a philosopher is to burden oneself with a quite excessive ambition. To affirm the possibility of an inquiry emancipated no longer from the authority of religion but from that of science, notably the human sciences, to undertake the restoration of meaning to something condemned on all sides as an enterprise both chimerical and defunct – this is sufficient cause for us to lose the modesty of the initial inspiration, sufficient cause for us to raise our voices by a tone or two.

The image of myself as teacher, so I concluded, pleased me because it placed me beneath myself. By accepting this name, I no doubt preserved the hope that I might surpass the definition. But the name of philosopher disturbed me, for it seemed to place me above myself.

Was this not a double error on my part? Would I not do better to moderate both my belittlement of the function of the teacher and my glorification of that of the philosopher? Should I not, furthermore, pay great attention to the interaction of the two – for can philosophy be altogether dissociated from teaching? This, surely, was a point deserving of further examination. Rather than undertaking it, I simply noted that my embarrassment was possibly no more than an effect of the very widespread feeling that there are fewer risks involved in adopting a humble image than in aspiring to a glorious one.

Nevertheless, I have long been aware of how people are only too ready to invoke psychological laws while taking no account of cultural determinations. Were these not at work in my own case? My initial reflection struck me as yet another evasion of the unexpected question that had crept in behind my interlocutor's innocent query. Would it not be better to accept that the teacher–philosopher duality had imposed itself upon me as the offspring of a duality imprinted upon the mind of modern Western man as fashioned by the Christian tradition? Had not the idea of a division between temporal and eternal life, between a natural, functional, mortal pole and one which was supernatural, mystical and immortal, given secret shape to my characterization – and this in spite of the fact that not since the end of childhood have I, consciously at least, embraced any religious faith? I wondered about this only half-seriously at first. But as I questioned myself in this way, my crucial reference to Socrates began to waver. I found my reluctance to call myself a philosopher pointing me in a fresh direction.

Why had this sudden swerve occurred in my thinking? It had been triggered off by the words *beneath* and *above myself*. For they reminded me of having read, a few years ago, Ernst Kantorowicz's book *The King's Two Bodies*. This work had aroused my interest, so much so that I had devoted an entire year's seminar to it. Before coming across it, I had in fact already begun to be interested in the representation of the body as the *body politic* in totalitarian ideology. This representation seemed to form itself as a reaction against democracy, against a type of society in which any notion of the organic unity of the social is dissolved at the same time as the hitherto established connection between the mystical unity of the people and the closed figure of a body whose members are like organs functionally related to each other.

Kantorowicz shed unexpected light for me upon the genesis of the image of the body politic during the Middle Ages and Renaissance – and more particularly upon that of the body of the King, a dual body at once natural and supernatural, functional and mystical, which itself was grounded in the first place upon the image of Christ's dual nature. One formula, shrewdly analysed by him, struck me most vividly. Applied to the Christian Emperor in the

Liber Augustalis, a book composed in the reign of Frederick II and addressed to him, it described him as *major et minor se ipso*. One can detect here a key representation of the modern prince, at one and the same time subject to the Law and above laws. In particular, Kantorowicz points out its efficacity in Dante's depiction of the universal monarch and in Shakespeare's tragedy of Richard II. This recollection prompted a new train of thought. Had my associations been guided by psychoanalytic considerations, I should have been alerted by my identification with a royal figure; but since I was seeking only to clarify my relationship with philosophy, I confined myself to noting that, while possibly reactivating a figure of thought which is impressed upon the matrix of our culture, I was developing a stubborn resistance to the image of the philosopher as substitute for the priest-king or to philosophy as the mystical body of philosophers. I would thus have trouble in calling myself or in allowing myself to be called a philosopher, not because of a fear of placing myself above my station, but because there is, in my view, no philosophy above life – no philosophy in the sense given to it both by those who fully uphold its reality and by those who claim to destroy it, namely in the sense of a figure of transcendence.

In fact, I concluded, there is a current way of either proclaiming the death of philosophy or of rallying to its banner that is reminiscent of the controversy between theology and atheism. Just as God was put to death in a manner that proved a testimony to his survival, just as atheism could provide none but a vain response to the certainty of the theologian who, supported by Revelation, claimed to give reality to an Other World, so the quarrel between philosophy and non-philosophy is a futile one. And the third option, which, in the wake of Marxism, consists in announcing the fulfilment of philosophy, both in life and in history, through its very destruction, is a no less futile revival of the belief prevalent in the early nineteenth century that God had become incorporated into humanity or that Christianity, as a separate religion, had become incorporated into social institutions. Surely I should finally acknowledge that, while I might harbour a contradiction within me, I still refused to materialize its terms into a *here* and a *beyond*, even though they might appear to have been freed of all religious connotations.

Why this train of thought leading me to recall '*major et minor se ipso*'? The answer came to me with the question. In fact, I was guided by something that I had read much more recently than Kantorowicz. Some weeks prior to the conversation to which I have referred, I had thought indeed that I had found an avatar of this theological-political formula, but used in this case with an altogether different intention, in a very fine text by Edgar Quinet. This historian, a contemporary and friend of Michelet, a poet and an author of philosophical essays, to whom we are most notably indebted for one of the boldest and most acute works on the French Revolution, is a writer who has inexplicably fallen into obscurity. Having become interested in his work, I came across a piece written by him in 1853 as a preface to his epic play *Les Esclaves*. In it he states, roughly, that it was the spectacle of slavery in ancient times and of slave revolts, in particular that led by Spartacus, which had led him to stage the universal drama of a humanity which he saw as torn by a dual movement debasing it and raising it alternately below and above itself. Returning to consult this volume, I at once retrieved two passages which I had marked. The first ran

Do you wish to be able to contemplate the fall of man? Look at this creature who, at the very apogee of his revolt, still does not even dream of seeking freedom; in each external emancipation he finds a fresh means to bind and circumscribe himself. *Ingeniously deriving servitude from the very midst of freedom*, see him return into the darkness by way of the path that guides others to the light. Rubble upon ruin, he overthrows slavery, without perceiving that he bears it within himself and recreates it with every breath.

The second ran as follows:

I believed that a new element could be infused into the drama by taking man there where he had not previously been sought, *beneath humanity*, distorted, denatured, annihilated within by slavery; then, having brought him back to life, restoring him through *heroism*. (my italics)

While exploiting the theme of man's being torn apart, it seemed to me that Quinet had nevertheless reformulated it: he summed up the paradox of the human condition as lying in a tension between servitude and heroism. What did he understand by servitude? That which La Boétie terms '*voluntary servitude*'. Indeed, this most enigmatic phrase is elsewhere quoted by him without acknowledgement of source, notably in the last chapter of his

French Revolution. As a warm admirer of La Boétie, and having
written an essay as afterword to the new edition of his famed
Discours some years previously, I was familiar with this source. I
had moreover worked my own way towards the idea of voluntary servitude through my study of ideology and totalitarianism.
I had been struck, in discovering La Boétie, to see this idea linked
with that of an attraction to the tyrant's *body*, or more generally to
that of the King or Master in whom the fiction of the social body
was incarnate; and no less struck to see it combined with the
notion of a spell emanating from the *name of One* who delivers his
subjects from the dread of division, the ordeal of the plural – the
riddle of the human institution of society. In short, I had found in
La Boétie a remarkable foreshadowing of what I had for so long
striven to formulate with regard to the totalitarian fantasy. Not
only this: I found myself enlightened and drawn by this thought
which had surfaced from the past, as if I had yet to attain it, as if it
were in advance of my own.

And what about heroism? What sort of significance did this
concept have for me? What did Quinet mean by it? That which his
friend Michelet, indeed, at the same period, was calling 'heroism
of the mind', translating and adapting Vico's phrase 'mente
heroica'. Despite the Neapolitan thinker's well-known circum-
spection and his care not to violate Catholic orthodoxy, this
formula applied perfectly to the philosophy of modern times. It
was coined to celebrate the risks of a search or research without
model, freed from the authority of established learning; to claim
the unbounded daring of a desire for thought over and above the
demarcations of the various disciplines of knowledge. But it must
also be said that Quinet or Michelet's use of the phrase was apt to
provoke or awaken in me a confused aspiration not to let myself
become confined within the frontiers of what conventionally
goes by the name of philosophy. I tried to work out the reasons
for this. In the end, they all amounted to the fact that the heroic
movement through which thought breaks away from the already
traced and separated out paths of knowledge can never allow itself
to be defined: there is no name for risk in thought, not even that of
philosophy.

My attention had been caught in the first place by the link
established between heroism and servitude. The latter, for
Quinet, was not the mark of a state of affairs brought about by *de*

facto conditions; it bore the mark of a desire. These words had impressed themselves deeply upon me: 'Look at this creature . . . ingeniously deriving servitude from the very midst of freedom.' They seemed to come straight out of the work of La Boétie. Both writers gave it to be understood that the desire which animated an indeterminate demand for independence and knowledge was, in inverted form, the same as that which put men in thrall to a master embodying the omnipotence of belief. La Boétie, for his part, suggests that the desire to be free or the desire to know amount in effect to freedom or knowledge in action, in short, that neither freedom nor knowledge constitute objects of desire, whereas, conversely, servitude is connected to the desire for something – for an 'I know not what' which would fulfil this desire, at once concretizing and exhausting it, just as in fantasy our vision is filled to extinction by the pseudo-visible. This 'I know not what' offers itself through the image of the Master, or through the sole spell of the *name of One* or some substitute for this spell. La Boétie also suggests that by this image, this name, this spell, serf-men acquire the illusion of their own unity, their own identity; even in suffering and sacrifice, they gain the pleasure of deliverance from the image of their separation. He suggests furthermore that servitude survives, for this very reason, by means of each individual's identification, at every stage in the hierarchy, with the Master before an inferior.

Quinet's argument follows the same insight, which also, indeed, inspires his critique of the French Revolution and his analysis of the re-establishment of despotism and servitude under Robespierre and Jacobinism in the wake of the institution of liberty. The conversion of the Revolution into counter-revolution was in his view none other than the effect of the reconstitution of a despotic power, embodying a phantasmatic unity and trampling upon the rights that had been so lately and heroically proclaimed. However, his thinking was distinguished for me by its emancipation from the opposition, still classically taken for granted by La Boétie, between a natural freedom and an unnatural servitude, in describing the contradiction of man as both *beneath and above himself.* He was no doubt speaking of the servitude which is 'derived from the very midst of freedom', but he also expressed his intention to 'take man there where he had not previously been sought, beneath humanity'. He spoke of this man as 'de-natured', yes, but he sought not so much to restore him to a nature as to restore him to life through heroism. So I asked myself again: what does heroism mean? Was it not – according to an idea I believe to have been common to a new generation of thinkers at the start of the nineteenth century – the power to claim a right which lacked any guarantee in nature, finding its truth in its very exercise; the attempt, in other words, to conquer or to re-conquer from servitude the terrain of desire, with no support other than the work accomplishing itself?

It would take too long to reconstruct the process whereby I had been led to scrutinize this notion of *heroism of the mind*. Let it suffice to note that, having resolved some years ago to devote my main seminar to the birth of democratic society and democratic sensibility in France at the beginning of the nineteenth century, I became interested in various writers, of varying political persuasion, who struck me as being similarly haunted by the 'impossible' task of disclosing that which is – the being of history, of society, of man – and of creating, of bringing forth through the exercise of a vertiginous right to thought and to speech, the work in which meaning makes its appearance. Far from endorsing the criticisms of certain contemporaries who condemn, under the name of Romanticism, the double phantasy of *revelation* and *creation*, it seemed to me that the nineteenth century witnessed the formation of an enigma which confronts us still and which lies at the heart of our modernity, detaching us from the classical tradition. Indeed, it seems to me that this enigma was best formulated by a thinker who is still close to us, Merleau-Ponty: 'Being is that which demands of us creation in order that we may experience it.'

When I observed, then, that the words which had come to mind – *beneath, above myself* – caused me to waver in my allusion to Socrates, I had no more than an inkling of the fact that the experience of an internal contradiction between the lapse or the relapse of desire under the lure of the figure of the One and the conquest or re-conquest of desire in the immoderation of freedom and of thought, in the unknowable exercise of the work of creation – that this experience cuts us off from any guarantee of human nature. There is nothing here, I reflected, to stop one finding in Socrates or, say, in La Boétie, exemplary instances of heroism of the mind – but only if one holds a conception of their task differing from their own. Nor does this lead, as some muddled contemporaries would have it, to the proclamation that Reason, Nature or Man 'do not exist'; but it does mean that we can decipher the signs of whatever exists, of whatever occurs, only at an infinite risk of thought, speech or action. In becoming aware of this risk, I felt justified in wondering whether it was legitimate to base the definition of philosophy upon it . . .

This question faced me again from another angle. The remarks of Quinet which had led me back to those of La Boétie testified to a connection between the demands of philosophy and those of politics, that is, between the demand for thought, which would take responsibility for an inquiry into the very essence of thinking, and the demand for intervention in public life through speech or action – no matter which – that would take responsibility for our relationship with what used to be called the City. In my view, this connection has always been unbreakable.

In the afore-mentioned preface, Quinet's hero was Spartacus, who represented for him the very image of the philosopher– warrior. It had previously struck me in reading Machiavelli that his hero, as Leo Strauss had already pointed out, was Epaminon- das, who stands, far more explicitly and in line with a firmly established tradition, for the type of the philosopher–captain. Should I not acknowledge, then, that my own heroes were think- ers who had devoted all their energy to trying to analyse and modify the conditions of the political régimes of their day? There was Machiavelli himself, to whom I had devoted a study which took me I dare not say how long to complete, La Boétie, Spinoza and, for some few years past, a handful of French writers who fought valiantly for the cause of democracy or socialism, Michelet and Quinet in the forefront. I nearly left out Marx . . . a strange oversight , for no other work, apart perhaps from that of Machiavelli or that of a contemporary and teacher of mine who was himself haunted by politics, Merleau-Ponty, has done so much to open up the way for me in my own questions. This omission was not accidental, however, for at the time when I thought of myself as a Marxist I was at least partially concealing from myself the problem that was subsequently to be posed for me by the relationship of philosophy to politics. In fact, this was just the problem with which I found myself increasingly con- fronted, refusing to allot a definite place to philosophy, but no less reluctant, as I have said, to cross it out in favour of politics. No

doubt I may raise a smile by talking about my 'heroes'. The image
came to me in the course of my train of thought; it had never
imposed itself upon me before. I have never consciously vener-
ated a hero – the very word used to disturb me. The fact is,
nonetheless, that in recalling the works which had most power-
fully attracted me, I noticed that they were *hybrids* and that
according to academic standards some of them were not even
recognized as having philosophical status.

But why, indeed, only mention my debt to a certain type of
thinker? I have never dissociated the work of interpretation involved in my studies of writings of the past from that to which I
found myself inescapably committed, both in the examination of
contemporary events – in the French context, for example, the
war in Indochina, the Algerian war, the emergence of Gaullism,
the creation of the Union of the Left; and above all in the Euro-
pean context, the revolts which over the last twenty-five years
have rocked the Communist countries, or again the development
of Stalinism in the U.S.S.R. and Krushchev's attempts at reform
– and more generally in my inquiries into the principles of modern democracy and of totalitarianism. I have never held the view
that there is one specific space for works of thought and another
for 'socio-historical reality'. I did not study the works of, say,
Machiavelli or Marx in order to extract from them a system of
thought, still less in order to catch them out in their contradictions. In either case, such an approach would have led me to
interest myself less in what was actually written in the work than
in the reconstruction of a hypothetical body of statements. On the
contrary, I have always taken pains to restitute not only that
which is deliberate and organized in a writer's thinking, but also
that which shows itself to be beyond his control, which constantly carries him off or away from the 'positions' he has adopted
– whatever, in short, makes for the adventures of thought in
writing, adventures to which the writer consents and which
commit him to losing sight of himself in order to be brought back
to the work.

It was just these ordeals and adventures that bound me most
closely to an author's writing: they became for me signs of the
place and time of the work's formation, signs of an experience, of
a world of representation out of which the work was extracted
and which had given rise to it. It was my awareness of these trials

and adventures which led me both to read in the work the questions for which it assumed responsibility, and to perceive or to reformulate the questioning that lies within my own time. I never, moreover, conceived of my analysis of modern democracy or of totalitarianism from the objectivist point of view of the sociologist or politologist who sets himself to define and compare institutional systems. I was trying to understand the point of a totalitarian enterprise, whether of the Fascist or the Communist kind, over and above the goal of the destruction of bourgeois democracy. Convinced that the emergence of totalitarian régimes is not to be explained by reference to transformations in the mode of production, I have endeavoured for more than twenty-five years to demonstrate the existence of a mutation of a symbolic nature.

But how could I have sought to make possible an assessment, or myself assessed, the significance within totalitarian systems of the denial of social divisions – the division between State and civil society, class divisions, the division between different sectors of independent activity – or that of denying the difference between the order of power, the order of law and the order of knowledge (a difference which is constitutive of democracy), without guarding myself simultaneously against providing a justification for the *de facto* divisions which characterize the régimes under which we ourselves live? How could I have tried to provide some glimpse of the way in which totalitarianism leads towards death without also seeking to dispel any misunderstanding which might allow of an acceptance of the conditions of inequality and oppression typical of those same régimes? Or again, how could I have embarked upon a critique of Marxism designed to reveal everything upon which the totalitarian fantasy has fed, without trying to reinstate, against the dominant ideology, the truth of the task of emancipation undertaken in his own time by Marx? In order to make readers alive to the dynamics of democracy, and to the experience which it establishes of an ultimate indeterminacy in the basis of social organization and of an interminable debate upon Law, I have always had to try to shake not only their prejudices but also their most intimate relationship to Knowledge, to try to awaken in them some sense of the questioning which might resign them to relinquishing the image of 'the good society', while at the same time freeing them from the illusion that whatever appears as the

real, here and now, must be one with the rational. Whether this is
a philosophical or a political way of proceeding, I cannot say. One
thing is certain: the intention which gradually took form within
me has imposed a way of writing which I never chose to adopt,
which merges with my way of being and which is not commonly
imputable to the register of philosophy.

At this stage in my reflections, I had to admit that my doubts as
to the possibility of circumscribing philosophy were not due
solely to the notion that the demands of politics must preclude it
from closing in upon itself. My interest in certain nineteenth-
century French thinkers is not only of a philosophical and political
nature. What attracts me to Michelet, to cite but one (although I
could easily produce a multitude of references), is that he eludes
determination. Shall we say that *The People* is a political work?
That *The French Revolution* is the work of an historian? *The
Origins of Law in France*, that of an anthropologist? *The Sorceress*,
that of a sociologist? Or shall we say that Michelet belongs above
all to literature? The truth is that such distinctions are misleading.
And that in fact historical criticism and literary criticism – even
that of Roland Barthes (or especially his, since he engages less
than any other in wondering *what makes Michelet think* and what *he
makes* of thought) – testify to the futility of certain ways of
proceeding prevalent among our contemporaries. Michelet possesses a sense of time as creation–destruction, a sense of universal
life and of death, a sense of Law as the expression of the human
establishment and of Right* as fierce contestation of all established institutions. He has a sense of unity and fragmentation, he
is the thinker of rootedness, the thinker of identity – we have
heard it often enough – but no less is he the thinker of the
'barbarous' spirit, nomadic, untameable; he combines the idea of
a humanity in the process of self-creation, communicating with
itself through the diversity of its works, with that of an impossible closing in of humanity upon itself . . .

Of all this it would be fruitless to seek a theory in Michelet's
works. But what I called the adventure of thought, as it is lived
and offered up in his writing, impresses itself upon the reader
through means which while they may not be those of philosophy
are no less efficacious, but differently so, as they awaken him in

---

* *Translator's Note:* The word *Droit* has the sense of both Law and Right.

like manner to the question, *what is it to think?* Since I can conceive of no more originary question, I am in ever-increasing doubt whether to sustain this question must necessarily involve naming it. And even if it must be named, does not its greatest force lie in the life of thought, in the way in which thought is engendered?

Philosophy, non-philosophy . . . where is one to draw the line? I was certainly not the first to ask myself this question. But it seemed inadequate simply to answer that there may be more philosophy in a history book, in a political work, in a novel or in a poem than there may be in a treatise bearing that name. Such an answer allows that which it should illuminate to remain obscure – namely, what are we to understand by philosophy? For as long as philosophy was considered definable by the way in which it differed from theology in the treatment of ultimate questions, some criterion was perhaps available. To speak only of the modern period, it seemed possible, as Léo Strauss suggested, to make a belief in Revelation the criterion of religion, whereas an untrammelled research, based upon trust in Reason, into the foundations of knowledge and human behaviour, would be that of philosophy. But the link between philosophy and theology has weakened to the point where it is permissible to doubt whether philosophy can any longer be conceived of as appropriation of the ultimate questions over which theology used to extend its jurisdiction. Nor is the relationship which has been established between philosophy and science of a kind to enlighten us much further. To say that philosophy researches the conditions of possibility for new ways of proceeding in science would be to reduce it to the limits of epistemology. To say that it seeks to formulate the questions generated by the ways of proceeding of these rising sciences does not necessarily mean that these questions have any ultimate value, that they are privileged, or more pertinent than the questions generated by the mutations affecting art or literature, or the conception of history or the sensitivity to history, or political thought, or, quite generally, the relationship of people to politics. It is clear, furthermore, that the fragmentation of philosophy into the philosophy of science, philosophy of politics, philosophy of art, etc. does no more than sanction the failure to think of philosophy as such.

What remains, then, of the demands of philosophy if we cannot relate them to an object? What remains that, precisely, encourages us to assert that these demands may be manifest in writings which are not consciously philosophical?

I should not as yet know how to reply to such a question; but it cannot be empty when it leaves me so disarmed. What I find empty is, as I have said, the discourse upon the destruction of philosophy. Yet this discourse is not itself without motive. Its only fault is that it turns a questioning into an affirmation (that is, in this case, a negation). I should add that this questioning is all the more insistent inasmuch as it does not concern philosophy alone; indeed it made itself apparent even earlier in other fields, particularly in those of literature and art – in painting, in music. It is a platitude to point out that painters, for some time now, have been ever-increasingly faced with the question, what is it to paint?, or that the idea of some painterly essence has vanished for them together with the visual essence to which it corresponded. Writers similarly give way to the vertigo of the question, what is it to write? The essence of literature and its counterpart, the essence of language, have vanished for them; while earlier confidence as to the nature of the novel or of poetry has dissolved.

In an essay entitled 'Indirect language and the voices of silence' (in fact a chapter taken by the author from an unfinished book, *The Prose of the World*, and modified by him), Merleau-Ponty had already drawn an illuminating analogy between the adventure of painting and literature and that of philosophy. He was particularly concerned to show that classical writers were haunted by the phantom of a pure language, but that we allow ourselves to become the dupes of their illusion when we forget that in their practice they were already devoted to a work of expression, a work which was creative, and whose success was in no way guaranteed by the nature of language. More generally, he remarked that, without being consciously aware of it, classical writers and painters were conducting research both into that which is sayable or seeable and into the nature of writing or painting as such; a research which later became ever more explicitly their aim. In the wake of these interpretations, I had myself wondered whether philosophy, over an even longer period, had not been haunted by the phantom of a pure thinking. And, following the same line of thought, I realized that in his practice the philosopher had always been devoted to a work of expression, to the production of a work, in which thought seeks itself through the medium of writing, at once disclosing and inventing itself; in this sense, thought had never been transparent to itself, the notion of such transparency being one which takes no account of the way in which thought actually proceeds. In the light of this realization, I concluded that this search, the question 'What is thinking?', bound up as it was with the question of writing, was becoming more and more the special province of philosophy in our time.

But should I not draw two consequences from this line of reflection? Firstly, that the philosopher is led to embrace his writer's vocation instead of denying it by the recognition of the bonds between philosophy and literature. Secondly, if the question which marks him out as a philosopher is indeed 'What is thinking?', then it cannot be circumscribed or defined in the traditional sense as a question of knowledge, one which puts a subject in sight of its object, a question inviting a return towards an origin in order to deploy and master the articulations of a field of consciousness. Rather, the question would be neither localizable nor determinable, a question accompanying every experience of the world, whether derived from the most sensitive and generalized relationships inscribed upon the organs of our body – which simultaneously open it to others and to things, and imprint them within it – or from relationships built up in us by the fact of our involvement in a culture and, beyond that, in the history of mankind. In this sense, what we called the *demands of philosophy* would spring or re-spring up everywhere, governed, for the writer–philosopher, simply by the call of the work within which the question remains in quest of itself, repeating itself from wherever its peculiar desire may have led it.

I have already quoted Merleau-Ponty's formula, 'Being is that which demands of us creation in order that we may experience it.' But should we preserve this term in the singular, Being? Can we still give the force of a name to what the word motions towards, if, as the same author once wrote – expressing a reservation about Heidegger – there can be none but an *indirect* ontology, to be found only in the deciphering of be-ings and the adventure of expression. And if to bring ourselves back to whatever makes us think and speak we must let ourselves be carried off by thought and speech, if it is the same movement which both uproots and enroots us, then should not whoever experiences the lure of philosophy lay claim to this wandering, should he not deliberately embrace this nomadic life, should he not wrap himself in the whirlwind which already constantly draws and blurs for each one of us, even though we may not know it, the lines between here and there, between within and without?

I was going to end here, when I remembered the reply with which I had evaded the question 'How did you become a philosopher?' I had immediately hastened to relate the circumstances of my meeting, towards the end of my secondary schooling, with a teacher who had seemed to me to be extraordinary and under whose influence my future direction was almost instantly settled. His name was Merleau-Ponty. I have never ceased to be guided by his inspiration, as must indeed be apparent from the handful of references I have made to him in these pages. I was, moreover, to devote to him a number of essays, which were collected into a book a few years ago. I could, certainly, have elaborated further to my interlocutor on the subject of this meeting. The questions with which Merleau-Ponty was dealing made me feel that they had existed within me before I discovered them. And he himself had a strange way of questioning: he seemed to make up his thoughts as he spoke, rather than merely acquainting us with what he already knew. It was an unusual and disturbing spectacle. In this teacher capable of extricating himself from the position of mastery, I found a master for the first time (although I was of too rebellious a temperament to realize it). It will be seen that had I done so, I would have been led to examine more closely the relationship between teaching and philosophy . . . But I found that in my reluctance to assume the name of philosopher I had made a yet more significant omission. My choice was not, in fact, simply the outcome of a meeting, however decisive. Well before entering the philosophy class in my last year at the *lycée*, I had been possessed by the desire to become a writer, a secret longing which dated from early adolescence. Like many other young people who have felt the same desire, I did not know what I wanted to write; my desire was without an object, waiting for its object. Philosophy did no more than to fix it by metamorphosis. Renouncing literature (although this was never a very settled decision), I became attracted by a writing which still bore the stamp of my original desire. This recollection brought me to a last question: has what I owe to my personal history led me to misjudge the 'essence of philosophy', or have I instead gained from it some ability to fathom the relationship of philosophy to writing? This, for the moment at any rate, is a question which I cannot answer.

As I remarked at the beginning, my reflections were to carry me a long way from my fragile point of departure. They finally carried me to where I could not but stand back before the point of view of the other. That they should now call upon a reader is perhaps thereby justified.

Translated by Lorna Scott Fox

EMMANUEL LEVINAS

Beyond intentionality

1. Does thought have meaning only through knowledge of the world – through the presence of the world and in virtue of our presence to the world – even when this presence is given in the horizons of past and future, temporal modes which are themselves also dimensions of re-*presentation* in which *presence* is after all recovered? Or, does not sense, in senseful thought, possess – perhaps prior to presence or to re-presentable presence, and to a greater extent than these – a meaning which is already *determined* and through which the very notion of sense comes to the mind before it is specified in terms of the formal structure of reference as it refers to a world unveiled, to a system, to an aim? Is not meaning *par excellence* that which would provide a justification for Being itself, that meaning the search for which is reflected in the now daily words of people who say they are concerned with the 'meaning of life'? Does Being provide its own reason for existing as the alpha and omega of intelligibility, first philosophy and eschatology? Does it not, on the contrary, carry on with its task of being, while still calling for a justification (as a question preceding every other question)? Is not the *for-the-other* (*pour-l'autre*) – which, in the guise of humanity, manages to disrupt the 'easy conscience' of the *conatus*, of the animal persistence of beings in Being, concerned solely for their own space and for the time of their own life – is not the *for-the-other* the opening of this question and the formulation of this meaning, *par excellence*? These problems make up the dominant theme of this essay.

It starts from certain standpoints found in Husserlian phenomenology, inasmuch as this is the conclusion to which one of the characteristic traditions of philosophy leads, according to which knowledge of entities and of their presence is the 'natural place' of the senseful and is equivalent to spirituality or to the psychic life of thought itself.

2. For Husserl – and for the whole venerable philosophical tradition which he completes or of which, at least, he makes certain presuppositions explicit – the 'bestowal of sense' (*Sinngebung*) is produced in a thought, understood as thought of . . . as thought of *this* or *that*; the this or that are taken as present to our thoughts (*cogitationes*) inasmuch as they are thought (*cogitatum*) to the point at which we are unable to determine or to recognize in reflection any thoughts without naming the *this* or *that* of which they are the thoughts. 'Meaning-bestowing' thought is constructed as the thematization (whether implicit or explicit) of *this* or *that*, more precisely, as knowledge. The very breath of the spirit in thought is held to constitute *knowledge*. This is what is expressed when it is said that meaning-bestowing con-sciousness (con*science*) is intentional, organized as the *noesis* of a *noema* where the noema is *concrete* in the intention of the noesis. By means of the *this* or *that*, which are ineliminable from the description of the *bestowal of sense*, a notion such as the *presence* of *something* appears with the emergence of sense itself. Presence of something: *Seinsinn*, the sense of Being, according to Husserl, which in Heidegger – descending through all the harmonics of the history of philosophy – becomes the Being of beings.

The 'bestowal of sense', constructed as knowledge, is understood in Husserl as a 'wanting-to-arrive-in-one-way-or-another-at-this-or-that', and reflection upon this thought as showing *what* thought *wants to get at* and *how it wants to get there*. Intentionality is thus an intention of the soul, a spontaneity, a *willing*, and the sense bestowed itself, in some way, what is *willed*: the way in which beings or their Being manifest themselves to thought in knowledge corresponds to the way in which consciousness 'wills' this manifestation through its own resolve or through the intention that animates this knowledge. Cognitive intention is thus a free act. The soul is 'affected', yet not passively, as it takes hold of itself again by taking responsibility for what is given in accordance with its own intention. It raises itself. Husserl speaks of a teleology of transcendental consciousness. In this way, thought thinking of Being, from which it distinguishes itself, is an internal process, a staying-in-itself: immanence. Here, in virtue of the 'bestowal of sense', there is a deep correspondence between Being and thought. There is nothing beyond the scope of intention in this sense: what is willed does not play games with the willing nor does it take the latter by surprise. Nothing enters thought 'without declaring itself', nothing is 'smuggled in'. Everything stands within the openness of the soul: presence is candour itself. The intentional distance – between Being and thought – constitutes also an extreme accessibility of being. Astonishment, the disproportion between the *cogitatio* and the *cogitatum* where truth is to be sought, subsides in the truth once it is found. Presence, the production of Being or its manifestation, is *given*, is a mode of being-given (*Gegebenheit*). Husserl describes this as filling a void, as satisfaction. He who himself lays stress on the role of human incarnation in the perception of what is given, and on the 'lived body' (*Leib*) as the organ of consciousness – since we must move around about things in order to grasp them, turning our head, adjusting our eyes and using our ears – will certainly authorize us to insist on the primary role played by the hand: Being is *bestowed* and this bestowal is to be understood in the literal sense of the word. The Bestowal is completed by the *hand that takes* (*la main qui prend*). It is therefore in this taking of possession (*mainmise*) that presence is 'presence proper', presence 'in flesh and blood' and not only 'in images': presence is produced as a *hand-holding-now* (*maintenant*). It is in the taking-in-hand that the 'thing itself' matches what the intention of thought willed and aimed at. The hand verifies the eye, for in it are performed the acts of grasping and assuming as one's own, which are irreducible to tactile sensation. This taking possession is not a simple sensing, it is a putting to the test. Before acting, as Heidegger would have it, as handling and use of tools, it is an appropriation. This is more fully and entirely presence, one would be tempted to say, than the presence given in thematization. It is precisely because of the way it allows itself to be grasped, to be appropriated – the way in which presence lets itself be given (*Gegebenheit*) – that presence is presence of a content, a content involving sensible qualities. This content can, of course, be classified in terms of generic identities and, in any case, in terms of the formal identity of *something* (*etwas überhaupt*), of a something which can be indicated and identified by an *index* as a determinable point within all which is present and gathered together: quiddity and identity of a thing, a solid, a term, a being. It is, no doubt, inseparable from a world out of which it is torn when it is first picked out and grasped, and yet such an act of separation is presupposed in every relation to or between things or beings. We may even go so far as to wonder whether the distinction between *Being* and *beings* is not an essential duality of presence, of that *Gegebenheit* which is sketched out in manifestation. Hands and fingers! The incarnation of consciousness, then, would be not a sorry accident befalling thought, cast down from the empyrean heights into a mere body, but rather the essential circumstance of truth.

To truth itself then, and not only to its use and abuse in a technological world, there belongs a primary technical success, that of the index which points at something and of the hand which grasps it. Perception is an apprehension and the concept, *Begriff*, a com-prehending. The adequation of thought and Being at every level to a restitution of the elementary conditions of its transcendental genesis. The idea of truth as a *grasp* on things must of the categorial and of the general to what is given directly (*schlicht gegeben*) is one of the basic intuitions of Husserl's *Logical Investigations*. Early on, Husserl outlines the thesis put forward in his *Formal and Transcendental Logic* according to which formal ontology refers back to a material ontology and, hence, to sensible perception. He also sets out the thesis, which recurs throughout his entire work, that every notion is to be carried back, while fully respecting the characteristics peculiar to its own level, to a restitution of the elementary conditions of its transcendental genesis. The idea of truth as a *grasp* on things must necessarily have a non-metaphorical sense somewhere. In things, which support and prefigure every superstructure, *to be* signifies *to be given* and *to be rediscoverable*, to be some *thing*, and hence an entity. For every theme which finds its focus in 'some one thing', the concept of this 'some one thing', though logically empty as the concept of *etwas überhaupt*, never fails concretely to refer to whatever it is that the hand grasps and holds – content and quiddity – and to what the finger points at – this or that. Positing and positivity which are confirmed in the theses – the positional acts – of conceptual thought.

Presence – and Being conceived of as presence on the basis of knowledge – is therefore openness itself and givenness (*Gegebenheit*). Nothing turns up to contradict the intention of thought, nothing emerges from hiding to foil it; there is no chance of an ambush, planned and set up in the darkness or in the mystery of a past or a future refractory to presence. The past is but a present that once was. It remains on a par with the presence of the present, with that manifestation which is perhaps only its emphatic perseverance. It re-presents itself. If the past were to have meaning without being the modification of a present in which it may have commenced, if it were to signify an-archically – this would undoubtedly indicate the rupture of immanence. Immanence connotes this gathering together of the diversity of time in the presence of representation. This ability of the diverse not to reject synchrony, but rather to allow its very diversity to be brought under the unity of a genus or a form – is a logically necessary condition for synchronization or for the results of synchronization. In the present – in the completed present, in the present of ideality – everything allows itself to be thought together. Temporal alteration itself, examined in the sensible realm which fills time and which endures in or thanks to it, may be interpreted on the basis of the metaphor of a flow (made up of drops distinct from and yet resembling each other *par excellence*, 'like two drops of water'). Temporal otherness (*altérité*) is thus to be conceived of as inseparable from the qualitative difference of the contents or of spatial intervals, distinct yet equal, discernible yet traversed in a uniform movement. This is a homogeneity, which constitutes a predisposition to synthesis. The past is representable, retained or remembered or reconstructed in an historical narrative; the future, is 'pro-tension', anticipated, presupposed by hypo-thesis.

The temporalization of time – temporal flow – would still be intentional, its diachrony could be synthesized in the representation of qualitative contents bound to time. One might, however, wonder to what extent the properly dia-chronic difference may not pass unrecognized within that which appears as indissociable from the contents and which makes us think of time as if it were composed of instants – atoms of presence or entities – designatable as terms which pass before us. This is but the differentiation of the Same (*le Même*) lending itself to synthesis, that is, to the synchrony which may be held to justify or to give rise to the psyche as re-presentation: memory and anticipation.

In this psyche, capable of apprehending presence, the subject or the self would be, precisely, the agent or the common ground of re-presentation, the possibility of gathering together that which is dispersed. Thus, Brentano was able to maintain that psychic life consists in re-presentation or is supported by re-presentation in all its various forms – theoretical, affective, axiological and active. Similarly, Husserl maintained to the very end that there was a logical stratum in all intentionality, even the non-theoretical sort. *Spirit was held to be presence and relation to being.* Nothing concerning it was alien to truth, to the appearance of Being.

In truth, thought thus moves out of itself towards Being, without thereby ceasing to remain in its own proper sphere (*chez elle*), always equal to itself, never losing its measure, never exceeding it. Thought *satis*fies itself in Being, which as a first move it begins by distinguishing from itself; it *satis*fies itself in adequation. The knowledge in which thought displays itself is a thought thinking 'to satiety', always within its own limits. Language, no doubt, suggests a relation *between* thinkers over and beyond this represented content, always identical to itself and thus immanent. However, the rationalism implicit in knowledge interprets this otherness as the mutual rediscovery of interlocutors within the *Same*, a Same of which they are the untoward dispersion. In language, diverse subjects can enter each into the thought of another and so coincide in reason. Reason on this view is the true inner life. The questions and answers which make up an 'exchange of ideas' could just as well be held within a *single* consciousness. The relation between thinkers would have no special meaning of its own and would count only as a transmission of signs, thanks to which a multiplicity was reunited around one and the same thought; the multiplicity of consciousnesses in relation with one another should be seen as nothing but the deficiency of a prior or final unity. Would not the proximity of one consciousness to another take on the sense of a failure of coincidence between them? Language would thus be entirely subordinated to thought, even if in its immanent functioning, the latter would have to have recourse to verbal signs in order to understand – to encompass – and to combine ideas and to preserve what had been acquired.

The rigorous correlation between what is manifested and the *modes* of consciousness enables Husserl to affirm both that consciousness bestows sense and that Being commands the modalities of consciousness which reach it, that Being controls what appears as phenomenon. This final phrase receives an idealist interpretation: Being is immanent in thought and thought does not transcend itself in knowledge. Whether knowledge be sensible, conceptual or even purely symbolical, the transcendent or the absolute, claiming, as it does, to be unaffected by any relation, can in fact bear no transcendental sense without immediately losing it: the very fact of its presence to knowledge signifies the loss of transcendence and of absoluteness. In the final analysis, presence excludes all transcendence. The intentionality of consciousness lies precisely in the fact that the sense of the sensible comes from appearance, that the very perseverance of a being in its Being is manifestation, and that Being as appearing is thus encompassed, equalled and, in some way, *carried* by thought. It is not through some degree of intensity or firmness which would remain unmatchable or unmatched in relation to the principle of noetic identification – nor through the axiological modalities which the Being as posited may be held to possess – that transcendence or absoluteness might be capable of preserving a sense which would remain unaffected even by its presence in manifestation. The energy of manifestation – that is, the noetic identification required for *appearance* – is held to have all the intensity or all the firmness required to persist in Being; of this persistence, manifestation would simply constitute the state of ultimate emphasis. Understood properly, the notion of intentionality signifies at once that Being commands the modes of access to Being and that Being is in accordance with the intention of consciousness. Intentionality signifies an exteriority in immanence and the immanence of all exteriority.

However, does intentionality exhaust all the ways in which thought is meaningful?

3. Does thought have meaning only through consciousness of the world? Or is not the potential surplus of the world itself, over and beyond all *presence*, to be sought in an immemorial past – that is, irreducible to a bygone present – in the trace left by this past which, perhaps, marks it out as a part of creation, a mark we

should not be too quick to reduce to the condition of a causal effect and which, in any case, presupposes an otherness representable neither in terms of the correlations of knowledge nor in terms of the synchrony of re-presentation. It is precisely a possible approach to this otherness which this study attempts to describe – a study which, by uncovering in Being, above and beyond its ontological contingency, its putting into 'moral question' and its call for a justification, would involve it in the ethical intrigue of otherness.

Is not the significance of thought nothing other than thematization, and so, re-presentation, and, thus, the bringing together of temporal diversity and dispersal? Is thought from the very outset braced towards the adequation of truth, towards the grasp of what is given as phenomenon in its ideal identity as 'something'? Would not thought then be senseful only in the face of pure presence, fulfilled presence, which, in the eternal realm of ideality, no longer 'passes by' or 'passes on' as in time? Is all *other*ness (*altérité*) only qualitative, a diversity that allows itself to be collected under genera and forms and brought back to the Same, in the same way as would be permitted by a time that lent itself to synchronization through the re-presentations of knowledge?

A deeper reflection on what is specifically human may, however, lead us to doubt the appropriateness of this line of thought. The self identifies itself independently of any particular characteristic quality which might distinguish one self from another and in which it would recognize itself. As 'pure selves', different selves are, precisely, indistinguishable. The otherness of the indiscernible cannot be reduced to a mere difference of 'content'. So the relation of one self to another is not the bringing together of beings in a world like that found in re-presentation or in the synchronization produced by way of knowledge. Otherness in the case of 'indiscernibles' does not refer them back to a common genus nor to a time that might be synchronizable in re-presentations through memory or history. Would these indiscernibles, then, be impossible to gather together and so simply remain separated? *Unless, of course, their gathering together be something quite different from synthesis, that is, unless it be proximity, face-to-face and society.* Face-to-face: the notion of the face that imposes itself here is not that of a datum empirically added onto the prior notion of a plurality of selves, of psyches or of interiorities to be totted up to form a total. It is the face which commands a gathering – or a proximity – quite different from that involved in the synthesis which unites phenomena into a world. It commands a thinking that is more ancient and more aware than knowledge or experience. I can, no doubt, have an experience of another person, but without, precisely, discerning in him his indiscernible difference. Thought alert to the face of the other is the thought of an irreducible difference, a difference which is not a thematization and which disturbs the equilibrium of the impassible soul of knowing. The alertness should not be directly interpreted as intentionality, as a *noesis* matching – whether the intention be fulfilled or remain empty – its *noema* and simultaneous with it. An irreducible otherness is strong enough to 'resist' this synchronization of the noetico-noematic correlation and to signify what is immemorial and infinite, balking at presence and at re-presentation, balking at immanence where otherness would fall away, even if re-presentations were to be limited to nostalgia or to a symbolism. As we have just stated: I can, no doubt, have an experience of another and 'observe' his face, and yet the knowledge gained in this way would be, if not actually misleading, nevertheless truncated as if the relationship with another were lost in the knowledge, which, here, can occur only through 'appresentation' and 'empathy' (*Einfühlung*), to use Husserl's expressions. For Husserl, indeed, the sense of the *other* is still meaningful in knowledge, which itself can be preceded by nothing else. Truncated knowledge. Indeed, in 'appresentation', I constitute the other on the basis of the perceived behaviour of a body analogous to the one I inhabit. However, this 'knowledge' of another self lacks any direct mode of access to this life, lacks the means to pierce the secret of his inner life and his personal identity, the *forever-indirect* knowledge of the un-knowable. What is at issue is, in fact, an otherness that cannot be reduced to the grafting of a specific and characteristic difference onto a fundamental identity, itself common to a diversity that is already synchronous, or synchronizable, a diversity thus assured of the common formal ground, the ultimate homogeneity necessary for every relation involving knowledge – but a common ground upon which the other would have lost his radical and indiscernible otherness and be brought back to the level of things in the world.

What we take to be the secret of the other man in appresentation is precisely the hidden side of a meaning other than knowledge: awakening to the other man in his identity, an identity indiscernible for knowledge, thought in which the proximity of one's fellow is a source of meaning, 'commerce' with *the other* which cannot be reduced to experience, the *approach* of the other, of the first comer.

This proximity of the unknown lies in the meaningfulness of the face, which from the outset carries meaning over and beyond that of the surface plasticities which cover it with their presence in perception. Before any particular expression – and under every particular expression – there lies an extreme rectitude; a pointblank rectitude, perhaps the ethical source and 'latent birth' of geometrical straightness, the straightness of the arrow's flight or of the projectile that kills. This is the extreme uprightness of that which does not appear simply in the context of an ensemble gathered beneath the sun and within the shadows of a horizon; in other words, that which strictly speaking does not appear, is not a phenomenon. In speaking of this uprightness – stretched by its exposition to . . . to the point of nudity, destitution, without defence or recourse to any possible digression – we have said elsewhere that the face of the other man is for me at one and the same time a temptation to kill and the 'thou shalt not kill' by which I am already accused or suspected, but which also already *summons me*. It is a concrete expression of mortality: the break up of plastic forms, a nakedness starker than any other in the uprightness of an exposition to the invisibility of death, to the mystery of death, to the never to be resolved alternative between Being and not Being. But this involves, certainly, even more: an alternative between this alternative and a third possibility, one that is excluded and unthinkable, but due precisely to which death is a mystery extending *beyond* the unknown. A beyond excluded both from knowledge and from ignorance and yet giving rise to the question in which just what is problematic in the question is to be found – the question *par excellence* in virtue of the uprightness of the face, but a question in which *I am summoned* as well. The face itself constitutes the fact that *someone summons me* and demands my presence. Ethical proximity begins here: in my response to this summons. This response cannot be conceived of as the communication of information; it is the response of responsibility for the other man. In the approach to others *indebtedness* takes the place of the grasp or the comprehension of knowledge.

Beyond surface plasticities. Not in any sense an experience of the beyond, not the knowledge of another presence, which, if it were to be attributed to the beyond, would be quite absurd, reducing this beyond to a mere continuation of intentionality, extending into a mythological other-world. Instead, a 'beyond' that is the break-up of presence, and, consequently, of synchronizable time. A relation between non-synthetizables, between non-synchronizables, a relation of the Same to the Other: ethical thinking or human fraternity. The singular character of this fraternal thinking among all the relations based upon presence and upon the synchronizable time of re-presentation and of the world is shown in the strange lucidity whereby two men born of the same maternal womb may suddenly recognize themselves as sufficiently foreign each to the other for the brother to be no longer his brother's keeper. Fraternity is precisely the relation across the abyss that is itself unbridgeable by mere knowledge of human otherness, and which, as responsibility, is neither a diminished knowledge nor a consequence of knowledge. I am responsible for others whether or not we share a common present. I am responsible for others above and beyond anything I may or may not have done in their regard, beyond anything that may or may not concern my own acts. It is as if, in virtue of this fraternity, my relation to the other no longer went back to a prior intimacy of what had once been *mine*, what I had once appropriated, to what Heidegger as early as Paragraph 9 of *Sein und Zeit* calls *Jemeinigkeit*, a concept that in his thought dominates the entire theory of authenticity, of *Eigentlichkeit*. Rather, it is as if my very self were constituted only through a relation to others, a relation that was gratuitous with respect to accounting for what may be mine and what another's. Responsible without being culpable, I am as if open to an accusation which the alibi of my otherness cannot excuse. A brother despite my strangeness! Fraternity, accusation and my responsibility come before any contemporaneousness, any freedom in myself, out of an immemorial-non-re-presentable-past, before any beginning to be found in myself, before any present. I respond to a question more ancient than 'my consciousness', a question that my consciousness could not have perceived yet which commits me, in accordance with the strange schema evident in a creature that must have been able to respond to the *fiat* of *Genesis*, before ever having been of the world and in the world, before having been capable of hearing. Dia-chrony as relation: non-relation which is relation. Non-relation in that diachrony is the multiplicity of the unassemblable which could never be counted together, whereas the terms of a relation share at least a common time and can be thought of simultaneously. Non-relation, too, because no preposition could ever convey the orientation of time without betraying it; relation whose unique figure is the very diachrony of time itself; and consequently, non-relation which is relation.

Proximity of the other man, meaningful in a different way from that through which appresentation draws its knowledge; yet meaningful also in a different way from that of the representations and direct experience that another man has of himself. Is it certain, however, that the ultimate and peculiar sense of man lies in what is exhibited, in what is manifested or in manifestation, in unveiled truth or in the noesis of knowledge? This is what the opening lines of our study left open: what is *sense*? Is it certain that man has no sense beyond, precisely, what man can be and what he can show himself to be? Does not this sense reside, rather, in his secretness as 'first comer', in his strangeness as other, inasmuch as it is precisely this strangeness which underlies the way in which he thrusts himself upon my responsibility, the way in which he places me under his command? Does the sense of another man lie in his manifestation? Is the way in which the stranger thrusts himself upon me not the very manner in which a God who loved the stranger and who put me into question by summoning me would 'enter on the scene'?

The meaning of this ineffaceable strangeness of the other within my responsibility for him or this 'difference between indiscernibles' lacking any common genus – myself and the other – coincides with a non-in-difference in myself with regard to the other. Is this not the very meaning of the face, of the primordial speaking that *summons me*, questions me, stirs me, provokes my response or my responsibility, which – before any knowledge I may have of myself, before any reflexive presence of myself to myself, and beyond my perseverance in Being and my repose in myself – would be the *for-the-other*, whereby the psychic life of humanity would be brought down to earth, and to a break with Heideggerian *Jemeinigkeit*?

The face 'signifies' beyond, neither as an index nor as a symbol, but precisely and irreducibly as a face that *summons me*. It signifies *to-God* (*à-Dieu*), not as a sign, but as the questioning of myself, as if I were being summoned or called, that is to say, awakened or cited as myself. In this summons, the *question* harkens back to its primordial, underived meaning. It finds it, evidently, not in its original state as a modality or as a moment of the doxic apophantic modality, such as doubt, probability, or pure possibility which remain immanent in thought. Although we are accustomed to the leading role of the question in the theoretical realm, the question, unlike knowledge, is not indifferent as to its expression; the latter is determined by factors outside the semantic content of knowledge, since already by virtue of its very meaning the question breaks out of the immanence of thought. Its problematical character is itself a summons and a call to others. It marks the point at which language in some sense tears thought open, and thought, which in intentionality is still 'transcendence in immanence', moves towards others. However, when it comes to the question of death, the question *par excellence*, I am summoned as though in the egoism of my *conatus* I were thereby to leave the other man alone to face the hazard of the death that puts him into question. My being put into question and my relationship-to-God (*à-Dieu*) seem to point up a certain foreignness of the *esse* where Being would take on a meaning in virtue of my responsibility for the other.

These interrogations and these conditionals do not, of course, constitute a return to the great psychoanalytic thesis according to which the analyst sees more accurately into the other man than he himself sees in his spontaneous and reflective consciousness. In this case, it is a question neither of seeing nor of knowing. We are asking rather whether man's humanity is to be defined solely by what he is or whether, in the face which *summons me*, a different – and more ancient – meaning than the ontological one is not taking shape and awakening a thinking other than knowledge, a thinking which constitutes probably the very pulsation of the Self. The sense of the human is not to be measured by presence, not even by self-presence. The meaning of proximity exceeds the limits of ontology, of the human essence, and of the world. It signifies by way of transcendence and the relationship-to-God-in-me (*l'à-Dieu-en-moi*) which is the putting of myself into question. The face signifies in the fact of summoning, of *summoning me* – in its nudity or its destitution, in everything that is precarious in questioning, in all the hazards of mortality – to the unresolved alternative between Being and Nothingness, a questioning which, *ipso facto*, *summons me*.

The Infinite in its absolute difference withholds itself from presence in me; the Infinite does not come to meet me in a contemporaneousness like that in which noesis and noema meet simultaneously together, nor in the way in which interlocutors responding to one another may meet. The Infinite is not indifferent to me. It is in calling me to other men that transcendence concerns me. In this unique intrigue of transcendence, the non-absence of the Infinite is neither presence, nor re-presentation. Instead, the idea of the Infinite is to be found in my responsibility for the Other.

Thought of the unencompassable, thought of the transcendent, thought of an otherness that refuses to admit of presence and simultaneity. Yet this refusal is not pure negation, it isolates one in the solitude of an inalienable responsibility, it is a refusal by way of responsibilities conferred. This negation constitutes the finiteness of the finite precisely in terms of responsibility, but a responsibility which is also the interweaving of the Infinite with the finite: the *In* of Infinite signifies at one and the same time, the *not* of the Infinite, the transcendence of the finite, and the overflow of the Infinite *in* the finite.

The transcendence of the movement towards God (*à-Dieu*) moves as if across a gap that no genus, not even an empty form, can ever span and both this transcendence and the relation to the Absolute or to the Infinite have an ethical significance, that is to say that their meaning is to be found in the proximity of the other man, he who is a stranger and who may be naked, destitute and undesirable; but also in his face, that undesirable face which *summons me*, which concerns me, which puts me into question – none of this should be taken as a 'new proof of the existence of God', a problem that, most likely, has a sense only within the world. All this describes only the circumstance in which the very meaning of the word 'God' comes to mind, even more imperiously than a presence, a circumstance in which this word signifies neither Being, nor persistence in Being, in which it signifies no 'other' world – nothing could be further from a world! – and yet, in which, precisely, these negations do not slip back into negative theology.

The singular signification of God is tied to responsibility for the other man. We should like to recall in this connection an apologue recounted in old Jewish texts concerning a well-known biblical passage at the beginning of chapter 18 of *Genesis*, where Abraham is visited by three angels. The first verse of this biblical text, in the Hebraic version, opens with a verb that expressly signifies Revelation: 'Revealed Himself to him, did the Lord, in the plains of Mamre, while he was sitting at the entrance to his tent during the heat of the day.' And the Doctors of Israel have commented on this in the form of a parable: the Lord revealed Himself to Abraham while he was sitting at the entrance to his tent, watching for passers-by tired by the heat and whom he wanted to invite into the shade of his lodging. Second verse: 'As he raised his eyes and looked, he saw three persons standing before him. And seeing them, he ran to them from the doorway of his tent and prostrated himself on the ground.' If these three figures who – we later learn – are angels, but who in the eyes of Abraham, following the obvious sense of the text, can only be three passers-by worn out by the journey and by the desert dust, if these three travellers to be welcomed are taken to represent what is meant by the revelation of God spoken of in the first verse, this would already be not at all a bad interpretation as an illustration of the idea of a God inseparable from the face of the other man, and from the *summons* that this face signifies. But there is a third verse: 'And he said, Lord, if I have found grace in your eyes, do not pass by this way before your servant.' Addressing his invitation to the three travellers, Abraham pronounces the word 'Adonaï', which means Lord, in the singular. Whom is he addressing? There are three travellers. The Jewish commentator first looks for the natural sense of this vocative that can indeed be understood in the singular: Abraham is supposed to be addressing the most important or the oldest among the three men in order to invite, through him, the entire group, of which the oldest is probably the leader. The term 'Adonaï' by which he addresses him is, of course, used to invoke God, but it can perfectly well carry a profane sense and concern a man. This is a textual meaning that is quite acceptable. But here is the sense that the passage calls for – the parabolic sense – of this singularity and of this singular: verse three should follow verse one, and verse two become verse three. 'The Lord revealed Himself to him in the plains of Mamre, while he was seated at the entrance to his tent during the heat of the day. And he said, Adonaï, if I find grace in your eyes do not pass by this way before your servant. As he raised his eyes and looked, he saw three persons standing before him; he ran to them from the doorway of his tent and prostrated himself on the ground.' In this version, Abraham asks the Eternal who is appearing to him not to leave but to wait for him, for it is important to him to run out to the travellers whom he wants to welcome under his tent. Was Abraham thereby lacking in respect to the Eternal who was revealing Himself to him or might it have been of greater urgency to greet the travellers than to listen to the Revelation? Or might there have been more revelation of God in greeting the travellers than in the tête-à-tête with the Eternal?

The singular epiphany of God in the face of three men wandering in the desert! One can, of course, separate out of this or isolate from it the idea of God. One can think it or know it while forgetting the circumstances. Religions and theologies thrive on this abstraction just as mystics do on this isolation. But so do wars of religion.

Translated by Kathleen McLaughlin

JEAN-FRANÇOIS LYOTARD

Presentations

I

R.J.M. and/or A.M. have asked J.F.L. (as they have each of the other French philosophers)[1] to say (1) what J.F.L. thinks he has said (= written); (2) what he believes to be the audience and the context of his writings; (3) what he knows to be the objections, or possible objections, to his writings and what he considers he should reply to these objections; (4) what, in his writings, he judges to offer the greatest difficulty to the French-speaking and non-French-speaking audience.*

This request is a request for a presentation.[2] The words *think, believe, know, consider, judge* indicate that J.F.L. is asked to present here and now not his objects and themes of reflection, his audiences, his adversaries and his readers in difficulty, but rather the images he forms of these.

Let us suppose that this request be answered by a narrative. We should see that the constraint contained in the request (the constraint of presentation) would be conveyed in the form of prescriptions concerning the narrative mode and voice.[3] The prescribed narrative mode could only be that of 'internal' focalization in which the narrator (the signatory of these lines) adopts, in principle and in order to tell the story, the point of view of the hero, a French philosopher of the same name, to the exclusion of any other point of view. As for the properties required for the

---

* *Editor's Note:* R.J.M. are the initials of Jeremy Mynott of the Cambridge University Press, A.M. those of Alan Montefiore, the editor of this collection of essays, and J.F.L., of course, those of Jean-François Lyotard himself.

narrative voice, we should remark, in distinguishing both the level and the person, that to be considered 'presentative' a narrative would have to be extradiegetic and homodiegetic respectively. The first property is that of a narrative in which the narrative act (in this case, the present presentation) is not included among the events it recounts (J.F.L.'s works and their fates). The second property names the narrative voice of a tale in which the narrator (the signatory) is also a character in the story he is telling (a French philosopher in the story of continental thought . . .).

The imagined narrative would therefore present phrases such as: *'For the continentals, philosophy of the modern period . . .'*; and *'He'* (J.F.L.) *'then decided temporarily to withdraw from every undertaking of the sort . . .'* The first phrase provides an example of internal focalization (continental philosophy is seen through the hero's eyes), and the second is an example of extra-homodiegesis (the hero of the narrative is its narrator, but he is not the hero *qua* narrator).

While, however, these properties stem from the nature of the request made by R.J.M. and/or A.M., the type of discourse in which they are to be displayed is itself in no way laid down. Now, apart from narratives like the *Discourse on Method* or the end of the *Theodicy*, philosophy has an overabundance of types of discourse in which it can choose to present itself: fictional written dialogue, the tale or didactic poem, the course notebook, intellectual autobiography, the metaphysical journal, the treatise *more geometrico*, the reflective essay, speculative epic, a collection of aphorisms, manuals, the résumé of real or fictitious lectures, the doctoral thesis, the pamphlet, the collection of articles or notes, and one could go on.

Here, while imposing on the signatory the mode and voice of his discourse, the editors leave him nevertheless a certain latitude in his choice of genre, provided only that the prescribed requirements be satisfied. If, for example, one decided to reply to their request by an extract from a philosophical journal, one could equally well satisfy the stated conditions; one of the rules of this genre is, in fact, that the sender (whether or not he be the author) be neither more nor less knowledgeable than the hero – this is the internal focalization condition – and that what is talked about (the referent, the hero) be nothing other than the sender – this is the homo-diegetic condition. Another clause, one that is not

customary in the genre of the philosophical journal, must, however, be added, namely that the act of writing the journal is not
to figure among the events related in the journal itself – the
extra-diegetic condition.

If one chose to reply to the editors' request by means of a
written philosophical dialogue, the twofold condition of voice
and mode would constrain the signatory to efface all traces of his
own address to the addressee (in order to ensure his own extra-
reference), for example by entrusting to a third party the task of
reporting to the addressee (to you, honourable reader, or to one of
the parties in the dialogue) a discussion supposed to have taken
place (the homo-diegetic condition), between one or more parties
and himself on the subject of the questions posed by R.J.M.
and/or A.M. The condition which may seem difficult to fulfil
would then be that of internal focalization; for should not a
dialogue in principle have a multiple focus (as many foci as
participants)?

It is possible to get round this difficulty, however, as many
Platonic dialogues have shown. The term 'Plato' (as sender–
author) is placed in hetero- and extra-reference in all the dialogues; and yet, with the exception of a few dialogues or segments
of dialogues in which there is very probably a counter-focus on a
non-Platonic interlocutor (Protagoras, Parmenides), the inner
focalization, that is, the bringing into perspective of the worlds in
question in the dialogues, whether the socio-political world, the
mythological world, the aesthetic world, the world of ideas – not
to speak of the scene of the dialogue itself – always takes place
'with' Plato, from the point of view of the hidden addressor–
author of the written dialogues.

The signatory of these lines could thus respond to the editors'
request by means of a written dialogue, which might work somewhat along the following lines:

Prologue (R.J.M. and A.M.):
R.J.M.: Have you heard of J.F.L.?
A.M.: I heard from him last summer . . .
Dialogue (A.M. and J.F.L.):
A.M.: You would be doing my compatriots a favour if you would be so
good as to explain your philosophy, its difficulties, the reception it finds,
the objections and oppositions it provokes.
J.F.L.: . . .

The latter might reply, for instance, by pronouncing the present discourse (in which case, continue reading by turning back to the first paragraph). This would then represent a (rather lengthy) reply extracted from a dialogue between A.M. and J.F.L. reported by A.M. to R.J.M. The fact that there were three actors on the stage of the dialogue would not alter the fact that each was doing no more than contributing to specifying J.F.L.'s point of view. The latter, however, would appear neither as the 'real' addressor (extra-diegesis) nor as the focus (hidden mode), at least in the universe of the dialogue.

If, however, the preceding paragraphs were part of the imagined reply, the extra-reference condition would not be fulfilled, since the question of the dialogue's addressor would then be discussed among the partners engaged in it and among these would figure one bearing the same name as its addressor–author.

It would be an interesting question to know whether the imagined dialogue constituted a part of these present reflections or vice versa. But this question can be left in suspense. According to the second hypothesis (dialogue 'containing', reflection 'contained'), the characters would pass more easily as 'real'; according to the first, they would be evidently imaginary.[4] If we must decide on their status (but this is in no way necessary), one thing alone is certain: another 'move' must be made, in a language game in which the difference between the real and the imaginary is relevant in relation to the rules of the game.[5]

There are thus a number of ways of 'linking up with'[6] a request for a presentation, even when this involves certain constraints on the relations between the various terms (addressor, addressee, referent, signified) presented by the sentence, the part of discourse or the discourse which will link up with the threads of the request. The request, however, is by itself a language game, belonging to the same family (prescriptives) as orders, prayers, instructions, supplications and so forth, which determines, in principle, the sort of 'move' expected from the addressee, namely that he perform the prescribed modification on the referent presented by the statement of the request (here, that J.F.L. write a presentation of his writings, etc.). But even if the *how* of the performance is in part indicated in the statement of the request, an appreciable latitude is left to the addressee when he finds himself in turn placed in the position of addressor in respect of the sentence (part of discourse or the discourse), by which he replies.

I have underscored the contingency of this linkage, even in the pragmatic situation of the obligation to offer a presentation.

II

In itself the mere fact of acknowledging this contingency is already to place the discourse that presents it (in this case, my own) at odds with Hegelianism. For the latter, this contingency results from the subjective illusion, which is the work of the logic of predication. It is dispelled provided that the following rules are admitted: (1) every term is equivocal, that is to say that it involves at least two signifieds: and this equivocity is at its perfection when the two signifieds are contradictory; (2) the subject is neither the subject of what is said nor that of the saying, but the continuing movement of the linkages themselves (Spirit, the Concept, movement); and the task of making the link consists first of all in the realization of (*ausmachen*) the term's equivocity by means of the dialectical syllogism whose form is that of a dilemma: if *signified 1*, then *not signified 1* (and even *signified 2*); if *signified 2*, then *not signified 2* (and even *signified 1*); (3) this work of dissolution (scepticism) has not only to be realized, but also to be expressed (*ausgedrückt*). Expression consists in the discovery of a new term (signified), which is the non-identical result (*Resultat*) of the realization of the equivocity of the first term; and this new term is itself equivocal.[7]

The linking up of this latter term to the first (or of the second sentence to the first – to Hegel the difference is of no account), bears the mark of necessity due to the second rule. The resulting aporia in reasoning, such as that attributed to a Protagoras by Diogenes Laërtius or to an Antisthenes by Aristotle,[8] is resolved by means of the third rule, that of expression. Thus the necessity of the interlinking is not caught up in the simple identity of the contents.

One sees that the speculative genre (or language game) does not present itself as one genre (or language game) among others. It runs through them all and grounds them, since it is the movement by which the object of reflection, split into two, dissolves and achieves expression. Presentation is philosophy. To affirm its contingency, as we have done, is to turn away from the task of speculation and to cease philosophizing.

The present presentation cannot therefore fail to be condemned by Hegelians and post-Hegelians (Marxists). And yet it arises out of the speculative genre, as its own contradictory result, and in this sense belongs to it. If it is true, as Adorno says, that after Auschwitz, neo-capitalism and Stalinism – let us add Maoism and Cambodia – it is no longer reasonable to seek to legitimize reality (terms, sentences) by reference to the necessary movement of the spirit in search of its own expression, and if philosophical discourse, as always the child of its time, must today 'show solidarity with speculative metaphysics at the moment of its downfall',[9] then how could this discourse maintain its claim to 'sublate' (*aufheben*) all the statements of knowledge, of art and of law in one necessary encyclopedia? When philosophy gives in to the metaphysical illusion of signifying the whole of everything, an illusion against which Kant had warned it, it gives rise to the destruction of all movement of spirit – to dogmatism according to Kant, to totalitarianism according to Adorno. Adorno's last words are to declare that the spirit takes refuge in the 'almost nothing', in the minute empty spaces and asides that escape the positive totalization of the system. Faced with 'macrology', philosophical discourse breaks up into 'micrologies', as already exemplified by the later works of the Frankfurt philosopher.

Adorno displayed an excessive despair with regard to the powers of language. He allots them only the task of protecting the spirit against the expansion of closed systems. This is a dualistic scenario; it is difficult to see how it can escape the critique levelled at dualism by Hegelian philosophy, even if this philosophy is declared to have been dethroned. Under the same name of micrology, we can also envisage a strategy of thought that is not merely defensive. If today we can no longer 'talk big', it is not because the grand discourse manages to signify everything, but rather the opposite: it is so simplifying, with its exclusive criterion of performativity, and with money as the exclusive unit of measure for evaluating performances, that it can only set itself up against the proliferating complexities of language games as an abstraction which feeds upon them, gives rise to them and kills them. After Auschwitz, but also in post-modern society, thinking can no longer take place in the realm of the speculative in

Hegel's sense; it has become foolish or suspect to allow that throughout all of its present, disastrous or sadly repetitive formations, spirit pursues its own self-expression. Thinking is accomplished in opposition to the speculative, in the micrologic.[10]

The micrologic, however, stands opposed to the speculative only as the small to the great or as the multiple to the one; and it therefore remains within it. The opposite of the speculative, in defining itself as its opposite, remains part of the speculative. The movement of spirit continues within the micrologic considered as a form of speculation opposed to speculation, but under this 'condition', it breaks the bond of necessity that links together the various formations of spirit and that made of Hegelian philosophy a great discourse and even a great narrative.[11] It preserves them under the name of language games. Among these there reigns much more than what Hegel called the unequalness of spirit to itself: the untranslatability of the rules of one game into those of another. In this way, experimenting thought, as that is the thought of today, is both stripped of the *aura* of 'experience',[12] and rid of the trappings of necessity. The linking of one sentence (which represents micrology, *par excellence*) to another, because this linking is contingent or at any rate slightly governed by failing institutions, hardly obeys the rule of the expressive *Resultat* (the third rule of the speculative system); it exhibits instead a divergent and powerful equivocity.

The 'downfall' of metaphysics does not inevitably result in positivism (whether logical, anthropological or political), nor can it be remedied by falling back upon the honeycomb of minor discourses whose existence positivism is prepared to admit. I am tempted to think that another perspective has been opened up through which it may be possible to measure up to the crisis and the reflective response it demands. This perspective is pointed to notably in writings of Wittgenstein, in particular in the *Philosophische Untersuchungen* and *Zettel*, under the programmatical name of *Sprachspielen*.

It remains to be shown how the manner of thinking language games is not a mere description of the positive experience of language, and in what way it leads into this speculative opposition to the grand speculative discourse of which our age is wanting. We shall content ourselves with two remarks which must suffice to indicate that this reading of Wittgenstein's writings is not entirely arbitrary.

To the request to define the notion of language games, the author of the *Philosophische Untersuchungen* replies by means of an objection, the reasoning of which seems to me perfectly speculative, namely that defining is in itself already one language game among others.[13] This argument reiterates, on its own level, the Hegelian critique of predicative logic by showing that the latter, if it is not unaware of the rules of its game, is indeed unaware of itself as a game. But, in Wittgenstein, this objection is also levelled against the reflective game itself, which is stripped of the primordial and necessary character accorded to it by Hegel: 'Reflection is part of the language game . . . The concept, in the language game, is in its element.'[14]

The element in which the concept bathes is not that of the necessary dialectic (and even less that of predication or the propositional function), but that of the language game. 'Language game' is to be taken in the plural. Language games are numerous, even innumerable.[15] They possess the property of obeying rules that are irreducible to one another, just as the rules of chess are irreducible to those of bridge.[16] A sentence is a move; this move can belong to a game which already exists, but it can also represent a 'paradigm for moves to come', because it establishes a new rule of the game (and so a new game).[17] We are worlds away from necessary linkages, but are at the heart of equivocity. The concept assumes responsibility for its paradoxical logic without seeking to cure itself of it.

These indications suffice to show how the 'micrologies' invoked by Adorno as the ultimate refuge in the face of totalitarianism can find a less defensive employment in the thought of language games. On the one hand, it is a thought that does not forget the great speculative rule according to which language (or spirit) wills its own expression and according to which, in order to do so, it possesses no reliable metalanguage but only the movement of willing this very expression, a movement that never ceases to destroy (*zerstören*)[18] its formations at the very moment that it expresses them. As a result language is always ahead of itself in respect of its realization (*ausmachen*) and behind itself in respect of its expression (*ausdrücken*); the language which speaks of games is itself a language game, whose stakes lie in establishing the ground rules and strategies of such games. This language game itself effects certain 'moves' on languages, and some of these 'moves' also belong to those which these games already allow, while others belong to games as yet unknown.

On the other hand, this thought is at the same time antispeculative, in that a move (a sentence, that which Hegel identified as term or as reasoning in contrast to the proposition) is in general deeply equivocal – indeed it is often played in several games at once, known and/or unknown. This equivocity is such that the task of expressing it, far from leading to another move (*Resultat*) which would synthesize the various signifieds that had been analysed, runs into an indefinite number of series of other moves belonging to an irreducibly heteronomous multiplicity of games.

Caught up into this collapse of 'big talk', but also in this blossoming of little local discourses, the question philosophical discourse poses to itself becomes the following: is *it* itself a language game? If one is to follow Wittgenstein, the response will be yes and no.[19] It is that speculative game which has as its referent the indefinite set of language games. But at the same time, it is no more one particular (metalinguistic) game than in Hegel the philosophical game is played outside and apart from those of ordinary language. It introduces into these an additional element of questioning, the effect of which is to allow the production of sentences (the making of moves) which test the rules, both known and unknown, of these games. This is why philosophical 'micrology' cannot fail to question itself on the subject of its questioning capacity: what is the nature of this additional force, and which one, of which it makes use? Why does it assign itself the task of experimenting with the rules? These questions call for a simple and non-edifying ontology (in that it begins by setting aside any recourse to the metaphysics of force),[20] which should permit the philosophy of language games to avoid the triviality of mere descriptions and the arbitrariness of the 'choice' of a 'perspective' on the problem of philosophical discourse today.

With regard to heteronomy (the untranslatability of one game into another) and to paralogy (the search for the limit between the tolerable and the intolerable by way of moves lacking any given model), contemporary arts over the past century offer abundant material. It suffices to cite a few great names – Schönberg and Cage, Mallarmé, Joyce, Gertrude Stein and Beckett, Marcel

Duchamp – to be persuaded that the object of these works is nothing other than that of testing different moves (forming series which themselves can constitute entire games) in music, language, painting, cinema and dance. Since these works do not conform to the supposedly immutable rules of fine arts, they can be seen as micrological paralogies which change the status of these rules: they display the 'playful' character of such rules by the mere fact that by virtue of their provisional 'bizarreness' they suggest the rules for another and equally possible game making use of the same material.[21]

Apollinaire used to say that contemporary artists have to make themselves inhuman. What they are testing out in their works is what Aristotle called *endechomenon*,[22] the possible in the sense of what can be tolerated; can a given genre, for example the theatre, tolerate 'cruelty' the way in which Artaud understands it? Can painting tolerate Malévitch's 'supreme'? Can literature tolerate Butor's 'book-object', or Gertrude Stein's 'paragraph'? By breaking down the boundaries of different genres, these works engender their confusion; this is the case, in particular, for the demarcation between the fictive and the theoretical.[23] In this way is constituted a universe of experimentation with forms, which can be termed satirical in the sense that the genres are mixed together (*satura*), and that the programme for each work is to saturate the tolerable. It remains to work out corresponding aesthetics.[24]

It does not follow from this that philosophy itself has to become an art.[25] Between bringing about paradox (or the intolerable) and finding the appropriate expression for it, the speculative difference remains. This is why the philosopher cohabits with the artist and why his commentary on works of art, in itself painful because of the need to produce an 'inhuman' expression worthy of the works themselves, exerts in return its own influence on the works of the artist in terms of the tension and attraction of new possibilities revealed by reflection. This re-examination of philosophical discourse in the light of a comparison with artistic 'moves' benefits greatly from the parallel examination of the new epistemology and the new history of science which have arisen out of the transformations undergone by scientific 'sentences' over the past century or more.[26]

Within the framework we have just outlined, the sketches of

several different presentations of the signatory's work may reasonably be proposed. The present presentation (par. II) could be termed *speculative*, whereas the first was *poetical* (par. I).[27] There follow the drafts of two other presentations, one *historico-political*, the other *ontological*.

III

For the continentals, the manner of philosophizing characteristic of the modern era is coming to an end. It had assigned itself the task of constructing a discourse in which the different branches of knowledge and different forms of practice would find their 'foundation' (their truth value and their justice value, respectively). Far from being one discipline among others, philosophy governed the rest; it analysed their conceptual contents, it elicited their presuppositions, it marshalled them within a necessary development, it offered its own speculative discourse as their end. This task was called speculation. The University of Berlin was created in 1811 to accomplish it, in accordance with a project of Schleiermacher taken up again by Humboldt.

An initial reversal (*Umkehrung*) of speculative thought and politics was the work of Feuerbach. He attempted to attribute to the existing, concrete human subject the founding task previously vested in Spirit or in Life itself.

The Feuerbachian reversal underwent a second reversal at the hands of Marx. The alienation of the concrete subject, notably in work, was for him the tangible expression of an inversion hidden in the substrata of social existence.[28] It was not enough to criticize the subordination of the concrete individual to Spirit, that is to God; the same subordination of the end to the means, of the producer to the produced, of production to reproduction, of the concrete to the abstract was perpetuated through the working of capital in the concrete subject himself. The foundational work performed by speculative thought had to be 'sublated' through the work of emancipation of the subject in relation not only to religion but to the economy as well.

The enterprise was presented as 'critical', that is to say, if not of Kantian at least of left-Hegelian inspiration. What was both manifested and hidden under this name was a return to the great Franco-American tale of emancipation, the *Enlightenment*, pursued and radicalized in the workers' movements, especially in France.

In this way two models, one critical, the other speculative, inhabited the thought and practice of Marxism. To the extent that Hegelian logic remained its 'rational core',[29] it turned out that the Marxist 'reversal' had not really damaged the metaphysics. It was no longer demanded that substance be conceived of 'also' as subject; the subject, the proletariat, had to accomplish its own concretization as substance, as 'material', *das Materielle*.[30]

In place of the working class, one class among others, substance without subjectivity, on the one hand, and in place of the party of emancipation, subject without substance, on the other hand, the proletariat had to be realized as substance–subject, that is, as a real historical development: that of communism.[31]

One can then see to what extent the question concerning the necessity of linkages, on which the fate of metaphysics depends, is also a political question. With its Hegelian dialectical core, Marxism preserved the necessary character of the *aufheben*. It differed from the Hegelianism of Berlin only in the substitutions of names: in place of the university, the party; in the place of the master (*Magister*), the party leader; in place of the student, the militant (the working class); in place of spirit, the proletariat; in place of absolute knowledge, the realization of socialism.

This necessitarian current gained the upper hand under a number of different, and at times conflicting, banners. In this sense German Social Democracy, Stalinist communism, Maoist Marxism–Leninism were not political errors; they were but so many symptoms of the fact that the speculative system, if it were not rid of the rule of the necessary result, restored life to metaphysics rather than contributing to its downfall and continued to produce excommunicatory effects with regard to everything that did not fall in step with what was deemed to be the ineluctable march of the historico-social process. It is not surprising that exclusions and eliminations have continually affected both Marxist and non-Marxist movements which, in the name of the emancipatory tradition, have criticized the bureaucracies held to be the owners of dialectical truth. Thus German Social Democracy annihilated Spartakism; Stalinism in Russia and throughout the world attacked workers' opposition movements, Trotskyism, Councilism, not to speak of anarchism; Maoism submitted its left-wing opposition to the same fate before sending its troops against its own rivals within the Chinese communist apparatus. With the extermination of part of the Cambodian people, the 'subject' has taken this logic to its bitter end: rather no 'substance' at all than a substance of which it is not the subject.

As to the critical aspect also contained in Marxism, it had found in the organization and the decisions of the Paris Commune a sort of paradigm of socialist society, designated as such by Marx himself. Given their *aufklärer* (bourgeois) origin, the forms of critical thought were in danger of sinking into mere humanism and into opportunism. By drawing upon the experience of workers' struggles, the Commune had provided the antidote to these errors, an antidote which later took the name of worker-management. Kant's thought had already arrived at the principle that the autonomy of the will is the sole guarantor of morality. But this was a critical transcendental principle. In his political writings, Kant feared that a collection of merely empirical subjects might end up by occupying the position of pure will. Although the worker-management current emancipated itself from the metaphysical illusion of necessary linkages, it remained a prisoner of the illusion mentioned in the Dialectic of the *Critique of Pure Reason*, that which confuses universality as a concept of reason and totality as a given intuition. And in this way, the current remained Hegelian, leftist though it might be.

Thus the conflict between the critical and the speculative continued within the workers' movement for a century-and-a-half of continental history. In France after 1948 one group[32] dedicated itself to the task of criticizing necessitarianism in its economic, social, political and theoretical forms by pushing to the forefront the question of revolutionary organization. It thought to contribute in this way to the reorientation of the workers' movement by giving it the means to free itself from political, syndical and cultural bureaucracies. The worker revolts of East Berlin (1953), of Poznań and of Poland (1956), of Hungary (1956) and, on a different level, the Algerian uprising (1954–62) marked stages in this work of reflection, publication and public discussion. Finally the signatory, who had dedicated himself to this work for twelve years, persuaded himself that it was not enough to 'begin the revolution afresh';[33] it was necessary to start thinking afresh without knowing, hence begin philosophy afresh. He decided therefore, two years before 1968, to withdraw for a while[34] from all efforts of a too directly political nature. . . .

IV

Here is a sample of cuttings taken from a work in progress:

1. There is a sentence: 'It is daylight', 'Give me the lighter', 'Was she there?', 'They fought to their last cartridge', 'May he escape the heavy weather!', 'The sentence "There is a sentence" is denotative', '$ax^2 + bx + c = 0$', 'Ouch!', 'But I just meant to . . .', 'You thought perhaps that I . . . ?' or many others.

1.1. As soon as there is one sentence, there are several. The one comes along with the multiple. A sentence is always caught up in at least one interlinking of sentences.

2. A sentence presents a universe. Regardless of its form, it involves a 'There is'.

3. In the sentences cited in 1 the presentation is not marked. In the sentence 'There is a sentence' it is marked by means of the expression 'There is'. 'There is' would thus be a mark of presentation in a sentence. Are there other marks of presentation in a sentence?

4. A sentence is the case, *der Fall*, a token, the event. The sentence-type is the reference of a sentence-event.

5. A sentence presents that which is in question (*ta pragmata, die Bedeutung*, the referent = Re), that which is signified by it (the sense, *der Sinn* = Se), that to whom (the addressee (*le destinataire*) = Da) and that by which, or in the name of which (the addressor (*le destinateur*) = De) something is signified with respect to the referent. These four terms may or may not be marked in the sentence.

6. The addressor and the addressee are terms, which may or may not be marked, presented by the relevant sentences. A sentence is not a message passing from an addressor to an addressee independent of it. Both are placed or situated in the universe presented by the sentence, together with its referent and its sense. Presenting sentences as messages is what a sentence does. It

presents the addressors and addressees of sentences as terms of communication. But the communication presented in this way is only one sort of sentential universe.

7. The universe which a sentence presents is not presented to something or to someone – as to a subject. A 'subject', whether addressor or addressee, referent or sense, is situated in a universe presented by a sentence. Even when the subject is declared outside the sentential universe *qua* addressor or addressee of the presentation, as in the case of the thinking subject in Descartes, the phenomenological Ego in Husserl or the subject of obligation in Kant – this subject is situated within the universe presented by the sentence which declares it to be outside. The metaphysical illusion consists in confusing presentation and situation.

8. The presentation is that there is a universe. The situation is that at the heart of a universe presented by a sentence, the relations indicated by the form of the sentence and by the form of the sentences which link up with it join the terms together. 'I saw it' is a sentence which situates in this way three of the terms (the term of addressee is not indicated by the sentence), and this situation consists notably in the determination of a tense. 'It is there that I saw it' determines notably a space-time in which the same three terms are situated. 'I tell you that it is there that I saw it' situates most notably the place of the addressee thanks to the illocutionary nucleon 'I tell you that . . .' (which is a constative in Habermas's terminology). The form of the sentences indicates the relationships of the instances to one another. The set of these situations forms the presented universe.

9. There are as many universes as there are sentence-tokens. And as many situations as terms, that is to say as many dispositions of universes as there are forms of sentences. The observation that two universe-dispositions are analogous and that two corresponding forms of sentences belong to the same sentence-type is the object of a sentence-token, which presents a universe in which the two sentences compared and their corresponding universes are situated.

12. The categories of Aristotle, of Kant and of others are kinds of relations between the instances presented in a sentential universe. It would be misleading to call them kinds of presentation

(or of Being). The presentation of a sentence does not permit of a determination by kind unless it is situated in the universe of another sentence, that is as presented presentation. This is why the kinds of presentation are presentable only as kinds of situation.

13. The presentation contained by a sentence-token is not presented in the universe it presents. It is not situated. However, another sentence-case can present it in another universe, and so situate it.

14. The presentation contained could be named: Being. It is *one* presentation, or: what in the sentence-token is the case. Being is a move, 'then' a move.

15. A presentation can be presented as an instance in the universe of a sentence: Being as a being. But this sentence itself contains a presentation which it does not present. Can we even say that this presentation is hidden or deferred?

19. The presentation contained in a sentence can be termed *absolute*. However, by so calling it we present it; it is placed in the universe presented by the sentence qualifying it, its quality of *absolute* is situated in this universe and is relative to it.

20. There are not two presentations contained. We may speak of two presentations, but they are presented in a statement whose presentation is not presented. There is no synthesis of the entirety of the presentations contained. Or: there is no transcendental time as ultimate unity of the diversity of the presentations contained. Or: a presentation is *one* presentation.

23. Augustine's God or Husserl's Living Present are presented as the name borne by the instance which synthesizes the 'nows'. But they are so by means of the sentences in which they are presented, and the 'now' of each of these sentences remains to be synthesized with the others, in a new sentence. God is for later, 'in an instant'; the Living Present is to come. They do not come. They only come by not coming.

24. The presentation contained in a sentence is forgotten by it. It is plunged into the Lethe. It is recovered only by another sentence, which presents it. Memory is lined with forgetfulness.

As one presentation forgets itself, another presentation holds onto it by presenting it and by forgetting itself. So that it is metaphysical to struggle against oblivion; ontology struggles for this.

25. This is why there is need of negation to present the contained presentation. It is presentable only as non-Being. This is what is meant by the word 'Lethe'.

26. That which is not presented is not. The presentation contained by a sentence is not presented, it is not. Or: Being is not. One can say: a contained presentation, when it is presented, is a non-contained presentation. Or: Being considered as being is non-Being. It is in this way that we are to understand the first chapter of the *Wissenschaft der Logik*. What Hegel terms determination and which provides the moving force of the passage from Being to non-Being is the situation of Being (or of presentation) in a sentential universe, that is to say, the passage from the presentation contained in the first sentence to the presentation (of the first sentence) presented by the second sentence. However, this 'dissolution' (the passage from Being to beings or to non-Being) is effective only if what is at stake in the second sentence is the presenting of the presentation; that is to say, if the language game played by this second sentence is the ontological game. It is one of the ground rules of this game which prescribes a linkage of this sort and the passage or the dissolution which results from it. But there are many language games in which the goal prescribed by the rules is not to present the presentation, and where, consequently, 'dissolution' is not necessary.

27. Everything can be presented, including a presentation, but only as presented. The presentation contained, the event, the 'There is' is a secret. This secret does not result from our not being able to say *everything*, it consists in our *having* to say everything. For if one asks: 'From whence do you take it that there is presentation (even if you make a non-Being out of it)?', one can only answer this: 'From the fact that it is capable of being presented and that it must be.' Or: 'From the fact that the ontological language game can and must be played, among others.'

28. 'Presenting' is not 'showing'. 'To show', 'to display', 'zeigen', 'montrer' are modes of presentation corresponding to

sentence forms which determine the situations of instances. 'Showing' is not opposed to 'saying'. It is then inappropriate to affirm, as Wittgenstein does, that 'What can be shown cannot be said'.

30. We must not say: 'That of which we cannot speak, we must condemn to silence.' We can speak of everything, including presentation. And what one has to do (what one 'must' do), is not to limit the capacity of sentences in presented universes, but to extend it. Not only can one speak of everything, but one must.

38. It is vain, though interesting, to wonder according to what rules a second sentence 'has to' link up with an equivocal sentence. Vain because there exists no model for such linking which will satisfy this 'having to' beyond that which a new sentence will present; interesting because this leads to formulating such a model in a new sentence, hence inventing a universe that will be a universe of interlinkings of sentences.

Translated by Kathleen McLaughlin

NOTES

1 In their letter of 17 April 1979.
2 In the sense of Habermas's *Präsentative*. See J. Habermas and N. Luhmann, *Theorie der Gesellschaft oder Sozialtechnologie – Was leistet die Systemforschung?*, Frankfurt am Main: Suhrkamp, 1971, p. 111.
3 G. Genette, *Figures III*, Paris: Seuil, 1972, pp. 206–11 and 238–61.
4 Thomas More's *Utopia* provides a good example of a dialogue containing a reflection which happens to be a descriptive narrative. The realistic function is ensured by the proper nouns of the dialogue; only one bit of information (the geographical position of the island) is lacking, smothered by a sneeze, for the narrative to be entirely 'realistic' (*The Complete Works*, New Haven and London: Yale University Press, 1965, pp. 22–3). Conversely, the dialogue between Theodore and Jupiter, then Pallas on the subject of Sextus in Par. 413 of Leibniz's *Theodicy* appears largely unrealistic, although it follows an actual dialogue taken from Laurent Valla, because of its inclusion within a speculative discourse.
5 The feature 'real/unreal' might characterize a family of language games: those of knowledge.
6 This term is borrowed from O. Ducrot, *Dire et ne pas dire: principe de sémantique linguistique*, Paris: Hermann, 1972; and 'Présupposés et

sous-entendus (réexamen)', in *Stratégies discursives*, ed. Berrendonner, Lyon: Presses Universitaires de Lyon, 1978, pp. 33–43.

7 See *Wissenschaft der Logik*, I, 1; *Phänomenologie des Geistes*, Vorrede. By the signatory, 'Essai d'analyse du dispositif spéculatif' (January 1980).

8 Diels–Kranz, *Fragmente der Vorsokratiker* II 80 A (1); Aristotle, *Rhetoric* II, 1402 a 5.

9 Th. W. Adorno, *Negative Dialektik, Gesammelte Schriften*, Vol. 6, Frankfurt am Main: Suhrkamp, 1973, pp. 354ff., in particular p. 400: 'im Augenblick ihres Sturzes'.

10 'Die Mikrologie ist Ort der Metaphysik als Zuflucht vor der Totale' (*ibid.*, p. 399).

11 J.-F. Lyotard, *La Condition postmoderne*, Paris: Les Editions de Minuit, 1979.

12 W. Benjamin, 'Charles Baudelaire' (1939), *Gesammelte Werke*, Vol. 2, Frankfurt am Main: Suhrkamp, 1974, p. 2. On experimental thought, see the signatory's *Les Transformateurs Duchamp*, Paris: Galilée, 1977.

13 *Philosophische Untersuchungen*, Pars. 65–88.

14 *Zettel*, Par. 391.

15 *Ph. U.*, Par. 23.

16 *Zettel*, Par. 320.

17 *Ibid.*, Par. 294.

18 Hegel, *Ph. G.*, Vorrede, G. Lasson and F. Hoffmeister (eds), Hamburg: F. Meiner, 1952, p. 51.

19 *Ph. U.*, Par. 68.

20 Metaphysics to which the signatory has made frequent recourse in a satirical book, *Economie libidinale*, Paris: Les Editions de Minuit, 1974.

21 See the signatory's *Des dispositifs pulsionnels* (1973), Paris: Christian Bourgois, 1980.

22 *Rhet* 1355 b 7–14: 'mechri hou endechetai, mechri toutou proagagein'; *Int* 12, 21 b 23; *Cat* 4 a 10–4 b 19.

23 See the signatory's 'Apathie dans la théorie', in *Rudiments païens*, Paris: U.G.E. 10/18, 1977.

24 See the signatory's 'Esquisse d'une esthétique à l'ère de la satire' (1979), Ottawa: National Gallery, forthcoming.

25 See Gerhard Höhn, 'Une logique de la décomposition. Pour une lecture de Th. W. Adorno', in *Presences d'Adorno*, Revue d'Esthétique, Paris: U.G.E. 10/18, 1975, p. 123. And the signatory's 'Dissertation sur une inconvenance', in *Rudiments païens*.

26 See, for example, P. Feyerabend, *Against Method*, London: N.L.B., 1975.

27 Poetics, says G. Genette, has as its referent not the text but the architext, that is, the set of relations between the text and literary

'universals' such as themes, modes, forms, genres. (*Introduction à l'architexte*, Paris: Seuil, 1979.)

28 See the signatory's 'La place de l'aliénation dans le retournement marxiste', in *Dérive à partir de Marx et Freud*, Paris: U.G.E. 10/18, 1973.

29 Postscript to second edition (1873), *Das Kapital*, Vol. 1, Berlin: Dietz Verlag, 1962, p. 27.

30 *Ibid.*

31 See for example Marx, *Ökonomisch-philosophische Manuskript* (1844), Drittes Manuskript, 'Kritik der Hegelschen Dialektik und Philosophie überhaupt', *Marx–Engels Werke*, Supplementary Volume 1, Berlin: Dietz Verlag, 1968, p. 583.

32 Who published the journal *Socialisme ou barbarie*, and the newspaper *Pouvoir ouvrier*.

33 This was the title of a programmatic article by C. Castoriadis in *Socialism ou barbarie*, 35 (1964), reprinted in *L'Expérience du mouvement ouvrier 2*, Paris: U.G.E. 10/18, 1974, pp. 307–65.

34 During this period *Discours, figure* (Paris: Kliencksieck, 1971) was written.

PIERRE MACHEREY

In a materialist way

What is it to do philosophy, today, in a materialist way?

In a materialist way: for to do philosophy in a materialist way is not at all the same thing as to produce a Materialist philosophy. To be materialist and to be a Materialist are not the same thing. A Materialist appears as the initiator or votary of a doctrine ranking alongside other doctrines of philosophy. It is, of course, in opposition to these other doctrines, since it is based on a different set of principles and tends towards different conclusions; but it shares with them the presupposition that the practice of philosophy consists in the possession and communication of a doctrine, that is, a particular body of knowledge; a doctrine, that is to say, a unified corpus of arguments, a system of answers based on proofs, providing a sufficient representation of the object with which it identifies the reality-to-be-known, which it identifies, indeed, as being reality itself. The condition of such a doctrinal conception of philosophy is that philosophy should have an object of which it provides the theory. In the case of a materialist doctrine, this object is material reality, or the materiality of the real, that can be designated by the concept of matter alone. Materialisms – for naturally there are several – are theories of matter.

'Dialectical Materialism', in the tradition of Soviet Marxism, represents one such philosophical system of knowledge. It enunciates, promulgates, and enacts 'general laws' of material reality – nature and history, considered in their joint transformations; and with regard to the development of the positive systems of knowledge which take over the various sectors of that reality, these laws have both retrospective and prospective significance.

This was the direction followed by Engels when in 1873 he embarked upon a work of investigation into the sciences of nature, which he pursued until 1883. In it he outlines a programme for a 'general theory of movement', synthesizing the findings of all preceding scientific knowledge and prefiguring, not to say orienting in a prescriptive manner, its subsequent research. But we must not forget that this approach, which Engels followed with Marx's avowed support, actually led him nowhere, and that he himself abandoned it. For *The Dialectic of Nature* is a theoretical fiction *a posteriori*, wholly made up on the basis of incomplete and contradictory drafts, which can only give the illusion of a completed work at the price of falsifying their content. If these philosophical texts by Engels are still of interest, as indeed they are, it is because they bear witness by their very incompleteness to the impossibility of putting materialism into dialectical form. For while the dialectic may be genuinely materialist, it is the very refutation of materialism; and if it is closely bound up with the fact of being materialist, this is precisely because it shows the impossibility of a materialist knowledge, a system of knowledge concerned with materialism. The essential lesson to be drawn, then, from Engels's attempt is that it is no longer possible to be a Materialist.

Today, therefore, we must start from another presupposition: that materialism be not a doctrine, not a theory, not a body of knowledge, but rather a manner of intervention, a philosophical 'position'.[1] A position is not the theory of an object, the discourse within which the latter is at once represented and constituted; it is the manifestation, the affirmation of an orientation, of a tendency, of a way of moving through, not 'reality', which is not an object of philosophy, but the philosophical field itself, grasped in the concrete complexity of its internal conflicts as the specific site of this intervention. The Kantian question is well known: how are we to find our bearings in the realm of thought? Let us turn it around and pose the materialist question: how are we to find our bearings in the realm of philosophy?

It must be immediately pointed out that this question does not bear upon some individual commitment engaged upon independently of its objective causes and effects, which go infinitely far beyond it. For one does not choose to take up a position in philosophy – and it is not only of materialists that this is true; all philosophical reflection, knowingly or unknowingly, is such a taking-up of positions. To do philosophy as a materialist, however, is to pose the question of this intervention; to question oneself as to its conditions, its stakes and the obstacles it encounters, insofar as it is an objective practice of intervention transforming the domain upon which, or rather within which, it acts; it is to change, not its object but its objectives, and so also to change the manner of its intervention.

This can be put as follows: there is no pure philosophical knowledge. Not that it is contaminated or deflected by pragmatic interests external to its domain, for such a category of exteriority is in reality devoid of content.

Instead of asking oneself what is the position of a work *in regard to* the relations of production of a given period, whether it is in agreement with them and therefore reactionary, or whether it aspires to their transformation and is therefore revolutionary – instead of this, or at least prior to it, I would propose a different question. I would ask: what is its place *within* these relations?[2]

We may take up this question formulated by Benjamin with regard to literary works in order now to assign to philosophical discourse its position *within* history.

In *The German Ideology*, Marx asserts that philosophy does not 'have' a history, in the sense of to possess or to have to itself; rather it belongs to the order of that which is historical. It is fashioned by an explicit and secret historicity forever carrying it beyond its immediate discourse, not only towards other discourses but into something other than the discourses that it holds to itself in order to acknowledge its own vocation and to settle its own destiny. If philosophy is measured against this alien, external 'other', against the specific movement of the reality that carries it along in tow, then from the standpoint of that history which possesses philosophy rather than being possessed by it, philosophy is no more than the expression of that movement, or merely one expression among others, a more or less adequate 'reflection', an authentic or dissembling utterance, in any case a whim or an illusion since its content and its truth lie outside itself. Thus reduced to the impalpable thinness, the unreal surface, of its own discourse (which is indeed no more than a discourse), philosophy as such is bereft of objective existence: it is annulled.

And yet there is philosophy, and it deals with history in a mode which is not that of external confrontation, of a cut-and-dried opposition between an objectivity in the fullness of its substantive reality and a representation empty of all but its own subjectivity. Philosophy is not this container without content, ever in flight from its own production towards a final self-abolition in an apparent and inoperative relation between itself and itself, fulfilled only in the private débâcle of an avowedly futile discourse, an utterance which is cut short the moment it is charged with the futility of that broken meaning which it pursues but can never reach.

To make philosophy admit its historicity is not only to denounce the scant reality of the discourse which it claims as its own and in which it is recognized, but it is also to determine that portion of reality, whatever it may be, which is the site of its own functioning as well as the place where it acquires its historicity. As utterance or thought that fits itself into the space of things and gestures whose obscure conflicts make up the common world, it starts neither at one extreme nor the other, being neither pure delirium nor the unshakeable truth of a knowledge impervious to any and every challenge, any and every summons to define itself by assigning to itself, and by identifying, the position which it occupies and which neither resembles nor is reducible to any other. For philosophy does not face reality as in some unequal confrontation between a thing and the discourse through which it is revealed or concealed. Philosophy is not merely a factitious, inactive reflection, powerless to act upon things, able only to speak about them while leaving them unchanged, giving way to their irresistible force, a force which would itself be acting upon it without genuinely acting within it, without involving it in the objectivity of its objectives.

There is no pure philosophical knowledge: this does not mean that such a knowledge would be subject to the external pressure of an objective reality independently developing its own movement. It means that such a knowledge integrates this objective relation, by itself developing in an unequal relationship to itself, which is the realization, or, to use a Hegelian phrase, the becoming-real of philosophy. This is why philosophy, inasmuch as it also has a connection with knowledge, is not reducible to the production of a system of knowledge: a system constructed around its principles, unified by its demonstrations, gathered together in its proofs. The materialist standpoint does not end up in such a theory, whatever its content might be; but it does bring a new dimension to the work of theoretical investigation by revealing that there are no independent theoretical effects. By this I mean not only that there are no theoretical effects unrelated to the material conditions of the practice within which they are produced and in which they are rooted, but also that no theoretical effect can itself be grasped in its isolated individual unity, independently of all the other theoretical effects together with which it is produced in a complex and conflictual field, the field of practice.

Here once again we come upon the dialectic and its fundamental category of contradiction, governing the materialist standpoint on practice. Contradiction, practice: these were the objectives of Mao Tse Tung's philosophical intervention in Yenan in 1936. Yet, surprisingly, this intervention separated the two objectives, and dealt with them each in itself in complementary 'essays', adding their effects together in an abstract and external way with no real fusion of their content – whereas contradiction is what determines practice, and practice is the form within which contradiction develops. The field of practice is thus not a neutral, homogeneous space substantially organized around a single principle functioning as its centre or its subject (man, for instance); rather it is torn by the concrete confrontation of unequal tendencies which develop along moving lines of force, between which any equilibrium will necessarily be unstable. The power of the negative: except that this materialist dialectic is a dialectic without teleology, since it corresponds to a genuinely complex and divergent movement, which is not steered *a priori* by the necessity for a one-way direction or meaning prefiguring, in exposition of the contradiction, the conditions of its resolution. The contradictions of practice are indefinitely open, insofar as they reconstitute themselves on ever-new grounds and in ever-changing conditions – they do not order themselves under the law of a universal form of contradiction, of whose model they would represent identical reproductions according to a univocal pattern of development. And practice itself, exposed to the play of these clashes, opens up a common objective space to philosophy and to history, the site of their debate.

Every theoretical effect is rooted in practice. It therefore cannot be disengaged from this active confrontation with adverse theoretical effects, to which it is linked as well as opposed in the concrete movement of the common production. In this sense, the material aspect of the Hegelian dialectic is represented by the thesis of the unity of opposites, which postulates the necessarily conflictual nature of all achievement: only by abstraction can these antagonistic elements, autonomous only in theory, be separated. In Hegel's work, of course, this materialist 'core' of the dialectic is covered over, 'wrapped' in a teleological discourse of a unitary nature affirming the ineluctable reconciliation of these opposites in their final fusion, the conditions for which are prefigured at the outset in the very terms of the contradiction it resolves. Thus, if one splits into two – the unity of opposites – so are two reconciled into one – the negation of the negation. This is the thesis which enabled Hegel specifically to realize the absolute as a knowledge, that is, to identify the real with the idea of which it is the manifestation. But the characteristic of Hegelian discourse, and that which gives it its peculiar efficacy, is precisely this interweaving of two adverse and irreconcilable theses, which cannot be reduced to their mere juxtaposition; indeed, far from cancelling out each other's effects – as they would if they were really independent – they work together in the space, at once theoretical and practical, that is opened up by their division.

Thus when Marx and Engels set out to salvage what seemed to them to embody the 'rational kernel' or 'method' in Hegelian thought, by stripping it of the 'mystical wrapping' of the 'system', in other words by dissociating these opposites, they had unwittingly abandoned the materialist standpoint on the dialectic at the very moment that they claimed to be setting it within a homogeneous materialist dialectic, purged of all idealist elements that had provisionally contaminated it. Their blunder corresponds precisely to the illusion of an independent theoretical knowledge, realized in the form of a doctrinaire materialism. There is nothing circumstantial about this mistake, however, and it is exemplary. It stands for the return of contradiction into the very discourse which claims to abolish it by resolving it. No interventions on this terrain are innocent, or free with respect to the conflictual conditions imposed by the practical field of their application.

More generally speaking, the materialist position as embodied in discourses of a theoretical nature is never to be found without an opposing position which may be called 'idealist'. This is not only because it finds itself face to face with it, like a kind of privileged interlocutor regularly sending back to it its image in reverse, and thus confirming it in its identity; but also because it is pervaded, in the very movement of its production, by this antagonism which works *within* it, and which takes the form not of abstract confrontation, indifferent and merely formal, but of an internal contradiction based upon the principle of the unity of opposites. If there is a 'struggle' between materialism and idealism, this is a struggle of tendencies,[3] set against one another in practice in a common combat to which all are equally committed, even if the conflict develops in unequal forms. It is not some external dialogue between two independent and divergent protagonists, the debate between whom might finally be settled in favour of one rather than the other. If materialism there is, then it is in the very development of idealism that it must be sought; similarly – although there is no formal symmetry here – the history of the materialist position is full of idealist revivals, which corrupt its factitious cohesion and which constantly provoke it into surmounting the temptation to turn into a stultified doctrine, a purely theoretical elaboration which in the end is always undone by practice. This is why, as I have maintained from the outset, there is no materialist knowledge, no materialism without contradiction, that could be fixed and isolated according to its specific theoretical content.

Consequently, if the idea of a struggle between materialism and idealism has any meaning for philosophy, this must not be reduced to some classificatory principle enabling us formally to sort out systems and their 'philosopher' authors according to whether they belong, implicitly or explicitly, to one or the other of these tendencies. There are no 'materialists' or 'idealists', except in the sense of a subjective tendency in accordance with which a given philosophy ends up by identifying itself with a univocal and independent principle of explanation, so as to construct from that basis a coherent explanation of reality – but such a project must inevitably be self-defeating. This is the theoreticist illusion *par excellence*, which makes for an abstract disengagement of philosophical work from its practical conditions, that is, from the conflictual field within which it takes shape. Materialism, with a capital M, is also Idealism: the materialist view of the dialectic allows us to envisage such a reversal and to draw out its critical significance.

But if we speak of materialism or idealism in the lower case, or suppressing, in French, the definite article which has the effect of freezing these philosophical tendencies into delimited theoretical concepts, which are necessarily incomplete and faltering in contrast to their totalizing subjective aspirations, we no doubt make progress. An essential difficulty, however, remains: why limit the confrontation of philosophical tendencies, or indeed the form of contradiction in general, to the conflict of two opposed terms? The discourse on dialectic remains haunted by the metaphor of the magnetic field, torn by the distance between its furthest poles which correspond to one another through the opposition of plus and minus: an image which in the abstract represents contradiction, brought down to the universal model of its exposition, as if there were such a thing as contradiction in general, whereas in reality there are only specific contradictions which have developed according to the objective conditions of their determination. The idea that one divides into two and only into two, in the purely theoretical reflection of a subject returning to itself in some speculative manner, also contains the idea of the reconciliation, the return of the two opposites into one; and through this latter idea the development of the contradiction is guaranteed *a priori* in the form of its final resolution. This speculation prevents us from examining other forms of contradiction, such as might not already be headed out on the beaten track of a finally unitary movement.

This leads us to a new conception of negativity: once detached from the naturalist temptation which brings it back to substantial form, the negative ceases to be the alternative to, or the exclusive contrary of, the positive. The desubstantialization of contradiction implies that it is no longer to be identified with that simple, abstract antagonism according to which negativity is a one-way power of obliteration – like the passage from the self-same to the other – since it only operates along one line of 'force', that which has already been laid down, in the opposite direction, by the positive of which it is the direct contestation. This is but a more or less veiled version of teleology, one in which all contradiction fits into a mechanical form constructed from the schema of action and reaction and supposed to contain the explanation for the whole of reality.

But to return to the struggle of tendencies in philosophy: in its practical extension, it is deployed in the indefinite totality of its concrete orientations and of the power-relations that give rise to it. This is what Althusser was thinking his way towards when he set out from the category of 'overdetermination',[4] whose primary role lies in the field of philosophical intervention. In the openness of this field the materialist position cannot be localized and enclosed once and for all in the strategic position that an already constituted, static knowledge would assign to it, after which it would only need defending and extending; this is why it does not find itself faced with a pre-established idealist position, similarly fixed once and for all in an adversary situation, a position the factitiousness of which it could simply go on to denounce. All philosophical positions are overdetermined, in that they are not determined once and for all on the basis of an *a priori* rational model that would prefigure their development and place them under the theoretical jurisdiction of a ready-made theory, of a knowledge pre-empting the practice of its own application and its own realization.

Let us go further: philosophy is something that cannot be applied outside itself in distinct effects which would constitute its realization in 'something else'. We referred earlier, in speaking of Hegel, to the becoming-real of philosophy: but this must not be taken to mean that philosophy, as an autonomous discourse, could be its own realization by virtue of some process of effectuation and objectification through which it would provide itself with its own 'matter' in an act of independent creation; rather, the philosophical enterprise is, from the very outset, a real process which has no need to be realized, let alone to realize itself, because it is part and parcel of a network of material determinations which forms the process of its exposition, or, if one prefers, its 'disposition'. A disposition in this sense is the putting to work of a position; it is the discursive deployment through which a position works itself out in practice, that is, in and through the conflicts which it resolves at the same time as it provokes in the situations in which it finds itself. By such a disposition, philosophical intervention tendentially produces its effects in the field of investigation which it has opened up for itself, without having to look outside itself for the instruments and criteria which would enable it to measure and to test its power.

To follow this course also implies giving up, as a standard for the assessment of these philosophical effects, the theoretical category of truth in favour of that of 'appropriateness' (*justesse*), a standard which belongs to the field of practice. This renunciation does not mean that one eliminates from philosophical discourse all mention of truth – quite the reverse; but it means that we should no longer invoke the model of truth as a criterion of the functioning of this discourse. A philosophical position is 'appropriate', not in terms of its knowledge, given once and for all as a definite speculative 'value', but in terms of the circumstantial effects which it produces upon the practical combination of circumstances within which it operates. This appropriateness depends on the adjustment (*ajustement*) of its disposition to the objectives which are set for it by the conditions governing its intervention.[5] Criteria of truth exist which limit, or claim to limit, once and for all the forms of existence of a theoretical discourse. But no criteria of appropriateness exist, insofar as appropriateness is a matter of concrete determination, linked to a particular conjuncture and not reducible to universal standards of evaluation. Appropriateness does not exist in itself; the appropriateness with which a position is taken up is not a delimited, substantial characteristic, fixed as such within its limits; rather, it is connected to the conditions of the transformation of practice, which itself consists of the constant calling into question of its own objectives. Appropriateness is thus an evaluation in concrete, but not in subjective, terms; it is relative to the actual conditions of its formulation, but not indifferently or equivocally. Appropriateness is appropriate neither for me nor for 'us', insofar as these terms denote forms of individuality. As the result of an adjustment, and subject to the perpetual demand for readjustment, appropriateness is a relationship: the modality of an intervention proceeding contradictorily within a situation torn by conflicting lines of force, between which it realizes, at its peril, a fresh balance – only to see it immediately toppled, displaced, if only because, by taking up a position within it, the intervention had contributed to its modification.

So the question with which we began – how are we to find our bearings in the realm of philosophy? – must be formulated anew.

It is philosophy itself – neither pure thought turned in upon itself, nor reflection of an inert material – which is this effort of orientation, philosophy which is orientation in itself; the objectives which it pursues, in the course of an ever-renewed movement, are not bestowed upon it from the outside according to the norms and constraints of some abstract conditioning, with reference to a model of truth, or to the mechanical determinism of an independent material reality. Philosophy as intervention, or as the taking up of a position organized in the discursive form of a disposition, is a material process; it develops its specific effects inside the problematic space opened up by the development of its own contradictions, which are made up of practically determined conflicts. Rather than the theory of practice – offering its 'proofs' as security against merely subjective commitment of either an individual or a collective kind – philosophy is the practice of a theory; as such it cannot be reduced to any doctrinal construction, or to the sort of systematic edifice to which the illusion of an independent knowledge would consign it.

The materialist view implies a fresh conception of the history of philosophy. This is not because it offers, as an explanation for the development of that history, some original causality that would be economically, politically or ideologically determined; nor because it brings this development down to the orderly course of an ineluctable progression leading to the ultimate advent of the materialist idea; nor because it selects from out of this evolution certain representative elements as the privileged expression of its own tendency, in which it might therefore recognize itself. The history of philosophy considered from a materialist point of view – rather than from the point of view of materialism – is that real, objective movement which discovers the overdetermined forms of its own materiality (a conjuncture, a stake) in the concrete disposition by which it is circumstantially organized. The historicity of philosophy is not reducible to that strictly chronological determinism which has each world-view correspond to the period that has given rise to it, as if it belonged once and for all to that period. It consists rather in the fact that there is already philosophy, always and everywhere, 'in the state of practice', in spontaneous or considered forms whose substance is not necessarily to be measured by their degree of theoretical elaboration. Philosophical intervention, then, never proceeds 'ab initio', as

professional philosophers would have it. It is resumed or continued, as the reflection of a movement already under way and that
lays down the antecedents as a sequel to which it must itself situate
itself; in this sense, philosophy is always self-critical. Philosophical discourse is never anything other than its own renewal, the
necessarily provisional response to a question which had been
posed to it from the outset and which at best it can do no more
than reformulate. Philosophy is to be found not only in what
philosophers say, or rather in what they write; it is essentially
deployed in the intermediary space separating their various systems, a space which does not pertain exclusively to the order of
discourse, of speculative discourse at any rate.

There is always philosophy everywhere, insofar as it is the
organization of conjunctures, the setting up of dispositions of
intervention which take account of the conflictual objectives of
the concrete situation, and find immediate expression in the concrete forms of an inorganic 'common sense'. Philosophy finds its
way about itself by 'reforming' these given data, these presuppositions of common sense[6] in relation to which it takes up its
own position. It renders their stakes explicit through the rules of
discrimination it imposes upon them or 'adjusts' to them, according to principles which are not those of an exclusively demonstrative order. Once restored to the conditions of such a practice,
philosophical discourses themselves appear to us as de-centred in
relation to their ostensible claims, to their system of 'proofs',
which are no more than elements of their production among
others in the indefinitely open space of their history.

As a materialist, one will approach the historical forms of
philosophy from a fresh angle. One can question a philosophy
with regard to its specific discourse, on the basis of its text, in
order to establish its theoretical content and the modalities
through which this content is set out, that is, both presented and
validated. One is then involved in the procedures of internal
analysis, procedures which exclusively favour the systematic
form of the discourse in question. Does this mean that one is thus
committed to entering philosophy just as one enters a monastery,
never to re-emerge except at the price of a recantation or a
conversion? Does the mastery of a given philosophical position,
the knowledge of it in its *de facto* historical singularity, imply the
de jure acknowledgement of the presuppositions that constitute

the guarantee of its truth-value, whether the latter is realized in all the rigour of its form or in all the exactitude of its content? We avoid this dilemma precisely by focussing not on criteria of truth, but on the concrete forms of appropriateness.

Historically, philosophy presents itself in a scattering of systems. We must take this presentation at its word, by bringing our interest to bear first of all on that which happens, or passes, between these systems – for it is also what passes or happens inside the systems themselves, in those interstices of discourse which simultaneously undermine and envelop them. In the light of this, the alternatives (whether to take a philosophy from the inside, at the cost of rational adherence to its principles, or whether to take it from the outside, always maintaining one's distance from the message it is supposed to carry) are seen to be false. The theoretical motivations that are the corner-stone of an historical philosophy, and the conceptual tools that serve to build it, do not constitute a centre closed around by its discourse and assured thereby of a stable and univocal meaning. Such a demand for coherence is never more than an individual form of truth, always signed with its author's 'proper' name, a banner rallying or excluding me, the reader. These motivations and instruments are more like the focal points through which a philosophical discourse is diffused and diffracted within itself, beaming out along divergent lines by which its meaning is concretely dissociated, arousing within its organization an inner distance with regard to itself, that detachment which is the concrete form of its self-calling into question: an open discourse, indefinitely prolonging itself beyond its explicit formulations, prior to which it had moreover already begun.

This indeed is the lesson to be drawn from the Hegelian conception of philosophy: no philosophy exists other than on the basis of its own internal contradictions, contradictions which disengage it from its immediate meaning, rendering it problematic and deploying it over the terrain of the other philosophies, all the other philosophies, with which it is involved. However, the contradiction specific to this theory, in the formulation which Hegel imposed upon it, is to have ideally mustered together this totality of determinations into a system of knowledge, an absolute knowledge, an infinite knowledge which yet remains only one knowledge among others, and no more than such a knowledge. To include all philosophies in one and the same conflictual development, as if they all belonged – together with the gaps that distinguish them from one another, while at the same time separating each from itself – to a single discourse, is to reintroduce the dimension of history into the very letter of its inscription; but it is also to maintain the philosophical element within this horizon of a purely theoretical truth, and to assimilate it to knowledge in a unilateral fashion, without reckoning with those practical forms of its determination through which its speculative purity is alloyed. This is a paradigm case of a philosophy that turns against the grain of its own fundamental commitments: Hegel outside Hegel, as he appears if we apply to him his own principle of the return of truth upon itself in a way that opposes it to itself, a truth that undoes itself in the very movement through which it makes itself.

Let us address this question from another angle: how are philosophical effects propagated? In a mechanical fashion, the problem frames itself as one of diffusion: the transmission of a meaning across a series of alien or familiar settings which assimilate or reject, alter or preserve it, according to the degree of connivance which it has entertained with them from the start; these settings determine the preliminary conditions for its reception. Yet on closer examination, this communication is seen to present two separate aspects. Historically a philosophy is recognized on the basis of its truth-content and of the manner of its exposition, insofar as these can be identified and recorded; but it gives rise also to effects of misunderstanding, such as errors of interpretation, through which it is no less of an active force. To the extent that it cannot be reduced to an exclusive, univocal meaning, the content of a philosophical discourse intertwines precisely these antagonistic elements. The distortions undergone by its 'message', whether these be the result of ignorances encountered, misunderstandings aroused or resistances to be overcome, are part of the content of this message, for which they serve as irreplaceable occasions of revelation. No thought is ever wholly innocent of the changes that it undergoes as a result of its conflictual confrontation with forms of practice to which its disposition is not, at first, appropriately adjusted. The disorder at the level of its own organization that is caused by the reproduction of a thought in an objective setting other than that in which it was originally elaborated is not accidental; rather it brings out whatever is most particular in its working order.

The meeting of the philosophies of Hegel and Spinoza[7] is a good example of the sort of distance that can separate two philosophical doctrines: they do not speak the same conceptual language, they aim at different objects, and they are based on incompatible forms of argument. And so the historical opposition of these two systems of thought prevents their mutual recognition in the sharing out of a common ground of truth. When Hegel reads Spinoza, however scrupulously he may keep to the text in which the thought is transmitted, he modifies its meaning insofar as he reinvests it in the development of his own discourse. Indeed, he assimilates it into his own discourse, if only by assigning to it the place of a privileged interlocutor, both as protagonist and antagonist, with whom he confronts his own project, the better to authenticate by thus distinguishing it. It is not hard, therefore, to pick out the blunders committed by Hegel as he interprets this adverse conception of things, which he constantly disqualifies by measuring his own conception against it. But these blunders are not mere mistakes such as might have been avoided or corrected. They are doubly symptomatic: they signify that for a consistent Hegelianism there is something unassimilable, something incomprehensible in Spinozist thought, and this is precisely what characterizes the two points of view when they are located as opposites in the space opened up by their common alternative: Hegel or Spinoza. In the distorting mirror held up to him by Hegelian philosophy, Spinoza is shown according to his effectual truth; conversely, in his relationship to Spinozism, Hegel himself acknowledges the limits that bound his own speculative enterprise. It is as if these two philosophies were acting together, no longer in that scattered order to which strict chronology would consign them; from the point of view of their objectives and their stakes, they share one and the same discursive field, within which they carry on their debate in the very movement by which they call one another into question.

Although a doctrine may precede in time the movement through which it is transmitted and in the course of which it earns the complicity or hostility of the various publics that accept or reject it, such an anteriority should not be interpreted in a one-way manner as a hierarchical relationship of priority. What we learn from a philosophy's posthumous history is that it is not complete at the moment when it is to all appearances concluded, because its author has written in the last word, since its real destiny, its historical becoming, is that it should continue to work itself out, while at the same time decomposing itself in the complex concatenation of the alien discourses which take it as their object and which cast an ever-novel light upon its content. For no philosophy is ever innocent of its history, as the theoreticist illusion would nevertheless have it to be; the content of a philosophy cannot be separated from the becoming through which its power to act is manifested.

How does a philosophy work? We shall not find the answer to this question in some technology of systems of thought, because the appropriate adjustment of a philosophical disposition supposes another kind of arrangement than that which links together the parts of a machine. There is no question here of some formal construct establishable *a priori* on the basis of a rigid schema, independently of the concrete situations in which it is to operate. Nor is it a question of the vital force with which an idea is infused and which pushes it to grow and propagate itself, while preserving its singular identity throughout the whole of its individual development. Neither a personal intuition nor a demonstrative structure, philosophy produces its effects in the material conditions of an historical practice which link it to all the other forms of social practice in relation to which it comes into play. This is why philosophy is never embodied in the shape of any one philosophy, but realizes itself through this common, forever unconcluded discourse, which moves between all philosophies without settling on any one of them and without ever managing definitively to resolve the real conflicts of which it is made.

To do philosophy as a materialist is first and foremost to allow this constant movement to unfold, without proposing to measure it against a theoretical standard of truth in order to isolate within it certain privileged segments, the elements of a definitive body of knowledge authenticated as such with the help of criteria of right. A materialist knowledge, if there is such a thing, consists in an acknowledgement of the inexorable nature of this history to which the practice of theory is dedicated: inexorable, not in the sense of its marching towards some fated destination according to a pre-established course which could be revealed, but in the sense of the necessity, for this practice to be possible, that there should be history – that is, in the last analysis, struggles, relations of power, issues at stake, the detail of whose interplay no knowledge can predict.

Philosophy does not have a history; it *is* history, it is all history, even if in its conscious reflection it is for the most part unaware of this nature, even if the pseudo-systems of knowledge in which it is exposed, and temporarily enclosed, have among other functions that of occluding the necessity of the movement which refutes them. Philosophy exists always and everywhere: not as speculation upon an external history with the aim of recuperating it or disavowing it or both, but as the historical practice of intervention, whose modalities are not determined by the rules explicitly laid down for it in the discourses of philosophers. This is why its inevitably circumstantial order depends neither on techniques of argument, nor on individual inspiration, that is to say neither on a formal nor on a subjective choice, choices modelled on the stereotypes of proof or personal commitment; it is an order that is required by all the forms of that historical reality from which philosophy derives its objectives and its stakes and which it exploits in an unequal manner, concentrating on some areas and spreading itself very thinly in others, and providing only more or less coherent accounts of the conditions of its own objective development. By a prejudice to which 'materialists' are by no means immune, one always tends to favour the mode of theoretical expression which lends the greatest appearance of rigour to philosophical 'play'; but does this not expose one to the risk of neglecting, perhaps of completely occulting that part of the matter of philosophy which eludes systematization? And by assigning to philosophical discourse strict limits to its domain, may one not also run the risk of cutting it off from the practical forms of intervention to which it is materially bound, in the name of preserving the ideal purity of its intellectual empire (to use yet another Hegelian formula)?

As a materialist, it is necessary to desist from installing or establishing philosophy within a domain of knowledge and truth reserved for the specialized competence of the initiated – that is, today, people with degrees, rightful members of a philosophical city haunted by the memory of the defunct heroes of thought; as Hegel put it, the history of philosophy is written in the present, and not in the past, the tense of rumination, nor in the future, the tense of prophecy. The history of philosophy is not written solely in the books of philosophers: these are merely particular forms of its expression. It is a history, a whole history, insofar as the paths it follows traverse every domain of social practice, a practice whose internal conflicts philosophy reflects without really suppressing them. This is its particular way of producing meaning, not in the exclusive order of a meaning which would be explicitly developed down to its last consequences 'and definitively guaranteed by its own self-instituted rules of validity, but in the scattered order of divergent symptoms indirectly expressing the specific characteristics of a concrete situation, an objective conjuncture of circumstances. These symptoms have to be interpreted; they do not bear on their face, in any immediately accessible way, the features that would allow us to identify them, to trace 'demarcation lines'[8] between them in order to bring to light the unstable network within which they form and vanish, exchange their positions and modify their presentation, constantly deviating from the course established for them by a momentary relation of power which is represented in merely provisional fashion in a rational construction.

The fact that, throughout its past history, philosophy should have devoted itself above all to the denial of its own practice – this denial taking the form of the various 'theories' in which philosophy has successively recognized itself – constitutes precisely one of these symptoms, perhaps the only one to which we may allow a certain degree of permanence. *Philosophia perennis*: might philosophy be unshakeable only in its myths, through which it seeks to evade its historical destiny? Everything goes to confirm us in this suspicion. It should not, however, encourage us towards an attitude of reprehension, that is, of retrospective resentment: Death to philosophy! This theme has already seen much service; indeed Marx himself flirted with it for a while. To pose the question of this denial is to redirect philosophy towards a new road, by modifying the internal economy of its field of intervention, by changing, as far as possible, the rules of its game. We may bet on its having nothing to lose from taking such a step, and much, perhaps everything, to gain.

Translated by Lorna Scott Fox

NOTES

1 Cf. the title of the volume published in 1976 by Louis Althusser: *Positions*.

2 Walter Benjamin, 'The author as producer' (talk given in Paris in 1934 at the Institut d'Etudes pour le Fascisme).

3 P. Macherey, 'L'Histoire de la philosophie considérée comme une lutte de tendences', *La Pensée*, 1976.

4 'Contradiction et surdétermination' (1962), reprinted in *Pour Marx*, Paris: Maspero, 1965.

5 L. Althusser, *Philosophie et philosophie spontanée des savants* (1967), Paris: Maspero, 1974.

6 In the sense accorded by Gramsci to this notion.

7 P. Macherey, 'Hegel on Spinoza', in the collection *Theorie*, 1979.

8 L. Althusser, *Lenine et la philosophie*, Paris: Maspero, 1969, p. 50.

LOUIS MARIN

Discourse of power – power of discourse: Pascalian notes

The intention of this volume lies in the directions laid down by its editor: that a number of French writers should explain to an English-speaking audience what they are doing (thinking, saying, writing) in the sphere of discourse which is called philosophy. These directions carry certain assumptions, the most significant of which amounts to the presupposition that, within or beyond differences of language, the field is divided by a national or cultural difference, a difference traced by a divergent history or histories of philosophy. Such a difference would suggest, as does the project itself, that the field of discourse called 'philosophy' is not singular but rather twofold, or again, that what they call 'philosophy' on the other side of the Channel (or elsewhere) is not the same as what we call 'philosophy' on this side. Here Pascal's formula finds a philosophical variation: truth on one side of (the Pyrenees) a frontier, error beyond; truth which is error, error which is truth according to the geographical, national, historical and cultural position, on one side of the frontier or on the other, occupied by the speaker of the formula: two philosophies or two ways of philosophizing, two truths or two ways of speaking the truth.

At the same time, the project and its guidelines carry the assumption that this frontier can be crossed. Translation, in more than one sense of the word, is seen as both possible and desirable, and indeed at present realizable – a translation at once of philosophy from one national and cultural location into the other, of (philosophical) discourse from one sphere into the other, and of language from one philosophical currency into the other. And it is precisely inasmuch as this translation is understood to be desired and desirable that it is seen as both possible and realizable. Equally, such an assumption involves a wager which, while it may pay off, carries stakes of the greatest concern to philosophy itself: for example, the claim that the difference between languages is not irrelevant to philosophy, or that this 'translation' may provide an opportunity to explore in philosophical terms the relationship between languages and language, or, again, that this relationship has a bearing on truth and on the manifestation of truth.

The directions request each contributor to 'write about what you are doing in the sphere of discourse which is called philosophy'; but they comprise a further directive in the form of a warning:

Write about your work in philosophy for an audience of English readers; that is, bear in mind as you go along that your contribution is to be translated and that it is intended – and this is the whole point of the project – to cross the frontier. It will not be doing so by way of a supplementary bonus, over and above its having been written for the hithermost side; on the contrary, your contribution is to be made for this purpose and is commissioned under that condition. To cross the border of national, historical, cultural and linguistic difference, the border of the philosophical difference between philosophies and of different discourses of truth – this is to be its whole *raison d'être*.

The directions add:

Write about what you are writing in philosophy for (with a view to, for the sake of) this translation. Rewrite from the standpoint of difference (national, historical, cultural, linguistic) in philosophy and in truth. Rewrite, and as you do so supervise your writing as if from that other site – from the place, the sphere, the space (of thought, of language and of writing idiom) – which is not your own. Rewrite what you write as from the position of your addressee. Rewrite the same (that which you write in philosophy) from the site of the other.

By the same token the addressee is to supervise my rewriting before he has even read what I write. Let me put it another way: my instructions are to write about what I am doing (what I am writing in philosophy), but having placed myself in the position of a reader who is all the more limiting in that I do not know him or what he expects from a text whose be-all and end-all is that it be addressed to him; all the more threatening in that his image is blurred and indeterminate to me, and all the more perturbing in that I am ignorant of his criteria of judgement. In other words, the regulation of my philosophical discourse – that is, of the rewriting of that discourse – is to be under the control and supervision of an addressee whose expectations and standards are entirely unknown to me.

Insofar, then, as I understand the initial request which impelled this work, one immediate form of response would be to set down a kind of intellectual 'autobiography', a record of my own itinerary – but viewed with a degree of generality – in the field that we seem here to have agreed (although by virtue of none but an implicit convention) to call philosophy. But where exactly is this 'here'? Is it to be located in the text which I am writing now, in its relationship to and differences from the other texts contained in this volume? (It should then be noted that my text is not yet written, and that I have not yet seen the others.) Or in this text as against other works of mine, whether already written or that I should wish eventually to write? Or is 'here' simply a reference to the geographical location in which I write, namely Paris, a response which would be far from innocent given the positive and negative determinations inherent in it? For it is well known, after all, that Paris is not the provinces, and that there is a certain Parisian 'fashion' of philosophizing, that there are certain styles of writing in philosophy which, according to one's inclination, conviction or interest, may be characterized as avant-garde, fashionable, etc. . . . Or is 'here' France? Appropriate reading in this case would include Vincent Descombes's *Modern French Philosophy*. Or is it the continent of Europe perhaps, as in the recurring phrase 'philosophy in the continental sense'? This expression may have a meaning, although I doubt it. At all events, its effect on the discourse of the contexts in which it is used is first and foremost once again to mark out the frontier which I mentioned earlier and which divides the field of discourses which on either side are labelled philosophical, and which the text I am now in the process of writing is intended to cross by means of translation.

In the light of all this, what is required may consist in the first place of an answer to the following question: how have people come to be philosophers, in France, in Paris, here, between 1945 and 1980? If such an approach to the original question/direction presents itself as the simplest and most direct, it nonetheless raises a number of questions that may – tentatively at any rate – be ranked as philosophical. For instance: What is to be understood by the term 'philosopher' as used on the continent, in France, in Paris, in certain Parisian circles, between 1945 and 1980? What entitles me to such a name? (Indeed, is it a name, a title, a designation?) Would English-speaking philosophers, or more broadly an English-speaking public, concur without further preparation or ado in calling this philosophy? Perhaps the whole purpose of this volume is to seduce the English-speaking public into accepting such a designation, or to enable it to sort out the contributions which it will read in the light of its own presuppositions, admitting some into the category of philosophy while excluding others as ineligible. Some, no doubt, will be held up as borderline cases pending a more detailed investigation on the frontier of which I have spoken; such tolerance, liberalism or reservations as may become apparent in the process will be a function, so it seems to me, of an English assessment of contributions on a sliding scale of exoticism.

It is well known that to cross a frontier raises some delicate problems, even when the traveller's passport is in order and he possesses the relevant tourist visa or work permit. I even wonder whether the real issue behind the directions for this project might not be that of granting either a tourist visa or a work permit for the translation (traversal) of the frontier. In other words, will *that* which, *here*, bestows the right to the name or title of philosopher qualify one only for a pleasure trip over *there* or will it entitle one to a (philosophical) work permit? There have been precedents in both directions – Hobbes, Hume, Voltaire, Rousseau . . . Does 'that' – meaning an education, examinations sat and degrees awarded, all characterized as being in 'philosophy', but also a teaching activity, the writing of articles, the publishing of books – does that bestow a right to the name, title or quality of philosopher? And will this term, as accorded to all that over *here*, merit a tourist visa or a work permit over *there*? This question forces itself upon me with peculiar urgency in view of the fact that I myself wonder – only for myself, needless to say – whether what I am doing (thinking, saying, writing) *still* belongs to the realm of philosophy (in the continental, the French, even the Parisian sense), if only because I have belonged professionally for the past several years to an institution from which the word 'philosophy' has been outlawed, where it has a bad name – perhaps because it had a bad name outside – and where the terms 'human science' or, better still, 'social science' have been substituted for it. But does this really amount to a substitution? And if a substitution has indeed taken place, what does that mean? Is it not rather that the field of discourse called philosophy has shifted, and reconstituted itself in a different way? Such a question is not merely a semantic or an epistemological one; it has institutional, professional, social, political and ethical significance. Or to invert the issue and to reformulate it in terms of that intellectual autobiography which may well be what has been asked of me and which has led me to question myself (or rather, to question the very project of such an autobiography, its intentions and its aims): might not what I am doing today be philosophy under the label of science (human/ social)? A positive answer to this question might constitute a modern or post-modern variation on the theme of the philosopher in the mask, such as Descartes, or on that of the philosopher of the enlightenment, such as Voltaire or Diderot.

In a bid to stem this proliferation of queries diverting me from my beginning – as I write this here – let me suppose (speaking for no one but myself and in my own name, as one says) that what I have been *doing* for the last fifteen or twenty years is in a sense to question the institution of philosophy. More specifically, I realize, as I write this here, that philosophy is inseparable from an institution (or indeed several institutions). It is itself an institution, and a philosopher is such only inasmuch as he thinks, speaks and writes within and from these institutions that philosophy is and from which it cannot be separated; but also inasmuch as he does all these things so that he may question them. In the very act of so doing, the philosopher signifies that philosophy is after all separable from them, if only to a limited extent; that there is a degree to which it may step back from the institution that it is and from those within or out of which its discourse comes into being. This idea may be given any number of formulations; as a result there may be great variation in the issues at stake. Is philosophy perhaps this to-ing and fro-ing between the institutions in which it is practised and the institution (the 'discipline') that it is? Is it the questioning itself, in institutionalized form, of these institutions or of institution in general? Might it be the meditation of institution in general upon itself? Or alternatively the movement of thought, discourse and writing towards the exterior of institution in general and of the philosophical institution in particular, the exterior of those institutions from which philosophy is inseparable, but from which it must of necessity succeed in some way in separating itself in order to be philosophy – insofar, that is, as any institution whatsoever, and particularly the institution of philosophy, can ever be said to have an exterior?

Perhaps philosophy is no more than a certain way of trying to cross the frontier of institution in general without either a tourist visa or a work permit – or a kind of attempted desertion from the institution of philosophy.

My next step, then, should be to examine what I mean by institution, examine the institution of philosophy (philosophy as a discipline among other disciplines of knowledge) as it exists today and in its relationship to, for instance, French university institutions, and more generally to other social and political institutions. Only then will I be in a position to embark upon the sort of intellectual autobiography that is (so I suppose) required of me. This is, as one knows, a highly topical question, at any rate in France. Indeed, the various queries outlined earlier could all be regarded as so many political strategies – route, interrogation, reflection, sally – for countering the threat that hangs over the institution of philosophy in France, as a counter-threat to that represented by philosophy to political and social institutions in general. Or to take a no less topical example: has a lecture on Aristotle, given in Prague, in the flat of a professor of philosophy expelled from the University for political and ideological reasons been so analysed, in France, as to convey a thorough understanding of the threat it posed to the political establishment? Such an analysis strikes me as being no less philosophical an enterprise, *here*, than the lecture on Aristotle itself may have been in its own context, over there beyond another frontier. However, to remain within the bounds of the exercise that I suppose to be required of me, one might well ask whether it can still be called doing philosophy to inquire into the history of French philosophy since 1945 or into the sociology of those 'intellectuals' known as 'philosophers' during that period and, in the area of overlap of that history and sociology, to try to bring out and reflect on the position of a philosopher in all its successive displacements – the position, that is, of an individual, in this particular case myself, who feels himself to be a philosopher. This enterprise may well be of a philosophical nature; once carried out, however, it will certainly not represent what I have been doing for the last fifteen or twenty years, nor what I am doing at present. It might quite possibly be of interest to an English audience as an individual intellectual history, as both a history and a sociology of contemporary thought in France, or even as a social history of philosophy; but the question will remain of the philosophical credentials of this history. Perhaps it might achieve philosophical status at the precise point at which it enabled me to raise the issue of the historical and sociological determinants, not to say determinisms, of work (whether of thoughts, discourse or writings) which rightly or wrongly I hold to be philosophical; that is to say, at the point where I would pose the question of the conditions of philosophical discourse in general. I come back to my point of departure.

Question: 'So what are you doing now?' Underlying implication: 'Once you have explained it to us, allow us to judge whether or not your work is of a philosophical nature.' But precondition: 'Rewrite what you normally write from your own point of view, only this time from the position of the addressee of this volume' (even though I am ignorant of the expectations and criteria of judgement of this addressee, given that he comes from beyond the frontier of which I have already spoken).

To return to my starting-point, then, let me recount a short anecdote. During an official luncheon held in the sixties at All Souls, Oxford, in honour of the visit of a renowned French philosopher, the highly renowned English philosopher at my side inquired of me what I *did* – the very same question posed twenty years later by the project for this collection, to which I replied 'I am a philosopher'. This answer (which I know now, as I should always have known, to be both naive and presumptuous) led him to ask my specialization in the field of philosophy. 'French philosophy of the seventeenth century,' said I, only to find myself reproved with the very proper correction: 'I see: you are a historian of ideas.' To have corrected him in my turn, in order to rejoin the realm of philosophy from which I had been so summarily expelled, would have called for an analysis of French institutions of philosophy from the two angles indicated above: the institution of the teaching of philosophy, in its various sites, norms and standards, and the institution of the discipline known in France under the name of philosophy, in all its codes, rules and incumbent modes of discourse. This analysis might have shown how the discourses of philosophy and history (and indeed sociology) had come to stake out then and here – and no doubt even now – a space or field of problems named then and here 'philosophy'.

Of course, such a history or sociology becomes somewhat suspect to the extent that they are conceived and executed by someone partially or totally formed by them, or who has participated, however modestly, in their development. My correction would also have shown the need for an inquiry into the historical sub-discipline known as 'the history of ideas' in order to assess the extent of the shifts and the depth of the transformations which have affected at once its scope, its limits and its methods.

Like many other contributors to this volume, no doubt, I have frequently resorted in my text to the word *'discours'*. I wonder whether it is really translatable. It will need to be translated nonetheless, since discourses constitute the field of my research. Let us take them to be linguistic sets of a higher order than the sentence (while often reducible to a sentence) and *carried out* or *actualized* in or by means of texts. My own preoccupation with discourses revolves around the problems exposed above concerning the discourse which I am in the course of writing for this volume: how do discourses develop into institutions? What is the nature of the remarkable relationship between power and discourse, whose locus is the institution as discourse or the discourse as institution?

Discourse of power – power of discourse: the chiasmus affecting the two terms, power and discourse, points to a problematic in order to elicit a demonstration. However, simply to posit a definition of power and a definition of discourse, on which to base a subsequent examination of the double and inverted relationship linking them in this chiasmus would be the surest way to overlook, forget or misread this problematic. I would suggest a contrary procedure: to find out – or to invent – what happens to power and to discourse within the chiasmus that joins them. What happens to discourse when it is the discourse of power, or when it is itself power? What happens to power when it is spoken by discourse, or when it defines discourse itself? Is there, in the universe of forms of discourse, a discourse specific to power, when discourse in general possesses in and through itself a power 'peculiar' to itself? And what is the relationship between *this* power, 'peculiar' to discourse in general and power in general, with its taking over of an existent discourse and its enunciation within a discourse 'peculiar' to itself?

Two propositions:

I Discourse is the ideological mode of existence of force, an imaginary known as power.

II Power is the imaginary of force at the moment that it is enunciated as the discourse of justice.

In order for discourse, power and the chiasmus linking them in my original formulation to come into play, I have introduced into these two propositions the terms 'force' and 'justice', terms that produce a shift in those of power and discourse. The momentum of this displacement, its driving force, is imagination.

How does force turn into power? How can it survive as power except by *taking over* a discourse of justice? How does this discourse of justice then turn into power, *taking the place* of the effects of force? How does discourse in general produce effects of force which are *taken* to be just, to be justice itself?

Taking over the discourse of . . . taking the place of . . . to be taken for . . . these are the three stages by which the imagination has transformed discourse into power, that is to say, discourse strong of itself.

It was from this angle that I came to Pascal, and in particular to this *pensée* (on which the rest of my text is no more than a commentary):

Justice, force. It is just that what is just should be followed; it is necessary that what is the strongest should be followed. Justice without force is impotent; force without justice is tyrannical. Justice without force is contradicted, because there are always wicked men; force without justice is denounced. Justice and force must therefore be brought together, and to that end let us make it the case that that which is just be strong, and that which is strong be just.

Justice is open to dispute; force is easily recognizable and beyond dispute. Thus was force bestowed upon justice; because force has contra-

dicted justice, and has said that it was unjust, and that it was force itself
which was just. Thus, being unable to make what is just to be strong, we
have made what is strong to be just.   (103)

The text which follows is to be taken as a 'philosophical'
parable – or rather, since it is not a narrative but a discourse, as an
allegory: at first sight a mere contemporary gloss of another
man's thought of more than three centuries ago. Yet it could well
be that for those with ears to hear, the thought of 1658 as it
appears through this commentary speaks essentially of the present day. There is, to my mind, no way of speaking of and with
both justice and force *today*, or of fortifying justice *now*, other
than by the detour or distantiation here called allegory (elsewhere
known as the history of philosophy, history of ideas, critique
. . .). Otherwise, to speak in such a way will, *volens nolens*, always
turn out to be the speaking of the discourse of power, and he who
speaks it, the spokesman of a tyrant.

'It is just that what is just should be followed'; this is a categorical imperative, since justice prescribes its decrees by no other
authority than itself. A just prescription is not deduced from the
nature of Being, or of the Good, or from some theoretical or
speculative proposition. A just prescription is just, without reference to considerations of utility or what is agreeable. There are
no degrees of justice, no more or less just: it is a matter of all or
nothing. 'Justice and truth are two points so fine that our instruments are too blunt to touch them exactly. If ever they succeed,
they flatten the point and press all around, covering more of what
is false than of what is true' (82). Whatever does not coincide with
the fine point of justice is unjust. Indiscernible though it may be, it
admits of no gradual shading from the just to the unjust.

'It is necessary that what is the strongest should be followed.'
Force is a matter of necessity. It is impossible to do otherwise than
to follow the strong, by virtue of a necessity at once material,
mechanical and physical. Force does not carry any imperative – it
generates no obligation. Force is absolute constraint and violence
(or else we are dreaming, imagining, fantasizing). There are,
however, degrees of force: only the strongest is necessarily followed, and even then he must first manifest his strength. How
shall he do this other than by confronting the other forces and
annihilating them? Thus the strongest demonstrates, without

words, that he is, necessarily, the strongest. He achieves this position only at the close of the war of forces that leaves him sole force in the field, having reduced all other forces to naught. The strongest is only the strongest at the pure point of the actual manifestation of his strength, the abstract moment of the annihilation of all the other forces. Such would be the moment of the genesis of society, at once originary and instantaneous, according to the fiction of a state of nature.

The bonds securing the respect of men for one another in general are bonds of necessity: there must be varying degrees of respect, since all men seek to dominate while not all, but only a few, are able to. Imagine, then, that we can see them beginning to take shape. It is certain that men will fight one another until the strongest party has subdued the weakest
. . .   (304)

'Justice without force is impotent; force without justice is tyrannical.' It is just that what is just should be followed. But whence comes the obligation – how, indeed, can one make it obligatory even for oneself, by some act of autonomous self-obligation – to follow justice? For a just prescription has no authority to prescribe other than that inherent in its own justice. Justice is essentially impotent, for of and in itself it lacks any force that would be its own enforcement, outside the utopia of a justice whose force lay precisely in the absence of force. Such a utopia was realized *once* by someone:

It would have been superfluous for Our Lord Jesus Christ to descend as a King in order to be revealed in the splendour of His kingdom of holiness; but He came in the splendour of His own order. It is ridiculous to be outraged by the lowliness of Jesus Christ, as if His lowliness were of the same order as the greatness which He had come to show forth.   (793)

'Force without justice is tyrannical.' Justice is devoid of force, in and of itself it is impotent – the degree zero of force. Tyranny is an excess of force; without justice, mere strength is *overstrong*. Here, more accurately, is the point at which the essence of all force emerges as a fantastical desire to be the greatest force of all or, what amounts to the same thing, as a desire for the destruction of all other forces.

Tyranny consists in a desire for universal domination, unrestricted to its rightful order. There are separate chambers for the strong, the handsome, the intelligent, or the God-fearing, each with a master in his own house. But occasionally they meet, whereupon the strong and the hand-some contend for mastery over one another – foolishly, for their mastery is of different kinds. They cannot understand one another; the fault of each is that he seeks to reign over all. Nothing can do this, not even force, which is indeed as nothing in the kingdom of the learned, having mastery only over external action . . . Tyranny is the desire to obtain by one means that which one may have only by another . . .   (332)

Two definitions of tyranny, that is, of that force without justice which is *pure* force; absolute violence. The boundless desire of the strong to be the absolute degree of force – a paradox itself as infinite as that desire – amounts to the desire for pure homogen-eity, that is, the desire for the destruction of all heterogeneity. Thus all force is by its essence tyrannical, a movement towards universal entropy (or death). 'Justice without force is contra-dicted, because there are always wicked men; force without jus-tice is denounced.' This is the key moment of the reversal of the apparent symmetries between force and justice – the negative moment of a leap into the domain of discourse. Justice, which is non-violent and devoid of force, which is the degree zero of force, is contra-*dicted* (contre-*dite*). Discourse states the opposite of what the just prescription, which has no foundation to its prescriptive authority other than itself, prescribes. In a single phrase, it says that what is just is unjust. Fact, accident or event: the just pres-cription is reversed in and through the enunciation of this newly apparent discourse. And why? Because *there are always* wicked men. The accident or event of this singular discourse has always already occurred. It has always already happened, without ex-planation or justification. There have always been wicked men. A discourse of evil, a *de facto* presence of evil in its discourse is always already *there*. This is no speculative or theoretical fable, such as that of Descartes's Evil Spirit, which would permit of a founda-tion for justice and its prescriptions. The discourse of evil has always been in existence. But evil is merely a discourse, and powerless as such to damage the just prescription or its innate justice. Evil is that discourse which gainsays or contradicts jus-tice.

Force without justice is denounced. Another, parallel, dis-course exists to match that of the wicked who contradict: a discourse through which the strongest are charged with their crimes, a discourse of accusation of tyranny. Two discourses, then, which confront one another: that which contradicts justice and that which denounces force. But if we know who, from time immemorial, has contradicted justice without force – the wicked, we yet do not know who denounces force without justice. The just man who is crucified before a tyrant on his throne – could it be him? Or perhaps the only possible denunciation of tyranny is lodged in the silence of the accuser . . . perhaps this silence in the act of denunciation is actually the secret, inaudible sign of a just man?

And Jesus stood before the governor: and the governor asked him, saying 'Art thou the King of the Jews?' And Jesus said unto him 'Thou sayest.' And when he was accused of the chief priests and elders, he answered nothing. Then said Pilate unto him, 'Hearest thou not how many things they witness against thee?' And he answered him to never a word; insomuch that the governor marvelled greatly. (Matt. 27, 11–14)

'Justice and force must therefore be brought together, and to that end let us make it the case that that which is just be strong, and that which is strong be just.' Conclusion. Up to this point, the two themes of strength and justice have been developed independently of one another out of the two original propositions that 'It is just that what is just should be followed; it is necessary that what is the strongest should be followed', that is to say, out of the opposition between justice and necessity, the consequences of which were twice formulated in two propositions through the double exclusion of justice by force and force by justice. This double exclusion, however, which conforms to the general principles of Pascal's method of reasoning via the negation of what is not the truth to be demonstrated, has led us to the perception of a double displacement. In the first place, whilst as regards justice (lacking or exclusive of force) we came up against the fact that it is absolutely devoid of force, we found that force (which excludes justice) is a universal desire for domination in every respect. In other words, justice without force *cannot* make justice manifest – it is impotent – whereas force without justice manifests itself as force outside its own 'proper' domain as constituted by external actions. In the second place, we have entered the realm of discourses, that which contradicts justice and that which denounces force, two discourses which work a remarkable reversal of each other's modalities. For the discourse of contradiction inverts the original prescriptive proposition 'One must follow what is just, because it is just' into a descriptive one 'The just is non-just', 'The just is unjust', whose implicit consequence would be the negation of the original prescription: 'That what is just should be followed, is unjust (since the just has been called not just)', or 'The just must not be followed, for it is unjust (or non-just)'. Likewise and conversely, the discourse of denunciation performs a reversal in the opposite direction, implicitly transforming the original statement of the necessity of following the strongest into a negative prescription: 'That the strongest should be followed, is unjust.'

Hence Pascal's conclusion (in the form of a pragmatic principle and consequence) designed to dispel the confusion and disorder inherent in the discourses of contradiction and denunciation. For to contradict the just is in itself *contradictory* ('It is unjust that the just should be followed'), and the denunciation of the strongest is itself – *qua discourse* – a transgression of order, perfectly homologous to the tyrannical transgression committed by force. When it converts the statement of a necessity into a negative prescription ('It is unjust that what is necessary should be followed'), the discourse of denunciation becomes, to borrow Pascal's word, *ridiculous*. 'Justice and force must therefore be brought together', since reasoning along the lines of contraries has shown that justice without force and force without justice end up either in contradiction (in the case of the discourse of contradiction) or in the ridiculous (in the case of the discourse of denunciation). Both necessary force and categorical justice are silent. Once they have been displaced into discourse in general – that of force without justice and that of justice without force – then this absurdity is revealed: in the contradiction of a discourse of force and in the ridiculousness of a discourse of justice. The bringing together of justice and force should thus make it possible to avoid both these absurdities.

It is noteworthy, however, that in the Pascalian discourse this conclusion is voiced as a prescription: 'Justice and force must therefore be brought together . . .', a prescription which is to be accomplished by means of an act, a 'making': 'and to that end let us make . . .'

What is the nature of this prescription? It is both ambivalent in its presentation and weak in what is presented. Ambivalent, because it represents at once a rational, epistemic demand aimed at resolving the contradictoriness of the discourse of contradiction (whose subject is force without justice), and a moral or ethical obligation to seek to rescue from the ridiculous the negative prescription of the discourse of denunciation on the subject of tyrannical force. Weak in what it presents, for it does no more than to bring together force and justice, while leaving them, in their very conjunction, as terms external to one another.

Nevertheless, it is equally noteworthy that it is in the act of realization, the 'making' which is at once the consequence of the principle that 'justice and force must therefore be brought together' and the means of its accomplishment, that both the reason behind the ambivalence and the force behind the weakness become apparent. Let us reread the passage: 'Justice and force must therefore be brought together, and to that end let us make it the case that that which is just be strong, and that which is strong be just.' This is indeed a pure principle, which, thanks to the ellipse of the grammatical form of obligation in French (*il faut*), belongs both to the realm of ethics and to that of operational instruction; it is an imperative command which contains within itself the cognitive conditions for the success of the task, undertaking or action which it demands. And this task, undertaking or action aims at nothing less than an identification of the two terms which the principle had placed in juxtaposition to each other while yet maintaining them in their relations of mutual exteriority. It is at this point, however, that the original opposition between the categorical imperative of the just man and the mechanical necessity of the strongest reappears. It reappears in the shape of two propositions which are mutually and exclusively disjunctive of the process of identifying force and justice. The identity to be forged is not inert, the conjunction is not static; '$x = y$' is not equivalent to '$y = x$'. The identification of force and justice is a dynamic process which can work from either of two mutually exclusive orientations, two contrary directions; either force becomes an attribute of justice, or justice becomes a determining quality of force. Yet even this may be misleading, for, in the operation called for both by an ethical command and by a technical instruction, we are no longer dealing with entities or essential notions such as 'force' or 'justice'. The task to be undertaken is concerned with qualities, and the process of identification of 'force' and 'justice' is none other than one of reduction of qualities or attributes, the existence of whose substance-subjects are in suspense: '. . . make it the case that that which is just be strong, and that which is strong be just.'

'Justice and truth are two points so fine that our instruments are too blunt to touch them exactly . . .' '. . . could we love the substance of a man's soul, in the abstract, regardless of the qualities it possessed?' Would we have justice to be force, or force justice? 'It cannot be, and would be unjust. Therefore it is never a person we love, but only qualities' (323). Thus we operate never on essences or substances, but only on qualities and by exchange or substitution of qualities. Which of the two exchanges, between what is strong and what is just, is possible? Which substitution is realizable?

Demonstration: 'Justice is open to dispute; force is easily recognizable and beyond dispute.' Justice is interminably arguable. Justice, the idea of justice, is the object of polemical debate. Why is this? Justice is, no doubt, categorically imperative: 'It is just that what is just should be followed'; but what *is* just? It seems that the very nature of the just description as deontic 'tautology' must imply an inquiry into the ontological determination of justice. This inquiry leads in turn, necessarily so it seems, towards a deduction of the just prescription from a theoretical, speculative statement positing the Being of justice as the Good, as Nature, or as God:

Why should I divide my ethics into four parts rather than six? Why should I ascribe four parts to virtue, rather than two, or one? Why as 'desist' and 'resist' rather than by 'following nature' or by 'discharging your private business without injustice', like Plato, or anything else? – But, you will say, here is everything encapsulated in a phrase. – Yes, but that is of no use unless explained, and no sooner does one uncover, to explain it, the precept that encloses all others, than they tumble out in the very confusion that one had sought to avoid. And when they are all enclosed in one, they remain hidden and useless as though in a safe . . .

(120)

Philosophical discourses, polemical discourses: discourses at war and in confusion, interminable dispute as to the ontological determination on which the imperative of justice might depend for its full validity as imperative. Its ought-to-be would find its 'ought' in a Being. But how may this be determined without falling into dispute? 'Justice and truth are two points so fine that our instruments are too blunt to touch them exactly . . .' Yes, indeed, the just (by its very nature as a value), the just prescription, has no other foundation than itself, granted. But fine and almost indiscernible point that it is, it appears that a discourse will always seek to determine the just as a 'palpable quality', the ontological predicate of the Being of justice. Thus justice can never be exempt from the fray, or avoid becoming the butt of mutually opposed and belligerent philosophical discourses.

Force, on the other hand, is easily recognizable and beyond dispute. It is impossible not to notice it, for it compels recognition by its very manifestation – such is the mechanical necessity of the strongest. By the same token, and of necessity, force cannot be an object of discourse. Force is not a topic of conversation; one either wields it or yields to it. – But, you may object, surely we can denounce the tyranny of force? – No doubt, but such a discourse is ridiculous because it is 'literally' without object, that is, without effect upon that of which it speaks. It is an impotent discourse, forever open to the ultimate threat, the threat of death: 'Silence, or I shall kill you, because I am the strongest.' The argument of the strongest invariably prevails, and the wolves will always carry off into the depths of the forest, there to devour without trial, any lambs who have been too eloquent in denunciation of the tyrant.

'Thus was force bestowed upon justice . . .' A somewhat surprising conclusion is here under way. Lo, rejoice! force has been given unto justice! Men, mankind, societies, have had the power to subjugate force and to deliver it into the hands of justice! Justice is henceforth strengthened; policy has turned into morality and politics has become indistinguishable from ethics. Alas, no . . . We have misread. Once more: 'Justice is open to dispute; force is easily recognizable and beyond dispute.' We expect the conclusion, 'Thus was justice given, delivered unto force . . .' But that would constitute a transgression of order, as Pascal might say. The principal proposition that stands at the beginning of the sentence is in reality only an effect of the subordinate clause of causation that follows; the inversion of the true order is thus reproduced in the syntax. For politics to be identical with ethics implies, by an abrupt, instantaneous inversion, the contrary – a masterstroke of force in a stroke of discourse.

'Thus was force bestowed upon justice; because force has

contradicted justice, and has said that it was unjust, and that it was force itself which was just.' Force could be given to justice, because force, which simply *is*, and cannot be an object of discourse, has accorded itself the right to speak. It has set itself up as a subject of discourse, producing language, passing into the world of signs. Here is the 'true' degree zero of force: mute violence becomes, at a stroke, mutated into meaning without loss of its polemical character. Force takes possession of signs, language and discourse by way of that universal desire for infinite domination outside the bounds of the order (of external actions, external bodies) that constitutes its tyrannical essence. Seizing language, force becomes mirrored in discourse and represented in signs. It is converted into meaning. And we are left to wonder, with Pascal, whether discourse, all discourse in general, might not already and since time immemorial be force reflected and represented, reactive and reactivated within signs; whether signs themselves and the symbolic function in general might not be the retrodden tracks of force, its delegated representatives or authorized agents. As a subject of discourse, force speaks; and the force which is represented in signs is a force that sets itself up as autonomous and self-instituting – enacting the law (its law) in order to endow itself with legitimacy and authority. Its position is a self-positioning whereby the pure manifestation of force, in this movement of self-reflection, institutes itself as a legitimate and autonomous source of power; power of discourse/discourse of power, identity and mutual appropriation.

This discourse of force – a discourse of self-institution and self-legitimation and which *is* power – comprises a twofold dimension, two facets, one negative and one positive. It is a two-stroke machine, but simultaneously as it were. Force has contradicted justice and decreed it to be unjust. Force does not quibble about what justice, or the just, may consist of – that is the business of the interminable philosophical and speculative discourses. Force contra-dicts and with all the more assurance because it is easily recognizable and beyond dispute; with all the more certitude, since behind its representation or reflection in discourse the absolute threat is always looming, the possibility of a return to silence or to the inarticulate cry of wordless violence: 'Justice is unjust! I speak the truth and you shall acknowledge the immutability of my truth or else I shall kill you.' Force contradicts justice in the enunciation of a pure contradiction: A is non-A, the just is non-just, justice is unjust. But the contradictoriness of the contradiction is resolved without mediation, *immediately*, and in the absence of any dialectic, for when force asserts that justice is unjust, it is *simultaneously* asserting its own justice. In the act of uttering the contradiction, force takes possession of justice, what is strong appropriates what is just; the strong becomes literally just. And by virtue of this very same move, this single stroke of force which is a stroke of discourse, the strong(est) who calls himself just, *is* just. A happy performative, to be so favoured by its situation of utterance as to be incapable of being contradicted; for to contradict the discourse of force (i.e. power) is not only injustice but also self-exposure to force, to the strongest whom it is necessary to follow. At the degree zero where mute violence or the silence of force cancels itself out, power, the discourse of force, is the force of the discourse which by saying, makes to be; by saying that it is just, makes itself to be just. By the same token we discover who the wicked are who had been contradicting justice (devoid of force); they are the strong who begin to speak, to hold forth in discourse, instead of striking and killing. Evil, the fact of evil, is the discourse of the strongest, or power. Far from policy being transformed into morality, it is rather ethics which, in one stroke, becomes politics. There is no morality: there is only the political.

'Thus being unable to make what is just to be strong, we have made what is strong to be just.' The first conclusion is duplicated and displaced by a second. What the former had envisaged as a possibility (to endow justice with force), because force through its discourse, as ruling power, had become justice, is revealed by the latter as impossible, as a negative necessity. It is impossible to ensure that the just should be strong or to give force to justice other than in mere 'words', other than in an unhappy discourse that says without doing, an impotent and ineffectual, in short a ridiculous discourse. It is impossible to endow justice with force: this negative necessity is simply the obverse of the positive necessity, easily recognizable and beyond dispute, that the strongest be followed. Within power, within the discourse of strength, this necessity has become the power of discourse – the powerful and happy discourse that is the justification of force.

Our original statement of the necessity of following the

strongest has been transformed in and by the discourse of strength, in and by power (discourse of power, power of discourse) into a final prescription as follows: It is just that what is the strongest should be followed; for the strongest has called himself just, and it is just that the just should be followed. 'We have made what is strong to be just': that final 'made' is a performative of language, an act of discourse for which the conditions of success and pragmatic validity are being established throughout Pascal's entire thought. All politics is discourse (discourse of power) and it is very likely that all discourse is political (power of discourse).

Translated by Lorna Scott Fox

On interpretation

The most appropriate way of giving an idea of the problems which have occupied me over the past thirty years and of the tradition to which my way of dealing with these problems belongs is, it seems to me, to start with my current work on narrative function, going on from there to show the relationship between this study and my earlier studies of metaphor, psychoanalysis, symbolism and other related problems, in order, finally, to work back from these partial investigations towards the presuppositions, both theoretical and methodological, upon which the whole of my research is based. This backwards movement into my own work allows me to leave until the end my discussion of the presuppositions of the phenomenological and hermeneutical tradition to which I belong, by showing in what way my analyses at one and the same time continue and correct this tradition and, on occasion, bring it into question.

I

I shall begin, then, by saying something about my work in progress on narrative function.

Three major preoccupations are apparent here. This inquiry into the act of storytelling responds first of all to a very general concern, one which I have previously discussed in the first chapter of my book *Freud and Philosophy* – that of preserving the fullness, the diversity and the irreducibility of the various *uses* of language. It can thus be seen that from the start I have affiliated myself with those analytical philosophers who resist the sort of reductionism according to which 'well-formed languages' are alone capable of evaluating the meaning-claims and truth-claims of all non-'logical' uses of language.

A second concern completes and, in a certain sense, tempers the first: that of *gathering together* the diverse forms and modes of the game of storytelling. Indeed, throughout the development of the cultures to which we are the heirs, the act of storytelling has never ceased to ramify into increasingly well-determined literary genres. This fragmentation presents a major problem for philosophers by virtue of the major dichotomy which divides the narrative field and which produces a thorough-going opposition between, on the one hand, narratives which have a truth-claim comparable to that of the descriptive forms of discourse to be found in the sciences – let us say history and the related literary genres of biography and autobiography – and, on the other hand, fictional narratives such as epics, dramas, short stories and novels, to say nothing of narrative modes that use a medium other than language: films, for example, and possibly painting and other plastic arts.

In opposition to this endless fragmentation, I acknowledge the existence of a *functional* unity among the multiple narrative modes and genres. My basic hypothesis, in this regard, is the following: the common feature of human experience, that which is marked, organized and clarified by the fact of storytelling in all its forms, is its *temporal character*. Everything that is recounted occurs in time, takes time, unfolds temporally; and what unfolds in time can be recounted. Perhaps, indeed, every temporal process is recognized as such only to the extent that it can, in one way or another, be recounted. This reciprocity which is assumed to exist between narrativity and temporality is the theme of my present research. Limited as this problem may be compared to the vast scope of all the real and potential uses of language, it is actually immense. Under a single heading, it groups together a number of problems that are usually treated under different rubrics: the epistemology of historical knowledge, literary criticism applied to works of fiction, theories of time (which are themselves scattered among cosmology, physics, biology, psychology and sociology). By treating the temporal quality of experience as the common reference of both history and fiction, I make of fiction, history and time one single problem.

It is here that a third concern comes in, one which offers the possibility of making the problematic of temporality and narrativity easier to work with: namely, the testing of the selective and organizational capacity of language itself when it is ordered into those units of discourse longer than the sentence which we can call *texts*. If, indeed, narrativity is to mark, organize and clarify temporal experience – to repeat the three verbs employed above – we must seek in language use a standard of measurement which satisfies this need for delimiting, ordering and making explicit. That the text is the linguistic unit we are looking for and that it constitutes the appropriate medium between temporal experience and the narrative act can be briefly outlined in the following manner. As a linguistic unit, a text is, on the one hand, an expansion of the first unit of present meaning which is the sentence. On the other hand, it contributes a principle of trans-sentential organization that is exploited by the act of storytelling in all its forms.

We can term *poetics* – after Aristotle – that discipline which deals with the laws of composition that are added to discourse as such in order to form of it a text which can stand as a narrative, a poem or an essay.

The question then arises of identifying the major characteristic of the act of story-making. I shall once again follow Aristotle in his designation of the sort of verbal *composition* which constitutes a text as a narrative. Aristotle designates this verbal composition by use of the term *muthos*, a term that has been translated by 'fable' or by 'plot'. He speaks of 'the combination [*sunthesis*, or, in another context, *sustasis*] of incidents or the fable' (*Poetics* 1450 A 5 and I 5). By this, Aristotle means more than a structure in the static sense of the word, but rather an operation (as indicated by the ending *-sis* as in *poiesis*, *sunthesis*, *sustasis*), namely the structuring that makes us speak of putting-into-the-form-of-a-plot (*emplotment*) rather than of *plot*. The emplotment consists mainly in the selection and arrangement of the events and the actions recounted, which make of the fable a story that is 'complete and entire' (*Poetics* 1450 B 25) with a beginning, middle and end. Let us understand by this that no action is a beginning except in a story that it inaugurates; that no action constitutes a middle unless it instigates a change of fortune in the story told, an 'intrigue' to be sorted out, a surprising 'turn of events', a series of 'pitiful' or 'terrifying' incidents; finally, no action, taken in itself, constitutes an end except insofar as it concludes a course of action in the story told, unravels an intrigue, explains the surprising turn of fortune or seals the hero's fate by a final event which clarifies the whole action and produces in the listener the catharsis of pity and terror.

It is this notion of plot that I take as a guideline for my entire investigation, in the area of the history of historians (or historiography) as well as in that of fiction (from epics and folk tales to the modern novel). I shall limit myself here to stressing the feature which, to my mind, makes the notion of plot so fruitful, namely its *intelligibility*. The intelligible character of plot can be brought out in the following way: the plot is the set of combinations by which events are made *into* a story or – correlatively – a story is made *out of* events. The plot mediates between the event and the story. This means that nothing is an event unless it contributes to the progress of a story. An event is not only an occurrence, something that happens, but a narrative component. Broadening the scope of the plot even more in order to escape the opposition, associated with the aesthetics of Henry James, between plot and characters, I shall say that the plot is the intelligible unit that holds together circumstances, ends and means, initiatives and unwanted consequences. According to an expression borrowed from Louis Mink, it is the act of 'taking together' – of com-posing – those ingredients of human action which, in ordinary experience, remain dissimilar and discordant.

From this intelligible character of the plot, it follows that the ability to follow a story constitutes a very sophisticated form of *understanding*.

I shall now say a few words about the problems posed by an extension of the Aristotelian notion of plot to historiography. I shall cite two.

The first concerns historiography. It would appear, indeed, to be arguing a lost cause to claim that modern history has preserved the narrative character to be found in earlier chronicles and which has continued up to our own days in the accounts given by political, diplomatic or ecclesiastical history of battles, treaties, parcelling and, in general, of the changes of fortune which affect the exercise of power by given individuals. (1) It seems, in the first place, that, as history moves away not only from the ancient form of the chronicle, but also from the political model and becomes social, economic, cultural and spiritual history, it no longer has as its fundamental referent individual action, as it generates datable events. It therefore no longer proposes to tie together events with a chronological and causal thread; and it ceases, thus, to tell stories. (2) Moreover, in changing its themes history changes its method. It seeks to move closer to the model of the nomological sciences which explain the events of nature by combining general laws with the description of the initial conditions. (3) Finally, whereas narrative is assumed to be subject to the uncritical perspective of agents plunged into the confusion of their present experience, history is an inquiry independent of the immediate comprehension of events by those who make or undergo them.

My thesis is that the tie between history and narrative cannot be broken without history losing its specificity among the human sciences.

To take these three arguments in reverse order, I shall assert first of all that the basic error comes from the failure to recognize the intelligible character conferred upon the narrative by the plot, a character that Aristotle was the first to emphasize. A naive notion of narrative, considered as a disconnected series of events, is always to be found behind the critique of the narrative character of history. Its episodic character alone is seen, while its configurational character, which is the basis of its intelligibility, is forgotten. At the same time the distance introduced by narrative between itself and lived experience is overlooked. Between living and recounting, a gap – however small it may be – is opened up. Life is lived, history is recounted.

Secondly, in overlooking narrative's basic intelligibility, one overlooks the possibility that historical explanation may be grafted onto narrative comprehension, in the sense that, in explaining more, one recounts better. The error of the proponents of nomological models is not so much that they are mistaken about the nature of the laws that the historian may borrow from other and most advanced social sciences – demography, economics, linguistics, sociology, etc. – but about how these laws work. They fail to see that these laws take on an historical meaning to the extent that they are grafted onto a prior narrative organization which has already characterized events as contributing to the development of a plot.

Thirdly, in turning away from the history of events (*histoire événementielle*), and in particular from political history, historiography has moved less from narrative history than historians might claim. Even when history as social, economic or cultural history becomes the history of long time-spans, it is still tied to time and still accounts for the changes that link a terminal to an initial situation. The rapidity of the change makes no difference here. In remaining bound to time and to change, history remains tied to human action, which, in Marx's words, makes history in circumstances it has not made. Directly or indirectly, history is always the history of men who are the bearers, the agents and the victims of the currents, institutions, functions and structures in which they find themselves placed. Ultimately, history cannot make a complete break with narrative because it cannot break with action, which itself implies agents, aims, circumstances, interactions and results both intended and unintended. But the plot is the basic narrative unity which organizes these heterogeneous ingredients into an intelligible totality.

The second problem I should like to touch on concerns the reference, *common* to both history and fiction, to the temporal background of human experience.

This problem is of considerable difficulty. On the one hand, indeed, only history seems to refer to reality, even if this reality is a past one. It alone seems to claim to speak of events that have really occurred. The novelist can disregard the burden of material proof related to the constraints imposed by documents and archives. An irreducible asymmetry seems to oppose historical reality to fictional reality.

There is no question of denying this asymmetry. On the contrary, it must be recognized in order to perceive the overlap, the figure of the chiasmus formed by the criss-crossing, referential modes characteristic of fiction and history: the historian speaking of the absent past in terms of fiction, the novelist speaking of what is irreal as if it had really taken place. On the one hand, we must not say that fiction has no reference. On the other hand, we must not say that history refers to the historical past in the same way as empirical descriptions refer to present reality. To say that fiction does not lack a reference is to reject an overly narrow conception of reference, which would relegate fiction to a purely emotional role. In one way or another, all symbol systems contribute to *shaping* reality. More particularly, the plots that we invent help us to shape our confused, formless and in the last resort mute temporal experience. 'What is time?' Augustine asked. 'If no one asks me, I know what it is, if someone asks me, I no longer know.' The plot's referential function lies in the capacity of fiction to shape this mute temporal experience. We are here brought back to the link between *muthos* and *mimesis* in Aristotle's *Poetics*: 'the fable', he says, '[is] an imitation of an action' (1450) A 2).

This is why suspending the reference can only be an intermediary moment between the pre-understanding of the world of action and the transfiguration of daily reality brought about by fiction itself. Indeed, the models *of* actions elaborated by narrative fiction are models *for* redescribing the practical field in accordance with the narrative typology resulting from the work of the productive imagination. Because it is a world, the world of the text necessarily collides with the real world in order to 're-make' it, either by confirming it or by denying it. However, even the most ironic relation between art and reality would be incomprehensible if art did not both disturb and rearrange our relation to reality. If the world of the text were without any assignable relation to the real world, then language would not be 'dangerous', in the sense in which Hölderlin called it so before both Nietzsche and Walter Benjamin.

So much for this brief sketch of the paradoxical problematic of 'productive' reference, characteristic of narrative fiction. I confess to have drawn in here only the outlines of a problem, not those of its solution.

A parallel approach to history is called for. Just as narrative fiction does not lack reference, the reference proper to history is not unrelated to the 'productive' reference of fictional narrative. Not that the past is unreal: but past reality is, in the strict sense of the word, unverifiable. Insofar as it no longer exists, the discourse of history can seek to grasp it only *indirectly*. It is here that the relationship with fiction shows itself as crucial. The reconstruction of the past, as Collingwood maintained so forcefully, is the work of the imagination. The historian, too, by virtue of the links mentioned earlier between history and narrative, shapes the plots which the documents may authorize or forbid but which they never contain in themselves. History, in this sense, combines narrative coherence with conformity to the documents. This complex tie characterizes the status of history as interpretation.

The way is thus open for a positive investigation of all the inter-relations between the asymmetrical, but also the indirect and mediate, referential modalities of fiction and of history. It is due to this complex interplay between the indirect reference to the past and the productive reference of fiction that human experience in its profound temporal dimension never ceases to be shaped.

I can only indicate here the threshold of this investigation, which is my current object of research.

II

I now propose to place my current investigation of narrative function within the broader framework of my earlier work, before attempting to bring to light the theoretical and epistemological presuppositions that have continued to grow stronger and more precise in the course of time.

I shall divide my remarks into two groups. The first concerns the structure or, better, the 'sense' immanent in the statements themselves, whether they be narrative or metaphorical. The second concerns the extralinguistic 'reference' of the statements and, hence, the truth claims of both sorts of statements.

A. Let us restrict ourselves in the first instance to the level of 'sense'.

(a) Between the narrative as a literary 'genre' and the metaphorical 'trope', the most basic link, on the level of sense, is constituted by the fact that both belong to discourse, that is to say to uses of language involving units as long as or longer than the sentence.

One of the first results that contemporary research on metaphor seems to me to have attained is, indeed, to have shifted the focus of analysis from the sphere of the *word* to that of the *sentence*. According to the definitions of classical rhetoric, stemming from Aristotle's *Poetics*, metaphor is the transfer of the everyday name of one thing to another in virtue of their resemblance. This definition, however, says nothing about the operation which results in this 'transfer' of sense. To understand the operation that generates such an extension, we must step outside the framework of the word to move up to the level of the sentence and speak of a metaphorical statement rather than of a word-metaphor. It then appears that metaphor constitutes a work on language consisting in the attribution to logical subjects of predicates that are incompossible with them. By this should be understood that, before being a deviant naming, metaphor is a peculiar predication, an attribution which destroys the consistency or, as has been said, the semantic relevance of the sentence as it is established by the ordinary, that is the lexical, meanings of the terms employed.

(b) This analysis of metaphor in terms of the sentence rather than the word or, more precisely, in terms of peculiar predication rather than deviant naming, prepares the way for a comparison between the theory of narrative and the theory of metaphor. Both indeed have to do with the phenomenon of *semantic innovation*. This phenomenon constitutes the most fundamental problem that metaphor and narrative have in common on the level of sense. In both cases, the novel – the not-yet-said, the unheard-of – suddenly arises in language: here, *living* metaphor, that is to say a *new* relevance in predication, there, wholly *invented* plot, that is to say a *new* congruence in the emplotment. On both sides, however, human creativity is to be discerned and to be circumscribed within forms that make it accessible to analysis.

(c) If we now ask about the reasons behind the privileged role played by metaphor and emplotment, we must turn towards the functioning of the *productive imagination* and of the *schematism* which constitutes its intelligible matrix. Indeed, in both cases innovation is produced in the milieu of language and reveals something about what an imagination that produces in accordance with rules might be. This rule-generated production is expressed in the construction of plots by way of a continual interchange between the invention of particular plots and the constitution by sedimentation of a narrative typology. A dialectic is at work in the production of new plots in the interplay between conformity and deviance in relation to the norms inherent in every narrative typology.

Now this dialectic has its counterpart in the birth of a new semantic relevance in new metaphors. Aristotle said that 'to be happy in the use of metaphors' consists in the 'discernment of resemblances' (*Poetics*, 1459 A 4–8). But what is it to discern resemblances? If the establishment of a new semantic relevance is that in virtue of which the statement 'makes sense' as a whole, resemblance consists in the *rapprochement*, the bringing closer together of terms which, previously 'remote', suddenly appear 'close'. Resemblance thus consists in a change of distance in logical space. It is nothing other than this emergence of a new generic kinship between heterogeneous ideas.

It is here that the productive imagination comes into play as the schematization of this synthetic operation of bringing closer together. It is the 'seeing' – the sudden insight – inherent to discourse itself, which brings about the change in logical distance, the bringing-closer-together itself. This productive character of insight may be called *predicative assimilation*. The imagination can justly be termed productive because, by an extension of polysemy, it makes terms, previously heterogeneous, *resemble* one another, and thus homogeneous. The imagination, consequently, is this competence, this capacity for producing new logical kinds by means of predicative assimilation and for producing them in spite of . . . and thanks to . . . the initial difference between the terms which resist assimilation.

(d) If, now, we put the stress on the *intelligible* character of semantic innovation, a new parallelism may be seen between the domain of the narrative and that of metaphor. We insisted above on the very particular mode of *understanding* involved in the activity of following a story and we spoke in this regard of narrative understanding. And we have maintained the thesis that historical *explanation* in terms of laws, regular causes, functions and structures is grafted onto this narrative understanding.

This same relation between understanding and explanation is to be observed in the domain of poetics. The act of understanding which would correspond in this domain to the ability to follow a story consists in grasping the semantic dynamism by virtue of which, in a metaphorical statement, a new semantic relevance emerges from the ruins of the semantic non-relevance as this appears in a literal reading of the sentence. To understand is thus to perform or to repeat the discursive operation by which the semantic innovation is conveyed. Now, upon this understanding by which the author or reader '*makes*' the metaphor is superimposed a scholarly explanation which, for its part, takes a completely different starting point than that of the dynamism of the sentence and which will not admit the units of discourse to be irreducible to the signs belonging to the language system. Positing the principle of the structure homology of all levels of language, from the phoneme to the text, the explanation of metaphor is thus included within a general semiotics which takes the sign as its basic unit. My thesis here, just as in the case of the narrative function, is that explanation is not primary but secondary in relation to understanding. Explanation, conceived as a combinatory system of signs, hence as a semiotics, is built up on the basis of a first-order understanding bearing on discourse as an act that is both indivisible and capable of innovation. Just as the narrative structures brought out by explanation presuppose an understanding of the structuring act by which plot is produced, so the structures brought out by structural semiotics are based upon the structuring of discourse, whose dynamism and power of innovation are revealed by metaphor.

In the third part of this essay we shall say in what way this twofold approach to the relation between explanation and understanding contributes to the contemporary development of hermeneutics. We shall say beforehand how the theory of metaphor conspires with the theory of narrative in the elucidation of the problem of reference.

B. In the preceding discussion, we have purposely isolated the 'sense' of the metaphorical statement, that is to say its internal predicative structure, from its 'reference', that is to say its claim to reach an extralinguistic reality, hence its claim to say something true.

Now, the study of the narrative function has already confronted us with the problem of poetic reference in the discussion of the relation between *muthos* and *mimesis* in Aristotle's *Poetics*. Narrative fiction, we said, 'imitates' human action, not only in that, before referring to the text, it refers to our own pre-understanding of the meaningful structures of action and of its temporal dimensions, but also in that it contributes, beyond the text, to reshaping these structures and dimensions in accordance with the imaginary configuration of the plot. Fiction has the power to 'remake' reality and, within the framework of narrative fiction in particular, to remake real praxis to the extent that the text intentionally aims at a horizon of new reality which we may call a world. It is this world of the text which intervenes in the world of action in order to give it a new configuration or, as we might say, in order to transfigure it.

The study of metaphor enables us to penetrate farther into the mechanism of this operation of transfiguration and to extend it to the whole set of imaginative productions which we designate by the general term of fiction. What metaphor alone permits us to perceive is the conjunction between the two constitutive moments of poetic reference.

The first of these moments is the easiest to identify. Language takes on a poetic function whenever it redirects our attention away from the reference and towards the message itself. In Roman Jakobson's terms, the poetic function stresses the message *for its own sake* at the expense of the referential function which, on the contrary, is dominant in descriptive language. One might say that a centripetal movement of language towards itself takes the place of the centrifugal movement of the referential function. Language glorifies itself in the play of sound and sense.

However, the suspension of the referential function implied by the stress laid on the message *for its own sake* is only the reverse side, or the negative condition, of a more concealed referential function of discourse, one which is, as it were, set free when the descriptive value of statements is suspended. It is in this way that poetic discourse brings to language aspects, qualities and values of reality which do not have access to directly descriptive language and which can be said only thanks to the complex play of the metaphorical utterance and of the ordered transgression of the ordinary meaning of our words. In my work, *The Rule of Metaphor*, I compared this indirect functioning of metaphorical reference to that of models used in the physical sciences, when these are more than aids to discovery or teaching but are incorporated into the very meaning of theories and into their truth claims. These models then have the heuristic power of 're-describing' a reality inaccessible to direct description. In the same way, one may say that poetic language re-describes the world thanks to the suspension of direct description by way of objective language.

This notion of metaphorical re-description exactly parallels the mimetic function that we earlier assigned to narrative fiction. The latter operates typically in the field of action and its temporal values, while metaphorical re-description reigns rather in the field of sensory, affective, aesthetic and axiological values which make the world one that can be *inhabited*.

What is beginning to take shape in this way is the outline of a vast poetic sphere that includes both metaphorical statement and narrative discourse.

The philosophical implications of this theory of indirect reference are as considerable as those of the dialectic between explanation and understanding. Let us now set them within the field of philosophical hermeneutics. Let us say, provisionally, that the function of the transfiguration of reality which we have attributed to poetic fiction implies that we cease to identify reality with empirical reality or, what amounts to the same thing, that we cease to identify experience with empirical experience. Poetic language draws its prestige from its capacity for bringing to language certain aspects of what Husserl called the *Lebenswelt* and Heidegger *In-der-Welt-Sein*. By this very fact, we find ourselves forced to rework our conventional concept of truth, that is to say to cease to limit this concept to logical coherence and empirical verification alone, so that the truth claim related to the transfiguring action of fiction can be taken into account. No more can be said about reality and truth – and no doubt about Being as well – until we have first attempted to make explicit the philosophical presuppositions of the entire enterprise.

III

A hermeneutical philosophy

I wish now to attempt to reply to two questions which the preceding analyses cannot have failed to provoke in the minds of readers who have been brought up in a different philosophical tradition from my own. What are the presuppositions that characterize the philosophical tradition to which I recognize myself as belonging? How do the preceding analyses fit into this tradition?

As to the first question, I should like to characterize this philosophical tradition by three features: it stands in the line of a *reflexive** philosophy; it remains within the sphere of Husserlian *phenomenology*; it strives to be a *hermeneutical* variation of this phenomenology.

By reflexive philosophy, I mean broadly speaking the mode of thought stemming from the Cartesian *cogito* and handed down by

---

* *Translator's Note:* In French, the adjective 'réflexive' incorporates two meanings which are distinguished in English by *reflective* and *reflexive*. On the advice of the author we have chosen to retain the latter in order to emphasize that this philosophy is subject-oriented; it is reflexive in the subject's act of turning back upon itself. The other possible meaning should, however, also be kept in mind.

way of Kant and French post-Kantian philosophy, a philosophy which is little known abroad and which, for me at least, was most strikingly represented by Jean Nabert. A reflexive philosophy considers the most radical philosophical problems to be those which concern the possibility of *self-understanding* as the subject of the operations of knowing, willing, evaluating, etc. Reflexion is that act of turning back upon itself by which a subject grasps, in a moment of intellectual clarity and moral responsibility, the unifying principle of the operations among which it is dispersed and forgets itself as subject. 'The "I think" ', says Kant, 'must be able to accompany all my representations.' All reflexive philosophers would recognize themselves in this formula.

But how can the 'I think' know or recognize itself? It is here that phenomenology – and more especially hermeneutics – represent both a realization and a radical transformation of the very programme of reflexive philosophy. Indeed, the idea of reflexion carries with it the desire for absolute transparence, a perfect coincidence of the self with itself, which would make consciousness of self indubitable knowledge and, as such, more fundamental than all forms of positive knowledge. It is this fundamental demand that phenomenology first of all, and then hermeneutics, continue to project onto an ever more distant horizon as philosophy goes on providing itself with the instruments of thought capable of satisfying it.

Thus Husserl, in those of his theoretical texts most evidently marked by an idealism reminiscent of Fichte, conceives of phenomenology not only as a method of description in terms of their essences of the fundamental modes of organizing experience (perceptive, imaginative, intellectual, volitional, axiological, etc.), but also as a radical self-grounding in the most complex intellectual clarity. In the reduction – or *epoche* – applied to the natural attitude, he then sees the conquest of an empire of sense from which any question concerning things-in-themselves is excluded by being put into brackets. It is this empire of sense, thus freed from any matter-of-fact question, which constitutes the privileged field of phenomenological experience, the domain of intuition *par excellence*. Returning, beyond Kant, to Descartes, he holds that every apprehension of transcendence is open to doubt but that self-immanence is indubitable. It is in virtue of this assertion that phenomenology remains a reflexive philosophy.

And yet, whatever the theory it applies to itself and to its ultimate claims, in its effective practice phenomenology already displays its distance from rather than its realization of the dream of such a radical grounding in the transparence of the subject to itself. The great discovery of phenomenology, within the limits of the phenomenological reduction itself, remains intentionality, that is to say, in its least technical sense, the priority of the consciousness *of something* over self-consciousness. This definition of intentionality, however, is still trivial. In its rigorous sense, intentionality signifies that the *act* of intending something is accomplished only through the identifiable and reidentifiable unity of intended *sense* – what Husserl calls the 'noema' or the 'intentional correlate of the noetic intention'. Moreover, upon this noema are superimposed the various layers which result from the synthetic activities that Husserl terms 'constitution' (constitution of things, constitution of space, constitution of time, etc.). Now the concrete work of phenomenology, in particular in the studies devoted to the constitution of 'things', reveals, by way of regression, levels, always more and more fundamental, at which the active syntheses continually refer to ever more radical passive syntheses. Phenomenology is thus caught up in an infinite movement of 'backwards questioning' in which its project of radical self-grounding fades away. Even the last works devoted to the *life-world* designate by this term an horizon of immediateness that is forever out of reach. The *Lebenswelt* is never actually given but always presupposed. It is phenomenology's paradise lost. It is in this sense that phenomenology has undermined its own guiding idea in the very attempt to realize it. It is this that gives to Husserl's work its tragic grandeur.

It is with this paradoxical result in mind that we can understand how hermeneutics has been able to graft itself onto phenomenology and to maintain with respect to the latter the same twofold relation as that which phenomenology maintains with its Cartesian and Fichtean ideal. The antecedents of hermeneutics seem at first to set it apart from the reflexive tradition and from the phenomenological project. Hermeneutics, in fact, was born – or rather revived – at the time of Schleiermacher and of the fusion of biblical exegesis, classical philology and jurisprudence. This fusion of several different disciplines was made possible thanks to a Copernican reversal which gave priority to the question of *what it is to understand* over that of the sense of this or that text or of this or that category of texts (sacred or profane, poetical or juridical). It is this investigation of *Verstehen* which, a century later, was to come across the phenomenological question *par excellence*, namely the investigation of the intentional sense of noetic acts. It is true that hermeneutics continued to embody concerns different from those of concrete phenomenology. Whereas the latter tended to raise the question of sense in the dimensions of cognition and percep-tion, hermeneutics, since Dilthey, has raised it rather in those of history and the human sciences. But on both sides the fun-damental question was the same, namely that of the relation between *sense* and *self*, between the *intelligibility* of the first and the *reflexive* nature of the second.

The phenomenological rooting of hermeneutics is not limited to this very general kinship between the understanding of texts and the intentional relation of a consciousness to a sense with which it finds itself faced. The theme of the *Lebenswelt*, a theme which phenomenology came up against in spite of itself, one might say, is adopted by post-Heideggerian hermeneutics no longer as something left over, but as a prior condition. It is because we find ourselves first of all in a world to which we belong and in which we cannot help but participate, that we are then able, in a second movement, to set up objects in opposition to ourselves, objects that we claim to constitute and to master intellectually. *Verstehen* for Heidegger has an ontological sig-nification. It is the response of a being thrown into the world who finds his way about it by projecting onto it his ownmost possibili-ties. Interpretation, in the technical sense of the interpretation of texts, is but the development, the making explicit of this onto-logical understanding, an understanding always inseparable from a being that has initially been thrown into the world. The subject–object relation – on which Husserl continues to depend – is thus subordinated to the testimony of an ontological link more basic than any relation of knowledge.

This subversion of phenomenology by hermeneutics calls for another such action: the famous 'reduction' by which Husserl separates the 'sense' from the background of existence in which natural consciousness is initially immersed can no longer be con-sidered a primary philosophical move. Henceforth it takes on a derived epistemological meaning: it is a move of distantiation that comes second – and, in this sense, a move by which the primary rootedness of understanding is forgotten, a move which calls for all the objectivizing operations characteristic both of common and of scientific knowledge. This distantiation, however, presupposes the involvement as participant thanks to which we actually belong to the world before we are subjects capable of setting up objects in opposition to ourselves in order to judge them and to submit them to our intellectual and technical mastery. In this way, Heideggerian and post-Heideggerian hermeneutics, though they are indeed heirs to Husserlian phenomenology, constitute in the end the reversal of this phenomenology to the very extent indeed that they also constitute its realization.

The philosophical consequences of this reversal are considerable. They are not apparent, however, if we limit ourselves to emphasizing the finite character of Being which renders null and void the ideal of the self-transparence of a fundamental subject. The idea of the finite is in itself banal, even trivial. At best, it simply embodies in negative terms the renouncement of all *hybris* on the part of reflection, of any claim that the subject may make to found itself on itself. The discovery of the precedence of Being-in-the-world in relation to any foundational project and to any attempt at ultimate justification takes on its full force when we draw the positive conclusions of the new ontology of understanding for epistemology. It is in drawing these epistemological consequences that I shall bring my answers to the first question raised at the start of the third part of this essay to bear on the second question. I can sum up these epistemological consequences in the following way: there is no self-understanding which is not *mediated* by signs, symbols and texts; in the last resort understanding coincides with the interpretation given to these mediating terms. In passing from one to the other, hermeneutics gradually frees itself from the idealism with which Husserl had tried to identify phenomenology. Let us now follow the stages of this emancipation.

Mediation by *signs*: that is to say that it is *language* that is the primary condition of all human experience. Perception is articulated, desire is articulated; this is something that Hegel had already shown in the *Phenomenology of Mind*. Freud drew another consequence from this, namely that there is no emotional experience so deeply buried, so concealed or so distorted that it cannot be brought up to the clarity of language and so revealed in its own proper sense, thanks to desire's access to the sphere of language. Psychoanalysis, as a *talk-cure*, is based on this very hypothesis, that of the primary proximity between desire and speech. And since speech is heard before it is uttered, the shortest path from the self to itself lies in the speech of the other which leads me across the open space of signs.

Mediation by *symbols*: by this term I mean those expressions carrying a double sense which traditional cultures have grafted onto the naming of the 'elements' of the cosmos (fire, water, wind, earth, etc.), of its 'dimensions' (height and depth, etc.). These double-sense expressions are themselves hierarchically ordered into the most universal symbols, then those that belong to one particular culture, and, finally, those that are the creation of a particular thinker, even of just one work. In this last case, the symbol merges into living metaphor. However, there is, on the other hand, perhaps no symbolic creation which is not in the final analysis rooted in the common symbolical ground of humanity. I myself once sketched out a *Symbolism of Evil* based entirely on this mediating role of certain double-sense expressions, such as stain, fall, deviation, in reflections on ill will. At that time, I even went so far as to reduce hermeneutics to the interpretation of symbols, that is to say to the making explicit of the second – and often hidden – sense of these double-sense expressions.

Today this definition of hermeneutics in terms of symbolic interpretation appears to me too narrow. And this for two reasons, which will lead us from mediation by symbols to mediation by texts. First of all I came to realize that no symbolism, whether traditional or private, can display its resources of *multiple meaning* (*multivocité*) outside appropriate contexts, that is to say, within the framework of an entire text, of a poem, for example. Next, the same symbolism can give rise to competitive – even diametrically opposed – interpretations, depending on whether the interpretation aims at reducing the symbolism to its literal basis, to its unconscious sources or its social motivations, or at amplifying it in accordance with its highest power of multiple meaning. In the one case, hermeneutics aims at demystifying a symbolism by unmasking the unavowed forces that are concealed within it; in the other case, it aims at a re-collection of meaning in its richest, its most elevated, most spiritual diversity. But this conflict of interpretations is also to be found at the level of texts.

It follows that hermeneutics can no longer be defined simply in terms of the interpretation of symbols. Nevertheless, this definition should be preserved at least as a stage separating the very general recognition of the linguistic character of experience and the more technical definition of hermeneutics in terms of textual interpretation. What is more, this intermediary definition helps to dissipate the illusion of an intuitive self-knowledge by forcing self-understanding to take the roundabout. path of the whole treasury of symbols transmitted by the cultures within which we have come, at one and the same time, into both existence and speech.

Finally, mediation by *texts*: at first sight this mediation seems more limited than the mediation by signs and by symbols, which can be simply oral and even non-verbal. Mediation by texts seems to restrict the sphere of interpretation to writing and to literature to the detriment of oral cultures. This is true. But what the definition loses in extension, it gains in intensity. Indeed, writing opens up new and original resources for discourse. Thanks to writing, discourse acquires a threefold semantic autonomy: in relation to the speaker's intention, to its reception by its original audience, and to the economic, social and cultural circumstances of its production. It is in this sense that writing tears itself free of the limits of face-to-face dialogue and becomes the condition for discourse itself *becoming-text*. It is to hermeneutics that falls the task of exploring the implications of this becoming-text for the work of interpretation.

The most important consequence of all this is that an end is put once and for all to the Cartesian and Fichtean – and to an extent Husserlian – ideal of the subject's transparence to itself. To understand oneself is to understand oneself as one confronts the text and to receive from it the conditions for a self other than that which first undertakes the reading. Neither of the two subjectivities, neither that of the author nor that of the reader, is thus primary in the sense of an originary presence of the self to itself.

Once it is freed from the primacy of subjectivity, what may be the first task of hermeneutics? It is, in my opinion, to seek in the text itself, on the one hand, the internal dynamic which governs the structuring of the work and, on the other hand, the power that the work possesses to project itself outside itself and to give birth to a world which would truly be the 'thing' referred to by the text. This internal dynamic and external projection constitute what I call the work of the text. It is the task of hermeneutics to reconstruct this twofold work.

We can look back on the path that has led us from the first presupposition, that of philosophy as reflexivity, by way of the second, that of philosophy as phenomenology, right up to the third, that of the mediation first by signs, then by symbols and, finally, by texts.

A hermeneutical philosophy is a philosophy which accepts all the demands of this long detour and which gives up the dream of a total mediation, at the end of which reflection would once again amount to intellectual intuition in the transparence to itself of an absolute subject.

I can now, in conclusion, attempt to reply to the second question raised at the start of the third part of this essay. If such are the presuppositions characteristic of the tradition to which my works belong, what, in my opinion, is their place in the development of this tradition?

In order to reply to this question, I have only to relate the last definition I have just given of the task of hermeneutics to the conclusions reached at the end of the two sections of part II.

The task of hermeneutics, we have just said, is twofold: to reconstruct the internal dynamic of the text, and to restore to the work its ability to project itself outside itself in the representation of a world that I could inhabit.

It seems to me that all of my analyses aimed at the interrelation of understanding and explanation, at the level of what I have called the 'sense' of the work, are related to the first task. In my analyses of narrative as well as in those of metaphor, I am fighting on two fronts: on the one hand, I cannot accept the irrationalism of immediate understanding, conceived as an extension to the domain of texts of the empathy by which a subject puts himself in the place of a foreign consciousness in a situation of face-to-face intensity. This undue extension maintains the romantic illusion of a direct link of congeniality between the two subjectivities implied by the work, that of the author and that of the reader. However, I am equally unable to accept a rationalistic explanation which would extend to the text the structural analysis of sign systems that are characteristic not of discourse but of language as such. This equally undue extension gives rise to the positivist illusion of a textual objectivity closed in upon itself and wholly independent of the subjectivity of both author and reader. To these two one-sided attitudes, I have opposed the dialectic of understanding and explanation. By understanding I mean the ability to take up again within oneself the work of structuring that is performed by the text, and by explanation the second-order operation grafted onto this understanding which consists in bringing to light the codes underlying this work of structuring that is carried through in company with the reader. This combat on two separate fronts against a reduction of understanding to empathy and a reduction of explanation to an abstract combinatory system, leads me to define interpretation by this very dialectic of understanding and explanation at the level of the 'sense' immanent to the text. This specific manner of responding to the first task of hermeneutics offers the signal advantage, in my opinion, of preserving the dialogue between philosophy and the human sciences, a dialogue that is interrupted by the two counterfeit forms of understanding and explanation which I reject. This would be my first contribution to the hermeneutical philosophy from out of which I am working.

In what I have written above, I have tried to set my analyses of the 'sense' of metaphorical statements and of that of narrative plots against the background of the theory of *Verstehen*, limited to its epistemological usage, in the tradition of Dilthey and Max Weber. The distinction between 'sense' and 'reference', applied to these statements and to these plots, gives me the right to limit myself provisionally to what has thus been established by hermeneutical philosophy, which seems to me to remain unaffected by its later development in Heidegger and Gadamer, in the sense of a subordination of the epistemological to the ontological theory of *Verstehen*. I want neither to ignore the epistemological phase, which involves philosophy's dialogue with the human sciences, nor to neglect this shift in the hermeneutical problematic, which henceforth emphasizes Being-in-the-world and the participatory belonging which precedes any relation of a subject to an object which confronts him.

It is against this background of the new hermeneutical ontology that I should like to set my analyses of the 'reference' of metaphorical statements and of narrative plots. I confess willingly that these analyses continually *presuppose* the conviction that discourse never exists *for its own sake*, for its own glory, but that in all of its uses it seeks to bring into language an experience, a way of living in and of Being-in-the-world which precedes it and which demands to be said. It is this conviction that there is always a *Being-demanding-to-be-said* (*un être-à-dire*) which precedes our actual saying, which explains my obstinacy in trying to discover in the poetic uses of language the referential mode appropriate to them and through which discourse continues to 'say' Being even when it appears to have withdrawn into itself for the sake of self-celebration. This vehement insistence on preventing language from closing up on itself I have inherited from Heidegger's *Sein und Zeit* and from Gadamer's *Wahrheit und Methode*. In return, however, I should like to believe that the description I propose of the reference of metaphorical and of narrative statements contributes to this ontological vehemence an analytical precision which it would otherwise lack.

On the one hand, indeed, it is what I have just called ontological vehemence in the theory of language that leads me to attempt to give an ontological dimension to the referential claim of metaphorical statements: in this way, I venture to say that to see something as . . . is to make manifest the *being-as* of that thing. I place the 'as' in the position of the exponent of the verb 'to be' and I make 'being-as' the ultimate referent of the metaphorical statement. This thesis undeniably bears the imprint of post-Heideggerian ontology. But, on the other hand, the testimony to *being-as* . . . cannot, in my opinion, be separated from a detailed study of the referential modes of discourse and requires a properly analytical treatment of indirect reference, on the basis of the concept of 'split reference' taken from Roman Jakobson. My thesis concerning the *mimesis* of the narrative work and my distinction between the three stages of *mimesis* – prefiguration, configuration and transfiguration of the world of action by the poem – express one and the same concern to combine analytical precision with ontological testimony.

The concern I have just expressed brings me back to that other concern, which I mentioned above, not to oppose understanding and explanation on the level of the dynamic immanent to poetic utterances. Taken together, these two concerns mark my hope that in working for the progress of hermeneutical philosophy, I contribute, in however small a way, to arousing an interest in this philosophy on the part of analytical philosophers.

Translated by Kathleen McLaughlin

Notes on contributors

PIERRE BOURDIEU. Professor of Sociology at the Collège de France and at the Ecole des Hautes Etudes en Sciences Sociales in Paris. Having begun his career as an anthropologist in Algeria, he later turned to the sociology of culture and education. From his diverse empirical work on education, intellectuals, literature, art and power, particularly of the ruling class, he has developed a systematic theory of the social world. His books include *The Algerians*, 1962, *Outline of a Theory of Practice*, 1977, *Reproduction in Education, Society and Culture*, 1977, *Algeria 1960*, 1979, *The Inheritors*, 1979, and *La Distinction* (English translation forthcoming).

JACQUES BOUVERESSE. Born 1940. Studied at the Ecole Normale Supérieure. From 1969 to 1979 taught at the University of Paris I (Sorbonne), first as Maître-Assistant, then as Professor. Since 1979 Professor at the University of Geneva. Principal publications include *La Parole malheureuse*, 1971, *Wittgenstein: la rime et la raison – Science, éthique et esthétique*, 1973, *Le Mythe de l'intériorité – Expérience, signification et langage privé chez Wittgenstein*, 1976, and *Meaning and Understanding* (edited by Herman Parret and Jacques Bouveresse), Walter de Gruyter, Berlin and New York, 1981. Is at the moment completing a work on Frege and preparing a book on the philosophical and epistemological aspects of the work of Robert Musil.

JACQUES DERRIDA. Born 1930 in Algeria. Teaches the history of philosophy at the Ecole Normale Supérieure. Principal works include *Writing and Difference* (1967), Chicago University

Press, 1978, *Of Grammatology* (1967), Johns Hopkins University Press, 1976, *Speech and Phenomenon* (1967), Northwestern University Press, 1972, *Positions* (1972), Chicago University Press, 1981, *Dissemination* (1972), Chicago University Press, 1981, *Spurs: Nietzsche's Styles* (forthcoming). In addition the following have not yet been translated into English: *Glas*, Galilee, 1974, *La Vérité en peinture*, Flammarion, 1978, *La Carte postale*, Flammarion, 1979.

JEAN-TOUSSAINT DESANTI. Born 1914 in Corsica. Studied at the Ecole Normale Supérieure. Has taught for a long time in secondary education. Is at present Professor of Philosophy at the University of Paris I (Sorbonne). Principal works include *Introduction à l'histoire de la philosophie*, 1956, *Phénoménologie et praxis*, 1963, *Les Idéalités mathématiques*, 1968, *La Philosophie silencieuse*, 1975, *Le Philosophe et les pouvoirs*, 1976, and *Un destin philosophique*, 1982.

VINCENT DESCOMBES. Born 1943. At present Maître-Assistant at the University of Paris I (Sorbonne). Has taught philosophy at the Universities of Montreal and Nice. Visiting Professor at Johns Hopkins University, Baltimore. Principal works include *Le Platonisme*, 1971, *L'Inconscient malgré lui*, 1977, and *Modern French Philosophy*, 1979.

CLAUDE LEFORT. Born 1924. Director of Studies at the Ecole des Hautes Etudes en Sciences Sociales. Has edited the posthumous works of Merleau-Ponty, whose student he once was. Main early influences include Marxism and phenomenology. Was one of the founders of the far left review *Socialism ou barbarie* at the end of the 1940s. Undertook from an early stage a systematic criticism of totalitarianism in the Soviet Union, a criticism which he has since broadened into a renewed theory of democracy. Principal works include *Le Travail de l'oeuvre*, *Machiavel*, *Eléments d'une critique de la bureaucratie*, *Sur une colonne absente: Ecrits autour de Merleau-Ponty*, *Les Formes de l'histoire*, *Un homme en trop* (on Solzhenitsyn) and *L'Invention démocratique*.

EMMANUEL LEVINAS. Born 1905 in Kaunas, Lithuania. Studied in Strasbourg, Freiburg im Breisgau and Paris. Has been Professor of Philosophy at the Ecole Normale Supérieure Israélite de Paris and at the Universities of Poitiers, Paris X (Nanterre) and

Paris I (Sorbonne). Has undertaken many visits abroad. Principal publications in philosophy include *Théorie de l'intuition dans la phénoménologie de Husserl*, 1930, *De l'existence a l'existant*, 1947, *Totalité et infini*, 1961, and *Autrement qu'être ou au delà de l'essence*, 1974 – all of which have been translated into English; and *Le Temps et l'autre*, 1948, *En découvrant l'existence avec Husserl et Heidegger*, 1949, *Humanisme de l'autre homme*, 1973, *Noms propres*, 1975, *Sur Maurice Blanchot*, 1975, and *De Dieu qui vient à l'idée*, 1982. Has also published in the philosophy of religion *Difficile liberté – Essai sur le judaisme*, 1963, *Quatre lectures talmudiques*, 1968, *Du Sacré au Saint*, 1977, and *L'au-delà du Verset*, 1981.

JEAN-FRANÇOIS LYOTARD. Born 1924. Taught philosophy in the secondary sector from 1949 to 1959 and since then at the Universities of Paris I (Sorbonne), Paris X (Nanterre) and Paris VIII (Vincennes). At present Professor at the University of Paris VIII (Saint-Denis). Has been Visiting Professor in the United States (at the Universities of Johns Hopkins, California at San Diego, Wisconsin and Milwaukee), in Canada (the University of Montreal), in Brazil (the University of São Paulo) and in Italy. Member of the Editorial Committees of *Socialisme ou barbarie* (1956–64) and *Pouvoir ouvrier* (1964–6). Was an active supporter of the Algerian movement of liberation and took part in the movement of May 1968. Principal works include *La Phénoménologie*, 1954, *Discours, figure*, 1971, *Dérive à partir de Marx et Freud*, 1973, *Economie libidinale*, 1973, *Au juste*, 1979 and *La Condition postmoderne*, 1979. Has also published several essays in the philosophy of art and a number of fictions.

PIERRE MACHEREY. Born 1938. Teaches philosophy at the University of Paris I (Sorbonne). Has contributed to *Lire le Capital* together with Louis Althusser, E. Balibar, R. Establet and J. Rancière. Principal works include *Pour une théorie de la production litteraire* (English translation, Routledge and Kegan Paul, 1978), and *Hegel ou Spinoza*.

LOUIS MARIN. Born 1931. Studied at the Ecole Normale Supérieure. At one time Director of the Institut Français in London. Has been Professor in the United States at the Universities of California at San Diego, Johns Hopkins, Baltimore. Since 1977 Professor at the Ecole des Hautes Etudes en Sciences Sociales.

Principal works include *Utopiques, jeux d'espaces*, 1973, *La Critique du discours – sur la 'Logique de Port-Royal' et les 'Pensées' de Pascal*, 1975, and *Le Portrait du roi*, 1981.

PAUL RICOEUR. Born 1913. Professor of the History of Philosophy at the University of Strasbourg, 1948–56, Professor of Metaphysics at the Sorbonne, Paris, 1956–66, Professor of Philosophy at the University of Paris X (Nanterre), 1966–present day, John Nuveen Professor at the University of Chicago, 1970–present. Principal works translated and published in English include *Fallible Man*, Henry Regnery, Chicago, 1965, *History and Truth*, Northwestern University Press, 1965, *Freedom and Nature: The Voluntary and the Involuntary*, Northwestern University Press, 1966, *The Symbolism of Evil*, Harper & Row, 1967, *Freud and Philosophy: An Essay in Interpretation*, Yale University Press, 1970, *The Conflict of Interpretations: Essays in Hermeneutics*, Northwestern University Press, 1974, *The Rule of Metaphor*, University of Toronto Press, 1977.

DATE DUE